IRAN

Politics and Government Under the Pahlavis

An Annotated Bibliography

by
Dariush
Gitisetan

The Scarecrow Press, Inc.
Metuchen, N.J., & London 1985

Library of Congress Cataloging in Publication Data

Gitisetan, Dariush.
  Iran, politics and government under the Pahlavis,
an annotated bibliography.

    Includes index.
    1. Iran--History--Pahlavi dynasty, 1925-1979
--Bibliography.   I. Title.
Z3366.G58   1985   016.955   84-23587
[DS316.3]
ISBN 0-8108-1770-5

Copyright © 1985 by Dariush Gitisetan
Manufactured in the United States of America

To my family

and

to Lori

ACKNOWLEDGMENTS

This project was supported in part by the California State University Foundation, Northridge. I would like to express my gratitude to the members of the Faculty Research and Grants Committee for this assistance.

I would also like to thank Mr. Norman E. Tanis, Director of University Libraries at California State University, Northridge (CSUN) for his valuable comments on my original proposal.

I am grateful to Virginia Elwood and Misha Schutt of the CSUN's Interlibrary Loan Department for their fine spirit of cooperation.

Special thanks are also due to Irene Thorsell who has been a source of encouragement and support throughout this project.

I wish to express my appreciation to Dr. Frederick Holler of CSUN who has read portions of the manuscript and has made helpful suggestions, and to Mr. Dunning Wilson, the Near Eastern Bibliographer at UCLA who offered useful comments at the early stages of the project.

Sincere thanks also go to Tony Gardner, JoAnn Skowronski, and other friends and colleagues whose suggestions, encouragement, and support have made working on this project more rewarding and enjoyable.

Dariush Gitisetan
Los Angeles 1984

CONTENTS

Introduction ix

I. THE RISE OF THE PAHLAVI DYNASTY
  1. Reza Shah and the Establishment of the Pahlavi Dynasty 3
  2. Reconstruction, Reform, and Westernization Under Reza Shah 9
  3. WW II, Reza Shah's Abdication, and the Aftermath 13
  4. Mossadeq and Nationalization of Oil, 1951-1953 19
  5. Mohammad Reza Pahlavi (The Shah) and His White Revolution 26

II. POLITICAL CONDITIONS
  6. Political Parties and Ideologies 35
  7. Internal Politics and Governmental Administration 40
  8. National Security and Armed Forces 49
  9. Foreign Policy and General International Relations 54
  10. Iran and Her Neighbors 60
  11. Relations with the Persian Gulf and the Indian Ocean Regions 64
  12. Iran and the Soviet Union 71
  13. Relations with Europe 77
  14. Iran and the United States 80
  15. Relations with Other Countries 90
  16. Relations with Regional and International Organizations 93

III. ECONOMIC CONDITIONS
  17. Economic Planning and Development 99
  18. Monetary and Fiscal Policies 105
  19. Energy, Natural Resources, and Industrialization 109
  20. Oil Industry and Politics of Oil 112
  21. Foreign Economic Policy and Other Aspects of the Economy 120
  22. Agriculture and Land Reform 127

IV. SOCIAL CONDITIONS
  23. The Society and General Social Conditions 137

24.	Ethnic and Religious Minorities	142
25.	Women and Their Status	146
26.	Modernization and Its Obstacles	149
27.	Islam and Politics	153
28.	Human Resources and Education	157
29.	Legal System and the Administration of Justice	162
30.	Repression, the Secret Police (SAVAK), and Other Violations of Human Rights	164

V. THE FALL OF THE PAHLAVI DYNASTY
  31. Discontent, Opposition, and Revolution — 171

VI. GENERAL SOURCES OF INFORMATION
  32. General and Bibliographic Sources — 183

Name Index — 192

INTRODUCTION

The purpose of this bibliography is to bring together materials related to the politics and government in Iran during the Pahlavi dynasty. It developed as a response to the wide need for a bibliography on contemporary Iran providing scholars, librarians, students, and others engaged in research in this area with a basic reference tool.

The significance of Iran in world politics cannot be overemphasized. Her strategic location, oil reserves, and other economic resources make this country one of the most important areas of study for the Middle East area specialist.

Furthermore, major political events in Iran and an abrupt change from a more than 2500-year old monarchy to a political system of an Islamic republic have marked a turning point in the history of this country. These events have also drawn attention from all over the world and have made Iran one of the most important political centers.

Although the Pahlavi dynasty's period of governing Iran is short within the context of the country's historical background, its influence on Iranian politics, economy, society, and culture, as well as on international politics, has been substantial.

In terms of scope, this bibliography reflects a wide spectrum of subjects on Iranian politics and government dealing with the period 1925-1979, whether published during that time or later. In addition, relevant subjects on the social and economic conditions of the country are included, for political conditions are not isolated phenomena and can be best understood when studied within their social and economic contexts.

Monographs and periodical articles in English and other major Western languages such as French, German, Italian, and Spanish are included. The majority of the entries, however, are for works in English. Major government publications and dissertations are covered while pamphlets and other ephemeral items are excluded.

The basic organization of this bibliography is by subject with a chronological emphasis at the outset (Part I) in order to provide a historical perspective of the dynasty's rise to power. Entries under each subject are arranged alphabetically by author, editor, compiler, issuing agency, or by title where no such authorship responsibility is indicated. Where an entry covers more than one subject category, it is listed under the most appropriate one. Occasionally, however, an important entry has been repeated under another subject with a different annotation or a cross-reference.

The annotations are, with few exceptions, informative rather than evaluative. In some instances, brief background information has been provided, always keeping in mind the often-quoted words of Fredson T. Bowers that "a good bibliography can be read as well as consulted" and hoping to have approached this difficult-to-attain ideal.

Since the phrase "the Shah" is a generic title attributed to all Iranian kings, it should be mentioned, for the purpose of clarification, that in the text of the annotations this phrase has been used to refer only to Mohammad Reza Pahlavi, who was best known in the West by that title. His father, the founder of the dynasty, has been referred to as Reza Shah.

The criteria for selection of materials include relevance and quality of citations, balance of subject treatment, and, as mentioned previously, an effort to include materials which help provide an overall perspective of the period under survey.

A straightforward filing system--alphabetical word-by-word, disregarding internal punctuations--has been followed throughout. Initial articles (a, an, the) and their equivalent in foreign languages are disregarded for filing purposes. "Mc" at the beginning of surnames is filed as if spelled "Mac." Numbers and abbreviations are filed as if spelled out.

A standard bibliographic format has been followed in describing the entries. The components of the entries for periodical articles are: Author; title of the article; name of the journal; volume and/or issue number; pagination; date; and annotation. For monographs, the entry elements consist of: Author, editor, etc.; title; place of publication; publisher; date of publication; and annotation. Each entry has been assigned an entry number and the references in the index are to these numbers.

Transliteration (romanization) of Persian inevitably requires explanation, for none of the numerous methods are free from compromises. As an example, "Reza Shah" has been transliterated in various sources as: Risa Shah, Reza Scia, Riza Chah, Reza Schah, etc. A simplified system of transliteration without diacritics has been adopted and consistently used in the text of the annotations. For authors and titles, however, the forms used in the publications have been followed without diacritics. Names of a few authors have been transliterated differently in various sources. To ensure uniformity these have been entered under one form and cross-references provided for the variant spellings in the index.

Although an effort has been made to include as many impor-

Introduction xi

tant sources as possible in this bibliography, no claim is made as to its completeness. Resources of many large research libraries in California, including the University of California, Los Angeles (UCLA); the Hoover Institution on War, Revolution, and Peace, Stanford, California; the University of California, Berkeley; and California State University, Northridge have been utilized.

Finally, it must be emphasized that in the selection and collection of data for this bibliography, no value judgment has been made in regard to the period under study, nor has this been the intention of this bibliography.

I

THE RISE OF THE PAHLAVI DYNASTY

1

REZA SHAH AND THE ESTABLISHMENT OF THE PAHLAVI DYNASTY

1 Agabekov, G. OGPU: The Russian Secret Terror. New York: Brentano's, 1931.
   A member of the G. P. U., the Russian secret police, Agabekov came to Iran in 1927 ostensibly as an attaché of the Soviet Embassy, but actually as the Resident General of the G. P. U. In this memoir he reveals the Soviet subservice aims in Iran and names of many Persian agents. These revelations may have motivated Reza Shah's determination to drive foreign interests out of Iran.

2 "The American Financial Mission to Persia." Journal of the Royal Central Asian Society. 14:344-345, 1927.
   Discusses the resignation and departure from Iran of A. C. Millspaugh, the administrator-general of the Finances of Persia after five years of service. Some of the reasons behind this action are examined. Valuable for the study of Reza Shah's period.

3 Blücher, Wipert von. Zeitenwende in Iran: Erlebnisse und Beobachtungen. Biberach an der Riss: Koehler & Voigtländer, 1949.
   The author's personal observations and experiences during his services in Iran as a German officer and ambassador in Tehran from 1931-1935. Policies of Reza Shah and a variety of other subjects are dealt with.

4 Bullard, Reader William. The Camels Must Go. London: Faber and Faber, 1961.
   Memoir of a former British ambassador to Iran.

5 "The Dictatorship of Reza Shah." Central Asian Review. 10(4): 398-405, 1962.
   Summarizes the Russian scholar O. S. Melikov's Ustanovleniye Diktatury Reza-Shakha v Irane [The Establishment of Reza Shah's Dictatorship in Iran] (Moscow: Institut Narodov Azii, 1961.) Melikov discusses Reza Shah's coup d'état and the series of maneuvers by which he rose to power and established the Pahlavi dynasty.

6 Elwell-Sutton, L. P. Modern Iran. London: G. Routledge & Sons, 1941.
Following an introductory description of Iran's geographic location and history, the author devotes most of his attention to the Reza Shah's regime. Contains several useful appendices including the Factory Act of August 10, 1936 and Saadabad Pact of July 8, 1937.

7 _____. "Reza Shah the Great: Founder of the Pahlavi Dynasty." In: Lenczowski, George (ed.), Iran Under the Pahlavis. Stanford, California: Hoover Institution Press, 1978. Pages 1-50.
An essay by a prominent authority on Iran describing the life and career of Reza Shah. Born in 1878, Reza Khan was an officer in the Cossack Brigade. Highly intelligent and patriotic, he engineered a coup d'état in 1921 and became minister of war and later prime minister in the new government. Following a series of events and maneuvers by Reza Khan, in 1925 the Parliament declared the end of the Qajar dynasty and soon thereafter he was proclaimed Shah by the Constituent Assembly. He introduced major reforms in Iran until 1941 when following a series of events during WW II, he was forced to abdicate on behalf of his son, Mohammad Reza Pahlavi. Reza Shah died in exile in 1944. More detailed biographical accounts are contained in other sources such as the ones cited in entries 8-9, 26-29, and especially 38.

8 Essad, Bey. Reza Schah: Feldherr, Kaiser, Reformator. Wien/Leipzig: R. Passer, 1936.
Most biographies of Reza Shah, such as this one, are in reality accounts of his achievements and the biographical passages they contain are inaccurate and sketchy. This particular study is also somewhat weakened by the author's uncritical treatment of his subject.

9 _____. Reza Shah. London: Hutchinson and Co., Ltd., 1938.
Reza Shah's childhood as well as his achievements before and after he became king in 1925 are discussed. This important work describes Iran's political and economic conditions during that time.

10 Farmanfarmaian, Hafez. Fall of the Qajar Dynasty. Ph.D. dissertation, Georgetown University, 1954.
The political events that led to Reza Shah's rise to power are described.

11 Filmer, Henry. The Pageant of Persia: A Record of Travel by Motor in Persia with an Account of Its Ancient and Modern Ways. Indianapolis, Indiana: Bobbs-Merrill, 1936.
Henry Filmer is the pseudonym of James Rives Childs, an American diplomat visiting Iran in the 1930's who was

12 Grey, W. G. "Recent Persian History." Journal of the Royal
    Central Asian Society. 13:29-42, 1926.
        Text of a lecture delivered before the meeting of the Central Asian Society on November 12, 1925. The emphasis is on Reza Khan's (later to become Reza Shah) achievements just before the foundation of the Pahlavi dynasty. At the time of this lecture Reza Khan was prime minister and his efforts in establishing a republic in Iran, following Kemal Ataturk's model whom he admired, had been unsuccessful mainly because of the clergy's opposition to this idea and insistence on a monarchy. Almost one month later, a constituent assembly elected Reza Khan as Shah who adopted the dynastic name of Pahlavi.

13 Haas, William S. Iran. New York: Columbia University
    Press, 1946.
        An introductory work on Iran. A survey of Persian civilization since earliest times is presented. However, the reign of Reza Shah Pahlavi has received special treatment. Reprinted in 1966 by the same publisher.

14 Harding, Clifford H. The World Position of Iran as Affected
    by the Work of Reza Shah. Ph. D. dissertation, New York
    University, 1954.
        Describes Iran's condition before Reza Shah's rise to power. Examines his internal reforms as well as foreign policy which enabled Iran to gain respect abroad.

15 Hugessen, Hughe Montgomery Knatchbull. A Diplomat in Peace
    and War. London: John Murray, 1949.
        In this autobiography Sir Hugessen recalls his diplomatic activities in various countries. Chapter Eight, "Minister in Persia (1934-1936)" throws some light on the Reza Shah's period. He was British minister to Tehran during that period.

16 Kassin, A. M. "Le 'Réveil Nationaliste (Pehlevi)' en Perse."
    Revue du Monde Musulman. 61:163-204, 1925.

17 Knapp, Wilfrid. "1921-1941: The Period of Riza Shah." In:
    Amirsadeghi, Hossein (ed.), Twentieth-Century Iran. New
    York: Holmes & Meier, 1977. Pages 23-51.
        Describes the emergence of Reza Shah and Iran's condition prior to his rise to power. His establishment of order in the country as well as his internal and external achievements are discussed.

18 Kohn, Hans. A History of Nationalism in the East. New York:
    Harcourt, Brace and Co., 1929.

This is a translation of the German edition published in 1928. Chapter X entitled "Changes in Persia and Afghanistan" contains some information on Reza Shah's attempts to revive nationalism in Iran. Translated by Margaret M. Green.

19 Mahrad, Ahmad. Die Deutsch-Persischen Beziehungen von 1918-1933. Bern: Herbert Lang, 1974.
A detailed discussion of Reza Shah's foreign affairs including relations with Germany. Also discusses Reza Shah's coup d'état and his coming to power. Contains reproduction of several original documents.

20 _____. Dokumentation über die Persisch-Deutschen Beziehungen von 1918-1933. Bern: Herbert Lang; Frankfurt/Main: Peter Lang, 1975.
Supplement to the author's Die Deutsch-Persischen Beziehungen von 1918-1933.

21 _____. Iran unter der Herrschaft Reza Schahs. Frankfurt/Main; New York: Campus-Verlag, 1977.
Critical treatment of Reza Shah making extensive use of German as well as other sources. Includes documents in English, French, and Persian. A detailed bibliography accompanies the text.

22 Melzig, Herbert. Resa Schah: Die Aufstieg Irans und die Grossmächte. Stuttgart: Union Deutsche Verlagsgesellschaft, 1936.
This study of Reza Shah is weakened by the uncritical admiration and laudatory style in which the author treats his subject.

23 Millspaugh, Arthur C. The American Task in Persia. New York: Arno Press, 1973.
Contains information on Reza Shah's early career as the first Pahlavi king. (Reprint of 1925 edition published by Century Co.)

24 Monterisi, Mario. Iran. Milano: Istituto per gli Studi di Politica Internazionale, 1941.
A general history of Iran up to the early 1940's. Chapter IX is devoted to the Reza Shah period.

25 Moulvi, A. M. Modern Iran. Bombay: Saif Azad, 1938.
Contains some useful information on Reza Shah's period and his efforts to modernize Iran.

26 Pahlavi, Mohammad Reza. Mission for My Country. New York: McGraw-Hill, 1961.
In Chapter Two of this autobiography entitled, "My Father and His Revolution," a first-hand account of Reza Shah's life and achievements is given by his son and successor.

27 _____. Resa Shah der Grosse. Tehran: (?), 195-(?).
Biographical account of the founder of the Pahlavi dynasty, Reza Shah, by his son and successor. Translated into several other languages including French and English. See next two entries.

28 _____. Réza Chah le Grand. Tehran:(?), 196-(?).
Translated from Persian by M. Chahkar, this is the French version of the publication cited in the previous entry.

29 _____. Reza Shah the Great. Tehran:(?), 195-(?).
Translated from Persian by M. Varasteh. English translation of the same publications as the two previous entries.

30 "Persian Affairs." Journal of the Royal Central Asian Society. 14:177-178, 1927.
A report of events in Persia during the early period of Reza Shah's reign. Among subjects discussed are Reza Shah's coronation, development in the Sixth Majlis (the Iranian Parliament), suppression of rebellions in various parts of the country, and Millspaugh's activities in Iran.

31 "La Révolte du Khouzistan et du Fars." Asie Française. 30 (280): 176-179, 1930.
The confrontation of Reza Shah's government with uprisings in Khuzistan and Fars provinces is discussed. The latter, in which the Qashqai tribes were involved, is considered more serious.

32 Rezun, Miron. "Reza Shah's Court Minister: Teymourtash." International Journal of Middle East Studies. 12(2):119-137, 1980.
Leadership and activities of Reza Shah's Court Minister, Abdul Hossein Khan Teymourtash are discussed. Teymourtash played a key role in Iranian foreign affairs and negotiated many treaties as well as economic agreements.

33 "The Rise and Fall of Teymourtache." Journal of the Royal Central Asian Society. 21:93, 1934.
A short biography of Teymourtash, former court minister of Reza Shah. He died in prison in October 1933.

34 "Riza Shah Pahlevi, 1925-1941." Journal of the Royal Central Asian Society. 28:444-445, 1941.
This very brief article attempts to sum up the Reza Shah's accomplishments on the occasion of the end of his career as Iran's ruler and the succession of his son, Mohammad Reza Pahlavi in 1941.

35 Saklatvala, Phiroz D. The Rich Fields in Persia. Bombay: The Iran League, 1933.
Originally a Parsi and residing in the U.S. at the time of

writing this booklet, the author attempts to provide general information on Iran of the Reza Shah period.

36 Sheean, Vincent. The New Persia. New York: The Century Co., 1927.
Includes information on Reza Shah in his early career. Political and economic conditions of Iran during that period are also examined.

37 Smith, Douglas L. "The Millspaugh Mission and American Corporate Diplomacy in Persia, 1922-27." Southern Quarterly, 14(2):151-172, 1976.
Activities of Arthur C. Millspaugh, administrator general of the finances of Iran in the 1920's are discussed. His relations with Iranian leaders and his influence on foreign affairs are examined.

38 Wilber, Donald Newton. Riza Shah Pahlavi: The Resurrection and Reconstruction of Iran. Hicksville, New York: Exposition Press, 1975.
Biography of the founder of the Pahlavi dynasty. This is a useful and comprehensive source on the subject, especially in light of the paucity of materials in this area. The author makes use of many Persian materials in addition to other languages. An extensive bibliography is included with annotations provided for the Persian sources.

39 Wilson, Arnold T. Persia. New York: Charles Scribner's Sons, 1933.
Contains useful information related to the reign of Reza Shah.

40 Yapp, Malcolm E. "1900-1921: The Last Years of the Qajar Dynasty." In: Amirsadeghi, Hossein (ed.), Twentieth-Century Iran. New York: Holmes & Meier, 1977. Pages 1-22.
Describes Iran's condition during the pre-Pahlavi era including the weakness of the central government during the last Qajar king, Ahmad Shah, and other problems which motivated Reza Khan, an officer in the Cossack Brigade and Seyyed Zia al-Din Tabatabai, a pro-British journalist, to plan a coup which occurred on February 21, 1921.

RECONSTRUCTION, REFORM, AND WESTERNIZATION UNDER REZA SHAH

41 "Affairs in Persia." Journal of the Royal Central Asian Society. 15:84-88, 1928.
A report of social, political and economic developments in the second year of Reza Shah's regime. The Russo-Persian treaty of friendship and neutrality, the abolition of capitulations, and Reza Shah's efforts to Westernize Iran are discussed.

42 Amouzegar, Parviz. "The Influence of Kemalism on Reza Shah's Reforms." Journal of the Regional Cultural Institute. 7(1): 31-38, 1974.
The influence of Kemal Ataturk (1881-1938), the Turkish reformer, and his ideas on Reza Shah's actions are examined. Although this influence was great, Reza Shah did not go as far as Ataturk in implementing his reforms, for example, in his treatment of the clergy. Both leaders, however, created a strong sense of nationalism and pursued a foreign policy which emphasized independence.

43 Arfa, Prince. "Rapport sur le Statut International de la Perse." Académie Diplomatique Internationale. Séances et Travaux. 7-12:47-50, 1929.
A report on the international status of Iran in the late 1920's summarizing Reza Shah's achievements inside Iran and in relation with other nations. The country's membership in the League of Nations and having a seat on the council are emphasized.

44 Banani, Amin. The Modernization of Iran, 1921-1941. Stanford, California: Stanford University Press, 1961.
Based primarily on Persian sources, this study deals with the impact of the West on Iran and Reza Shah's attempts at Westernization. Following a background history, the Westernization of various sectors such as the army, civil administration, education, public health, and judiciary are discussed. However, some aspects of Westernization initiated by Reza Shah, for example changes in the status of women, are not covered.

45 Bonn, A. G. "The Trans-Iranian Railway." Journal of the Royal Central Asian Society. 25:219-227, 1938.
    Considered a major achievement of Reza Shah, the scheme for the Trans-Iranian Railway was approved in 1926 and the project was completed in 1938. This article gives a detailed account of its construction.

46 Bourke-Burrowes, D. "Changes and Development in Persia During the Pahlavi Regime." Journal of the Royal Central Asian Society. 18:39-49, 1931.
    A survey of internal changes and developments in Iran (known to the West as Persia until 1935) since the accession to the throne of Reza Shah on December 15, 1925 until 1931. Developments in the army, transportation, judicial, and financial systems which occurred during the first six years of Reza Shah's rule are examined.

47 Boyce, Annie Stocking. "Moslem Women in the Capital of Persia." Moslem World. 20(3):265-269, 1930.
    Discusses Reza Shah's efforts at emancipation of women. The unveiling of women in public is described as an example of these efforts.

48 Conolly, Violet. "The Industrialization of Persia." Journal of the Royal Central Asian Society. 22:454-463, 1935.
    An account of the author's observation during a visit to Iran. She is critical of the rapid industrialization going on under Reza Shah. Asserts that some Iranian leaders regard machinery as a means to achieve equality with great nations.

49 Forbes, Rosita. "British and Russian Relations With Modern Persia." Journal of the Royal Central Asian Society. 18:74-81, 1931.
    Although economic relations of Russia and Great Britain with Iran during the Reza Shah's regime is the subject of this article, the bulk of the material is devoted to the social and political developments of Iran during this period.

50 Furstenau, G. Das Verkehrswesen Irans. Sagan: Krause, 1935.
    This is the most complete monograph on the roads and communications of Iran during Reza Shah's regime.

51 Graefe, Axel von. Iran: Das Neue Persien. Berlin: Atlantis-Verlag, 1937.
    A brief text accompanied with over one hundred photographs showing the new and the old in Iran.

52 Hesse, Fritz. "Zur Abschaffung der Kapitulationen in Persien." Europäische Gespräche. 7(7):358-373, 1929.
    Abolition of capitulations is considered one of the major achievements of Reza Shah. This article discusses the agreement between Germany and Iran in 1929 regarding the abolition of capitulations.

53 Hopper, Bruce. "The Persian Regensis." Foreign Affairs. 13(2):295-308, 1935.
A brief and general discussion of Reza Shah and his reforms. The last section examines Iran's significance in world politics.

54 Lee, Lester A. The Reforms of Reza Shah: 1925-1941. Master's thesis, Stanford University, 1950.

55 "A Letter from Tehran." Journal of the Royal Central Asian Society. 21:89-92, 1934.
A report of events which occurred from November 1932 to November 1934. This report shows that Iran was moving rapidly toward industrialization and gaining self-sufficiency under Reza Shah's regime.

56 Migliorini, Elio. Strade e Commercio dell'Iran. Messina: Giuseppe Principato, 1939.
This work is especially important for its authoritative survey of the construction of the Trans-Iranian Railway, built during Reza Shah's reign.

57 "Persian Transport Development." World's Carriers. 25(296): 404-406, 1929.
Describes the efforts made by Reza Shah to improve roads and transportation in Iran. The famine in Tehran in the winter of 1925-1926 was averted through efforts of a trucking service organized by the American Financial Mission.

58 Polacco, Angelo. L'Iran di Rezà Scià Pahlavi. Venezia: Zanetti, 1937.
Social and economic achievements of Reza Shah are discussed. Contains a reliable survey of the construction of the Trans-Iranian Railway in which a number of Italian firms were involved.

59 "Railways in Persia: Trans-Persian Railway." Journal of the Royal Central Asian Society. 14:340-343, 1927.
A discussion of Reza Shah's efforts in constructing the Trans-Persian Railway is followed after a brief background history of railway construction in Iran.

60 "Recent Developments in Persia." Journal of the Royal Central Asian Society. 13:130-132, 1926.
A year after the foundation of the Pahlavi dynasty, this article is a report of certain developments under Reza Shah's new regime. Passing of the Railway Bill which provided for the engagement of American and German railway engineers, economic relations with Russia, and increasing American influence in Iran are among subjects mentioned. The last part of the article is a brief account of Reza Shah's characteristics and leadership abilities.

61 Rossi, Ettore. "La Riforma Linguistica nell'Iran." <u>Oriente Moderno</u>. 19(9):516-519, 1939.
   Useful for studying Reza Shah's campaign for purifying the Persian language and purging it of words of Arabic or other foreign origin. These efforts led to the foundation of an Iranian Academy or Farhangestan.

62 Setoudeh, Hassan. <u>L'évolution Economique de l'Iran et ses Problèmes</u>. Paris: Librairie Technique et Economique, 1936.
   Economic achievement of Reza Shah's government are outlined. Causes underlying Iran's lack of economic growth after the Safavid period are examined and Reza Shah's effort to alleviate them are discussed.

63 Siyassi, Ali-Akbar. <u>La Perse au Contact de l'Occident</u>. Paris: Ernest Leroux, 1931.
   A well-informed survey of Iran in international relations in modern times with a focus on Reza Shah's period. Cultural and political effects of contact with the West are examined. Originally presented as the author's thesis, University of Paris.

64 Stürzenacker, Walter. "Vom Bau der Transpersischen Bahn." <u>Bau-Ingenieur-Zeitschrift für das Gesamte Bauwesen</u>. 12(43): 759-764, 1931.
   Improvement in transportation in Iran under Reza Shah and the building of the Trans-Persian Railway are discussed.

65 Thompson, W.J. "Iran: 1939-1944." <u>Journal of the Royal Central Asian Society</u>. 32:34-43, 1945.
   Surveys changes and developments during World War II in Iran. Gives a detailed account of Reza Shah's social reforms.

66 Vassenhove, L. van. "La Politique Etrangère de la Perse." <u>Revue Politique et Parlementaire</u>. 145(433):419-433, 1930.

67 Wilson, Arnold T. "The Next Twenty Years in Asia: A Survey and a Forecast." <u>Journal of the Royal Central Asian Society</u>. 19(3):373-411, 1932.
   A survey of Asian countries including Iran during the early 1930's.

68 _____. "The Road to Isfahan." <u>Asiatic Review</u>. 26(85): 158-167, 1930.
   A description of roads in Iran during this period.

69 Young, T.C. "The Problem of Westernization in Modern Iran." <u>Middle East Journal</u>. 2(1):47-59, 1948.
   The impact of the West on Iran from the Safavid period to the end of Reza Shah's rule is examined.

WW II, REZA SHAH'S ABDICATION, AND THE AFTERMATH

70 Andrews, William R. "The Azerbaijan Incident: The Soviet Union in Iran, 1941-46." Military Review. 54(8):74-85, 1974.
    The Azerbaijan crisis after World War II and Stalin's attempt to establish a people's republic in that province are discussed. Final withdrawal of the Soviet troops and the United States' role in this crisis are examined.

71 Bullard, Reader. "Persia in the Two World Wars." Journal of the Royal Central Asian Society. 50:6-20, 1963.
    The events in Iran during the two world wars, in which she remained legally neutral, are discussed.

72 Churchill, Winston L. S. The Second World War. New York: Houghton Mifflin Co., 1948-50.
    Volume 3, Chapter 26 presents the most detailed and authoritative account of the circumstances leading to the occupation of Iran by the Allies in 1941.

73 Cottam, Richard. "The United States, Iran and the Cold War." Iranian Studies. 3:2-22, 1970.
    Asserts that American policy in postwar Iran was designed to thwart a Soviet thrust in the Persian Gulf area.

74 Doenecke, Justus D. "Iran's Role in Cold War Revisionism." Iranian Studies. 5(2-3):96-111, 1972.
    Examines the facts about the origins of the cold war and Iran's role in it from a revisionist point of view.

75 _____. "Revisionists, Oil and Cold War Diplomacy." Iranian Studies. 3:23-33, 1970.
    An evaluation of revisionist view of the origins of the cold war in Iran.

76 Eagleton, William. The Kurdish Republic of 1946. London: Oxford University Press, 1963.
    The Soviet-backed Kurdish Republic, formed in Iran shortly after World War II, is discussed in detail.

77 Elwell-Sutton, L. P. "Iran and the Modern World." Journal of the Royal Central Asian Society, 29:120-128, 1942.

Reviews the events in Iran during World War II and after abdication of Reza Shah. Iran's difficulties of adjustment in a period of transition are detailed.

78 Farboud, Homayoun. L'évolution Politique de l'Iran Pendant la Seconde Guerre Mondiale. Lausanne: Payot, 1957.
Political evolution of Iran during World War II is presented. Iran's historical background, her relationship with super powers as well as her internal affairs are discussed.

79 Fleming, D. F. The Cold War and Its Origins. Garden City, N. Y.: Doubleday, 1961.
Another revisionist view of the origins of cold war in Iran and Turkey.

80 Great Britain. Central Office of Information. Paiforce: The Official Story of Persian and Iraq Command, 1941-1946. London: H. M. Stationery Office, 1948.
The military record of Iran and Iraq in the Second World War from the British side.

81 Hamzavi, A. H. "Iran and the Tehran Conference." International Affairs. 20:192-203, 1944.
Discusses the significance of the Tehran Conference for Iran in which the Allied leaders, President Franklin D. Roosevelt, Prime Minister Winston Churchill, and Prime Minister Joseph Stalin, agreed in the Tehran Declaration to give economic assistance to Iran after World War II and to respect its independence, territorial integrity, and sovereignty.

82 _____. "Iran's Future: Some Lessons from the Past." Journal of the Royal Central Asian Society. 31:273-280, 1944.
Difficulties faced by Iran because of World War II are outlined and the future prospects after the war are examined. The Anglo-Iranian relation is emphasized.

83 _____. Persia and the Powers: An Account of Diplomatic Relations, 1941-1946. London, New York: Hutchinson, 1946.
Discusses Iran's role in the two world wars with an emphasis on her contributions to World War II. Outlines the developments in Iran after World War II.

84 Harbutt, Fraser J. The Fulton Speech and the Iran Crisis of 1946: A Turning Point in American Foreign Policy. Ph. D. dissertation, University of California, Berkeley, 1976.

85 Hess, Gary R. "The Iranian Crisis of 1945-46 and the Cold War." Political Science Quarterly. 89(1):117-146, 1974.
Reviews the 1945-46 Azerbaijan crisis and the role of the Soviet-American struggle for power in Iran. The role of United Nations in resolving the crisis is also emphasized.

86 Hindus, Maurice. In Search of a Future: Persia, Egypt, Iraq, Israel. New York: Doubleday, Doran, 1949.
This study includes a journalist's account of Iran in post-World War II era. Contains some valuable factual information about that period.

87 Hirschfeld, Yair P. "Irans Bedeutung für die Deutsche Kriegswirtschaft: Vom Beginn des Zweiten Weltkrieges bis zur Anglo-Russischen Besetzung Irans im August 1941." Jahrbuch des Institut für Deutsche Geschichte. 7:421-445, 1978.
The importance of Iran to the German war economy during World War II is examined. The author contends that Iran's contribution was not significant.

88 Iran. Ministry of Foreign Affairs. The Tehran Conference: The Three-Power Declaration Concerning Iran, December 1943. Iran: Ministry of Foreign Affairs, 1945.
"The text of the Triparties treaty, the Atlantic charter, and a brief account of the Moscow conference." Published in commemoration of the Tehran Conference.

89 Irani, Ghobad. American Diplomacy: An Option Analysis for the Azerbaijan Crisis, 1945-1946. Hyattsville, Maryland: Institute of Middle Eastern and North African Affairs, 1978.
An analysis of the U.S. policy toward the Azerbaijan crisis at the close of the Second World War.

90 Kazemzadeh, Hossein. Iran and Post-War Political Issues: Policy Reflections in the United Nations. Ph.D. dissertation, Princeton University, 1954.
Discusses how Iranian delegation to the U.N. has asserted itself on postwar political issues. As an example, one of the issues discussed in Chapter Five is the Anglo-Iranian Oil Company case of 1951 and the U.N.'s role in that case.

91 Kovac, John Eugene. Iran and the Beginning of the Cold War: A Case Study in the Dynamics of International Politics. Ph.D. dissertation, University of Utah, 1970.
This study deals with Iranian politics during World War II with an emphasis on the years 1944-1947.

92 Kuniholm, Bruce Robellet. The United States, the Northern Tier, and the Origins of the Cold War: Great Power Conflict and Diplomacy in Iran, Turkey, and Greece. Ph.D. dissertation, Duke University, 1976.
Attempts to demonstrate how the power conflict along the Northern Tier (the northern Middle Eastern countries on the border of the Soviet Union) was a major factor in the origins of the cold war between the United States and the U.S.S.R.

93 Lambton, A.K.S. "Persia." Journal of the Royal Central Asian Society. 31:8-22, 1944.

Discusses the effects of Westernization on Iran and analyzes some of the problems which led to the chaotic condition after Reza Shah abdicated in favor of his son Mohammad Reza Pahlavi.

94 _____. "Some Aspects of the Situation in Persia." Asiatic Review. 39:420-425, 1943.
    A brief discussion on internal developments in 1942 and 1943.

95 _____. "Some of the Problems Facing Persia." International Affairs. 22:254-272, 1946.
    Post-World War II difficulties facing Iran and problems arising from the relations with the Soviet Union and Great Britain are discussed.

96 Mahrad, Ahmad. Iran am Vorabend des II. Weltkrieges: Eine Materialsammlung Deutscher, Britischer und Sowjetischer Geheimberichte. Osnabrück: Eigenverlag A. Mahrad, 1978.

97 Mark, Edward M. "Allied Relations in Iran, 1941-1947: The Origins of a Cold War Crisis." Wisconsin Magazine of History. 59(1):51-63, 1975.
    The causes underlying the events during and after World War II in Iran, which led to conflicts between Iran and the Soviet Union and the development of a cold war crisis between the United States and the Soviet Union, are examined.

98 Motter, Thomas Hubbard Vail. The Persian Corridor and Aid to Russia. Washington: Office of Military History, Dept. of the Army, 1952 (United States Army in World War II. V. 7, Part 1: The Middle East Theater.)
    A history of the United States Army activity in the "Persian corridor" including Iran during the war years of 1941-1945 for the purpose of supplying the Soviet Union and the Allies with military aid.

99 Ramazani, Rouhollah K. "The Autonomous Republic of Azerbaijan and the Kurdish People's Republic: Their Rise and Fall." Studies on the Soviet Union. 11(4):401-427, 1971.
    The history of two Soviet-backed Communist regimes in Iran after World War II is presented.

100 "Recent Events in Persia." Journal of the Royal Central Asian Society. 37:81-82, 1950.
    A summary report of some of the events in Iran in 1950. Among the major events discussed are the visit of American technical and economic experts to Iran and the Shah's visit to the United States.

101 Roosevelt, Archie. "The Kurdish Republic of Mahabad." Middle East Journal. 1(3):247-269, 1947.

102 Rosenberg, J. Philip. "The Cheshire Ultimatum: Truman's Message to Stalin in the 1946 Azerbaijan Crisis." Journal of Politics. 41(3):933-940, 1979.
The author's response to James A. Thorpe's article (see entry 114). The author asserts that Thorpe disregarded archival information on this matter and tries to confirm the claim that Truman gave Stalin an ultimatum which forced the Soviet withdrawal from Azerbaijan in 1946.

103 Rossow, Robert. "The Battle of Azerbaijan, 1946." Middle East Journal. 10(1):17-32, 1956.
The occupation of the Northwestern Iranian province of Azerbaijan by the Soviet army on March 4, 1946 and the outcome of that event are detailed in this article.

104 Royal Institute of International Affairs. Chronology of the Second World War. London: Royal Institute of International Affairs, 1947.
A useful reference work for the study of Iran during the 1939-1945 war.

105 Sadr-Nabawi, Rampur. Die Wirtschaft des Iran während des Zweiten Weltkrieges. Heidelberg: Ruprecht Karl Universität, 1968.
Iran's economic conditions during World War II are discussed. Economic problems as well as the role of oil in Iranian economy are analyzed.

106 Sayre, Joel. Persian Gulf Command: Some Marvels on the Road to Kazvin. New York: Random House, 1945.
The military record of Iran in the Second World War from the American side.

107 Scarcia, Gianroberto. "La Persia Durante la Seconda Guerra Mondiale: Materiali e Documenti." Oriente Moderno. 46: 269-343, 1966.
Contains documents regarding Iran during World War II with an emphasis on her international position in 1941-45.

108 Schulze-Holthus, Bernhard. Daybreak in Iran. London: Staples, 1954.
Translation of Frühort in Iran. Translated by Mervyn Savill. See next entry.

109 _____. Frühort in Iran. Esslingen: Bechtle, 1952.
The author, a German officer in the intelligence section of the Wehrmacht, retells the story of his espionage activities in Iran during the Second World War.

110 Sherwen, Douglas S. The Persian Corridor: The Little-Known Story of Signal Corps in the Middle East During World War II. Hicksville, New York: Exposition Press, 1979.
Military activities of the 833rd Signal Service Company during the Second World War in Iran. Autobiographical.

111 Skrine, Clarmont P. World War in Iran. London: Constable, 1962.
A relatively detailed account of events in Iran during the Second World War and its aftermath including the Azerbaijan incident.

112 Steppat, Fritz. Iran Zwischen den Grossmächten, 1941-1948: Eine Historisch-Politische Studie. Oberursel, Taunus: Europa-Archiv, 1948.
A political and historical survey of Iran's struggle with superpowers during World War II. Also useful for its coverage of postwar crisis over Azerbaijan.

113 Thompson, W.J. "Conditions of Daily Life in Iran, 1947." Journal of the Royal Central Asian Society. 35:199-208, 1948.
The author, who was an Anglican bishop in Iran, attempts to give a picture of Iran in 1947 and the social and cultural developments that occurred in Iran after Reza Shah's rise to power.

114 Thorpe, James A. "Truman's Ultimatum to Stalin on the 1946 Azerbaijan Crisis: The Making of a Myth." Journal of Politics. 40(1):188-195, 1978.
Attempts to disprove the claim that Harry S. Truman gave Stalin an ultimatum which forced the Soviet Union to withdraw its troops from Azerbaijan in 1946.

115 United Nations. General Assembly. 1st Session, 1946. Delegation from Iran. Compilation of Documents Prepared by the Representative of Iran for Convenient Reference in the Consideration by the Security Council of the Disputes Between Iran and the Union of Soviet Socialist Republics. New York: (?), 1946.

116 Van Wagenen, Richard W. and Young, T.C. The Iranian Case, 1946. New York: Carnegie Endowment for International Peace, 1952.
The role of the United Nations in resolving the dispute between Iran and the Soviet Union and the resulting withdrawal of the Soviet troops from Iran are presented.

4
MOSSADEQ AND NATIONALIZATION OF OIL, 1951-1953

117 Abbeg, L. "Als Augenzeuge im Persien Razmaras: Erdöl-Nationalismus und Kalter Krieg." Zeitschrift für Geopolitik. 22:168-176, 1951.
Useful for the study of post-World War II oil crisis in Iran.

118 Anglo-Iranian Oil Company, Ltd. A Report on the History of the Southern Oil of Iran: Presented by the National Oil Company of Iran to the Honourable Averell Harriman, Special Envoy of the President of the United States of America. Tehran: Bank Melli Iran Press, 1951.
A booklet presenting a very brief history of the Iranian oil industry. The last chapter is entitled: "The Dangers of Non-Execution of the Nationalisation Laws Concerning Oil."

119 Atyeo, Henry C. "Political Developments in Iran 1951-1954." Middle Eastern Affairs. 5:249-259, 1955.
The events which occurred in Iran during 1951-1954 are discussed. The government of Mossadeq, the fall of his government, and the events following his arrest are outlined.

120 Bayne, E. A. "Crisis of Confidence in Iran." Foreign Affairs. 29(4):578-590, 1951.
The political crisis in Iran during Mossadeq's regime is examined.

121 Bullard, Reader. "Behind the Oil Dispute in Iran: A British View." Foreign Affairs. 31(3):461-471, 1953.
Discusses Sir Reader's views on the Anglo-Iranian oil dispute of the early 1950's.

122 Carrère d'Encausse, H. "Le Conflit Anglo-Iranien 1951-1954." Revue Française de Science Politique. 15(4):731-743, 1965.
Reviews the Anglo-Iranian oil conflict and its consequences for both countries.

123 Cheng, B. "The Anglo-Iranian Dispute." World Affairs. 4: 387-405, 1951.
Studies the oil dispute between Iran and Great Britain according to international law.

124 "Dr. Musaddiq and After." World Today. 9(10):421-429, 1953.
The successes and failures of the Mossadeq regime are
examined. Mossadeq's relations with the Tudeh party are
analyzed.

125 Efimenco, N. M. "An Experiment with Civilian Dictatorship:
The Case of Mohammed Mossadegh." Journal of Politics.
17(3):390-406, 1955.
Discusses the downfall of Mossadeq's government and factors contributing to it.

126 Eisenhower, Dwight D. Mandate for Change, 1953-1956: The
White House Years. New York: Doubleday, 1963.
This memoir contains important information regarding the
American role in the Iranian oil crisis of the 1950's.

127 Engler, Robert. The Politics of Oil: A Study of Private Power
and Democratic Directions. New York: Macmillan, 1961.
American role in the Iranian oil crisis of the 1950's is
discussed. Claims that private American oil companies
pressured the U.S. government during the World War II to
assume an aggressive role in making policies regarding
Middle Eastern oil.

128 Fatemi, Nasrollah S. Oil Diplomacy: Powderkeg in Iran.
New York: Whittier Books, 1954.
Examines the Western power rivalries in Iran for the
control of Iranian oil.

129 Ford, Alan W. The Anglo-Iranian Oil Dispute of 1951-1952:
A Study of the Role of Law in the Relations of States.
Berkeley: University of California Press, 1954.
Analyzes the oil controversy up to July 1952, when the
International Court of Justice dismissed Great Britain's application to submit the dispute to the court. The author
takes this issue as a case study to draw conclusions regarding the role of law in the relations between states.

130 Foster, Austin T. "An Unanswered Legal Problem Raised by
the Suez and the Iranian Controversies." In: American Society of International Law. International Law and the Middle
East Crisis: A Symposium. New Orleans: Tulane University, 1957. Pages 63-78.
A paper originally delivered at the regional meeting of
the American Society of International Law on April 6, 1957.
This study uses the Anglo-Iranian case of 1951 to discuss
the issue of unilateral abrogation of concession contracts
by states and problems posed by such action. A history of
the Anglo-Iranian Oil Company (AIOC) is presented.

131 Fredborg, Arvid. "Streit um Persiens Öl." Internationales
Jahrbuch der Politik. 1:34-54, 1955.
Records the development of the Iranian oil fields.

Discusses the causes of the oil crisis in Iran, which was led by the Iranian nationalist, Mossadeq.

132 Ghosh, Sunil Kanti. The Anglo-Iranian Oil Dispute: A Study of Problems of Nationalization of Foreign Investment and Their Impact on International Law. Calcutta: K.L. Mukhopadhyay, 1960.
After presenting a background on the history of the Anglo-Iranian Oil Company, the author discusses the sources and legal aspects of the dispute. The existing rules of international law relating to expropriation of foreign investment in general are also examined.

133 Great Britain. Foreign Office. Correspondence Between His Majesty's Government in the United Kingdom and the Persian Government, and Related Documents Concerning the Oil Industry in Persia, February 1951 to September 1951. London: H.M. Stationery Office, 1951.
Contains texts of several documents including "Anglo-Persian Oil Company's Convention of 29th April, 1933" and "Persian Oil Nationalization Law, 1st May, 1951."

134 Guyer, R.E. "El Conflicto Anglo-Persa." Revista del Instituto de Derecho Internacional. 4(15):207-218, 1951.
Examines the history of the oil concessions and the dispute between the Anglo-Iranian Oil Company (AIOC) and the Iranian government.

135 Hidayati, Muhammad Ali. Situation Politique et Sociale de l'Iran en 1950-1951, Année de la Nationalisation du Pétrole. Neuchâtel: Messeiller, 1965.

136 Hoveyda, Fereydoun. La Nationalisation des Industries Pétrolières en Iran. Paris, 1951.

137 Huici Poyales, F. "Aspectos Técnicos y Económicos de la Crisis del Petróleo Persa." Cuadernos de Política Internacional. 7:109-123, 1951.
Examines Iran's significance in regard to oil production and the economic consequences of the Iranian oil crisis of the early 1950's.

138 International Court of Justice. Anglo-Iranian Oil Co. Case (United Kingdom v. Iran) Judgment of July 22nd, 1952. The Hague, 1953(?).

139 Iran. Embassy. United States. Some Documents on the Nationalization of the Oil Industry in Iran. Washington, D.C., 1951.
On March 15, 1951, the Iranian Parliament, Majlis, voted to nationalize the Iranian oil industry following a series of disputes with the British government. This publication contains some of the documents related to this major event.

140 Iran. Prime Minister. The Text of the Prime Minister's Report to Majlis on the Development of Saheb-Gharanieh Oil Conference, Submitted at the Session of 30th Mordad, 1330 (August 22, 1951). Tehran: Bank Melli Iran Press, 1951.
   An important report by Prime Minister Mohammad Mossadeq during the Iranian oil crisis and only months after the Majlis and the Iranian Senate had voted for nationalization of oil in Iran.

141 Kemp, Norman. Abadan: A First-Hand Account of the Persian Oil Crisis. London: Wingate, 1953.
   A journalist's account of events in the Iranian oil city of Abadan at the height of the Iranian oil dispute in 1951.

142 Kirk, George E. The Middle East, 1945-50. London: Oxford University Press, 1954.
   Contains information which presents insight into the Iranian oil crisis of the 1950's. Relates American aid to Iran to the Iranian nationalization of the Anglo-Iranian Oil Co.

143 Lavrent'yev, A. K. "Mosaddeq's Role in the Events of 1951-1953." Central Asian Review. 9(3):302-306.
   Discusses Mossadeq's activities during 1951-1953. Translated from the Russian.

144 Lentz, W. Iran, 1951/1952. Heidelberg: K. Vowinckel, 1952.
   Contains a discussion of political and economic aspects of Iran's oil crisis of 1951-1952.

145 _____. "Sondervollmachten für Mossadegh." Zeitschrift für Geopolitik. 23(11):680-698, 1952.
   A sympathetic account of Iranian oil nationalization in 1951 which was led by the Iranian nationalist, Mohammad Mossadeq. Iran's social and political structures during this period are also examined.

146 _____. "Die Verstaatlichung der Ölindustrie in Iran." Zeitschrift für Geopolitik. 23(10):608-631, 1952.
   A historical review of oil industry and oil exploitation in Iran is presented. The positions of Iran and Great Britain in the oil dispute involving the Anglo-Iranian Oil Company are discussed.

147 Levy, Walter J. "Economic Problems Facing a Settlement of the Iranian Oil Controversy." Middle East Journal. 8:91-95, 1954.
   Reviews the principles that have been proposed to Iran for the settlement of the oil crisis of the Mossadeq period.

148 Lockhart, Laurence. "The Causes of the Anglo-Persian Oil Dispute." Journal of the Royal Central Asian Society. 40: 134-150, 1953.

Discusses the dispute between Iran and Great Britain which led to nationalization of the oil industry in Iran in 1951. Attempts to survey some of the causes of that dispute.

149 Lockwood, Rupert. Persian Oil. Sydney: Current Book Distributors, 1951.
This very brief booklet is an attack against the Anglo-Iranian Oil Company and a call for a peaceful flow of oil from Iran.

150 Macciocchi, Maria Antonietta. Persia in Lotta. Roma: Edizioni di Cultura Sociale, 1952.
An Italian leftist journalist's observations of Iranian politics. Supports Mossadeq and attacks Anglo-American influence in Iran.

151 McCrea, William S. A Comparative Study of the Mexican Oil Expropriation (1938) and the Iranian Oil Nationalization (1951). Ph.D. dissertation, Georgetown University, 1955.
An attempt to compare the Iranian oil nationalization with the Mexican oil expropriation in order to show a parallelism between the two. The work is divided into two basic sections. The first deals with the causes and the second involves the effects of expropriation and nationalization. One of the conclusions reached by the author is that "the United States should have recognized the parallelism in the causes for Mexican and Iranian nationalizations ... and should have applied the experience gained in the Mexican case."

152 Magnus, Ralph H. Documents on the Middle East. Washington, D.C.: American Enterprise Institute for Public Policy Research, 1969.
See entry 547.

153 Mossadeq, Mohammad. Discours sur la Nationalisation du Pétrole en Iran [Speech Concerning the Nationalization of Petroleum in Iran]. Tehran: The University Press, 1951.
An important document concerning Iranian oil nationalization by the leader of the National Front, Mohammad Mossadeq. This is the translation of his speech deliverd on December 17, 1950 in the Iranian Parliament. Contains texts in English as well as in French.

154 Naamani, Israel T. "Iran and Her Problems." Middle Eastern Affairs. 2:203-212, 1951.
Some of the social and political problems of Iran in the early 1950's are discussed. Among these are the oil crisis, the feudal system, the Kurds, etc.

155 Noori, Hossein Shiekh-Hosseini. A Study of the Nationalization of the Oil Industry in Iran. Ph.D. dissertation, University of Northern Colorado, 1965.

156 Price, Philips. "The Present Situation in Persia." Journal of the Royal Central Asian Society. 28:102-111, 1951.
A report of the author's observations during a visit to Iran. Describes the general situation in Iran in 1950. The emphasis is on the lack of attention given by the Iranian government to problems of land tenure and peasant poverty.

157 Razwy, A. A. "The Anglo-Iranian Oil Dispute." Pakistan Horizon. 6(2):75-85, 1953.
Supplies background information on the nationalization of the Iranian oil industry in 1951 and the dispute with Great Britain over this issue.

158 Roosevelt, Kermit. Countercoup: The Struggle for the Control of Iran. New York: McGraw-Hill, 1979.
The author discusses the alleged role of the United States and his own involvement in the CIA-engineered operation AJAX (a cryptonym) in 1953 in order to overthrow Mossadeq's government and reinstall the Shah.
Copies of the 1979 edition of this publication were recalled and withdrawn. A new version which contained significant yet subtle changes was released in 1980. For an interesting account see: Gallagher, Nancy E. and Wilson, Dunning S., "Suppression of Information or Publisher's Error?: Kermit Roosevelt's Memoir of the 1953 Iranian Countercoup." Middle East Studies Association Bulletin. 15(1):14-17, 1981.

159 Sablier, E. "La Signification de l'Affaire du Pétrole Iranien." Politique Etrangère. 18(1):16-22, 1953.
Discusses the background and the significance of the Anglo-Iranian oil dispute of the early 1950's.

160 Shwadran, Benjamin. "The Anglo-Iranian Oil Dispute 1948-1953." Middle Eastern Affairs. 5:193-231, 1954.
Nationalization of Iran's oil industry, a history of the Anglo-Iranian oil dispute, and the role of the United States and Great Britain are discussed.

161 Sinclair, Angus. "Iranian Oil." Middle Eastern Affairs. 2:213-224, 1951.
Discusses the history of oil concession in Iran and the events which led to the nationalization of the Iranian oil industry.

162 Stocking, George W. Middle East Oil: A Study in Political and Economic Controversy. Nashville: Vanderbilt University Press, 1970.
Iranian oil crisis of the 1950's is discussed. Concludes that the United States policy was an "aggressive" one in this crisis.

163 Tully, Andrew. CIA: The Inside Story. New York: Morrow, 1962.

The alleged role of the United States government and the CIA in the 1953 coup d'état that overthrew Mossadeq's government in Iran is discussed.

164 Young, T. C. "The Social Support of Current Iranian Policy." Middle East Journal. 6(2):128-143, 1952.
The social structure of Mossadeq's supporters is studied.

165 Zabih, Sepehr. The Mossadegh Era: Roots of the Iranian Revolution. Chicago: Lake View, 1982.
Utilizing primary Iranian sources as well as materials which became accessible only after the Shah's overthrow in 1979, this important work gives a detailed account of Mossadeq's era, his rise to power, and his downfall. A brief postscript attempts to study Mossadeq's "legacy for the 1979 revolution."

MOHAMMAD REZA PAHLAVI (THE SHAH) AND HIS WHITE REVOLUTION

166 Ahmadi, Ashraf. 12 Years in Constructing a New Iran, 1953-1964. Tehran: Central Council, Celebration of the 25th Century of the Foundation of the Iranian Empire, 1964(?).
Discusses the social and economic development during the period 1953-1964. Contains numerous graphs and charts.

167 Bayne, E. A. Persian Kingship in Transition: Conversations with a Monarch Whose Office Is Traditional and Whose Goal Is Modernization. New York: American Universities Field Staff, 1968.
The author presents the Shah's views on various issues related to politics and government of Iran as well as religion and Iranian people.

168 Bill, James A. "Modernization and Reform from Above: The Case of Iran." Journal of Politics. 32(1):19-40, 1970.
Studies the social and political changes in Iran resulting from the Shah's reforms which began in 1963 and came to be known as the "White Revolution." The author concludes that there is a challenge to be faced by the political elite of Iran, namely to make this modernization program work despite the political and social demands of the intellectual and professional classes.

169 Blanch, Lesley. Farah, Shahbanou of Iran, Queen of Persia. London: Collins, 1978.
Life story of Farah Diba, the Shah's queen since December 1959 when they married following the termination of the King's previous marriage in 1958. See also entry 186.

170 Edmonds, I. G. The Shah of Iran: The Man and His Land. New York: Holt, Rinehart and Winston, 1976.
A biographical account of the Shah and the Pahlavi dynasty's accomplishments. It also gives an informal survey of Iranian history.

171 Esfandiari, Soraya. Meine Eigene Geschichte. Bern: Phoenix Verlag, 1963.
This is the autobiography of the Shah's second queen. In

her autobiography, Soraya Esfandiari recalls her life as empress to the Shah, Mohammad Reza Pahlavi. She was born on June 22, 1932 in Isfahan, Iran. Her father was a member of the nomadic tribe of Bakhtiari and her mother, Eva Karl, a German. She married the Shah on February 12, 1951 replacing his first wife, Fawzia, who had been divorced in 1948. Soraya was married to the Shah for seven years. No child was born of this union and it ended in March 1958.

172 _____. Mi Vida. Barcelona: Editorial Juventud, 1964.
Spanish translation of the original German: Meine Eigene Geschichte. See previous entry.

173 _____. Soraya: The Autobiography of Her Imperial Highness. Garden City, N.Y.: Doubleday, 1964.
English translation of the original German, Meine Eigene Geschichte, the autobiography of the Shah's second queen from 1951 to 1958. See entry 171. Translated by Constantine Fitzgibbon.

174 Fallaci, Oriana. Interview with History. New York: Liveright, 1976.
English translation of the author's original Italian Intervista con la Storia by John Shepley. See next entry.

175 _____. Intervista con la Storia. Milano: Rizzoli, 1974.
The book is an account of interviews with fourteen political figures by a prominent Italian journalist. Chapter Eleven is devoted to the results of the author's interview with and her impression of the Shah. Various topics are discussed, including the Shah's foreign policy, oil, his views of women, repression in Iran, etc. Other individuals interviewed by Fallaci include Henry Kissinger, Indira Gandhi, and Yasir Arafat.

176 Fisher, Commodore S. "The Shah's White Revolution." Muslim World. Part I, 54 (2):98-103, 1964; Part II, 54(3):195-199, 1964.
Iranian land reform and emancipation of women are discussed. The forces opposing these reforms are also examined.

177 Friedman, Bruno. "The White Revolution and Iranian Culture: Interview with Farah Pahlavi, Empress of Iran." Impact of Science on Society. 22(1-2):9-28, 1972.
In this interview, the former queen comments on various cultural and social changes in Iran including the changes in Iranian women's social and political status, negative impact of technology on Iranian life, and the status of cottage industry in Iran.

178 Gil Benumeya, R. "El Shahinshah Reza Pahlavi en la Actualidad Mundial." Revista de Política Internacional. 138:137-

146, 1975.
Discusses the role of the Shah in international politics.

179 Greaves, Rose. "1942-1976: The Reign of Muhammad Riza Shah." In: Amirsadeghi, Hossein (ed.), Twentieth-Century Iran. New York: Holmes & Meier, 1977. Pages 53-91.
Surveys events in Iran since 1941 when Mohammad Reza Pahlavi ascended the throne following his father's abdication and up to 1976.

180 Gregory, Lois. The Shah and Persia. Orpington; Kent: Orpington Press, 1959.
A flattering account of the Shah's achievements. The book deals with a variety of subjects such as economics, foreign trade, education, etc. The fourth chapter is the text of the Shah's press conference held September 1958.

181 Hoyt, Edwin Palmer. The Shah: The Glittering Story of Iran and Its People. New York: P.S. Erikson, 1976.
Biography of Mohammad Reza Pahlavi up to 1975. After a brief background about his father, Reza Shah, the book discusses in great detail the Shah's private and political life.

182 Iran. Vizarat-i Ittilaat va Jahangardi. The Royal Road to Progress: A Survey of Achievements of the Shah-People Revolution. Tehran: Ministry of Information and Tourism, Publications Dept., 1974.
A public relations-type document depicting the social and economic effects of the White Revolution, which was initiated by the Shah in 1963.

183 Iran Press Services. Coronation of His Imperial Majesty the Shahanshah Arya Mehr of Iran and Her Imperial Majesty Empress Farah Pahlavi, October 26, 1976. Tehran: Iran PR Services, 1967(?).
Formal coronation of the Shah and his wife, Farah Diba, occurred on his forty-eighth birthday -- October 26, 1967. This document was published on that occasion and describes the event.

184 "Iran: The White Revolution." Current Notes on International Affairs. 42(7):353-361, 1971.
A sympathetic and optimistic discussion of the Shah's reform programs initiated in 1963. Part of the outcome is reviewed.

185 Karanjia, Rustom Khurshedji. The Mind of a Monarch. London: George Allen & Unwin, 1977.
A highly flattering biographical account of the Shah based on the author's interviews with him. The book is in a question-and-answer format and except for a brief background history, the entire book is devoted to the Shah's achievements.

186 Kurth, Hanns. Farah Diba und der Schah von Persien: Nach zeitgenössischen Quellen Frei bearbeitet von Heinz Offermann. Düsseldorf: Deutsche Buchvertriebs- und Verlags-Gesellschaft, 1962.

In December 1959, the Shah, after two previous marriages which had ended in divorce, married Farah Diba whose family was from the provinces of Azerbaijan and Gilan. This book discusses Farah Diba's life with the Shah of Iran using contemporary sources.

187 Laing, Margaret. The Shah. London: Sidgwick & Jackson, 1977.

A biography of the Shah. After a brief discussion of the Shah's father and the foundation of the Pahlavi dynasty, the book retells the life story of the Shah and his role in the Iranian government.

188 Mattison, Georgia. "The Celebration of Power." Liberation. 16(7):16-19, 1971.

A discussion of the Shah's relationship with Iranian peasantry. The author contends that the Shah's power is on the increase and the opposition to his government is kept in constant suppression.

189 Pahlavi, Farah. My Thousand and One Days: An Autobiography. London: W. H. Allen, 1978.

In this autobiography, Farah Diba retells her life story and her responsibilities as empress. Born in Tehran on October 14, 1938 she married the Shah, Mohammad Reza Pahlavi, in December 1959. On October 31, 1960 she bore an heir, Reza Cyrus, who was proclaimed crown prince by imperial decree on November 1, 1960. Farah Diba was crowned as the empress or Shahbanu (wife of the Shah) at the coronation of Mohammad Reza Pahlavi on October 26, 1967. She was active in several charitable organizations including Farah Pahlavi Charity Organization which was operated under her direction.

190 Pahlavi, Mohammad Reza. Answer to History. New York: Stein and Day, 1980.

English translation of the Shah's last autobiographical account published before his death in 1980 under the title Réponse à l'Histoire. See entry 194.

191 _____. Iran: Philosophy Behind the Revolution: A Selection of Writing and Speeches of the Shahanshah. London: Orient Commerce Establishment, 1971.

The book is divided into three parts. The first part, "Ancient Traditions to Modern Era," is an extract from the Shah's previous book Mission for My Country published in 1961. The second part is the text of The White Revolution which he published in 1967. The third part, "Iran in an Inter-Dependent World," is a collection of his speeches given to various academic institutions and international organizations. In these selections the Shah discusses his political and social ideologies.

192 _____. Mi Gloria y Mi Caída. Buenos Aires: Editorial Atlántida, 1980.
Spanish translation of the Shah's Réponse à l'Histoire. See entry 194. Translated by A. Dellepiane Rawson.

193 _____. Mission for My Country. New York: McGraw-Hill, 1961.
In this autobiography the Shah, in addition to his life story, discussed Iran's social and political problems and his views on various issues, from land reform and education to the role of women and modernization. Born in Tehran on October 26, 1919 he was officially proclaimed crown prince at the coronation of his father, Reza Shah. Upon abdication of his father on September 16, 1941, the Shah ascended the throne. Following two previous marriages with Fawzia and Soraya Esfandiari which had terminated in divorce, in 1959 he married Farah Diba who bore an heir, Reza Cyrus, on October 31, 1960.

194 _____. Réponse à l'Historie. Paris: A. Michel, 1979.
The Shah's last autobiographical account, written before his death in 1980. He discussed his role in Iran's history. This book has been translated into English under the titles Answer to History and The Shah's Story. See entries 190 and 196

195 _____. Riposta alla Storia: Il Testamento Politico e Morale dello Scià. Milano: Editoriale Nuova, 1980.
Italian version of the original French Réponse à l'Histoire. See previous entry.

196 _____. The Shah's Story. London: M. Joseph, 1980.
Translation of the original French Réponse à l'Histoire. See entry 194.

197 _____. Die Soziale Revolution Irans. Düsseldorf; Köln: Diederichs, 1967.
A discussion of the Shah's White Revolution and social reforms. Translated from Persian by Issa Shehabi. See also entry 199.

198 _____. A Translation of the Historic Speeches of His Imperial Majesty Shahanshah Aryamehr. Tehran: College of Translation, 1973.
Translated into English by Abbas Aryanpur (Kashani). Includes several of the Shah's public speeches which emphasize his socioeconomic reforms.

199 _____. The White Revolution of Iran. Tehran: Imperial Pahlavi Library, 1967.
   The Shah describes the theory and principles as well as goals of his White Revolution: a reform program designed to build a modern Iran. Various areas of the reform such as land reform, Literacy Corps, nationalization of forests, etc. are discussed.

200 Pedrazzani, Jean-Michel. L'impératrice d'Iran: Le Mythe et La Réalité. Paris: Publimonde, 1977.
   A biographical account of Farah Diba, the Shah's third wife and queen of Iran 1959-1979.

201 Ramazani, Rouhollah K. "Iran's 'White Revolution': A Study in Political Development." International Journal of Middle East Studies. 5(2):124-139, 1974.
   Attempts to find the "meaning" of Iran's White Revolution. Discusses its goals as a social and economic reform.

202 Sahebjam, Freidoune. Mohamad Reza Pahlavi, Shah d'Iran: Sa Vie, Trente Ans de Règne (1941-1971). Paris: Berger-Levrault, 1971.
   A biographical account of the Shah of Iran. Documentary and well-illustrated.

203 Sanghvi, Ramesh. Aryamehr: The Shah of Iran: A Political Biography. London, Melbourne: Macmillan, 1968.
   A journalistic account of the Shah's role in Iranian history. Written in a laudatory style, it lacks critical analysis.

204 _____. The Shah of Iran. New York: Stein and Day, 1968.
   A "political biography and a biographical history." It is a highly flattering account of the Shah's role in Iran's history from an Indian journalist's point of view.

205 _____; German, Clifford; and Missen, David. The Revolution of the Shah and the People. London: Transorient, 1970.
   A discussion of reform programs initiated by the Shah in 1963 which later were called the "White Revolution" or "Shah-People Revolution."

206 Shamim, Ali Asghar. Iran in the Reign of His Majesty Mohammad Reza Shah Pahlavi. Tehran: Central Council Celebration of the 25th Century of the Foundation of the Iranian Empire, 1966(?).
   Surveys the Shah's reign since its beginning in 1941 up to the 1960's. Lacks critical and objective analysis and is written in a rather laudatory style. Chapter Five deals with foreign and international policy of Iran. (Translated into English by Aladin Pazargadi.)

207 Tripet, François. "Cinq Ans de Révolution Blanche en Iran." Etudes. 206-220, August/September, 1969.
Reviews the program of reforms initiated by the Shah in 1963 known as the White Revolution. Analyzes its results after five years and discusses the problems challenging the government in the future years.

208 Villiers, Gérard de; Touchais, Bernard; and Villiers, Annick de. The Imperial Shah: An Informal Biography. Boston: Little, Brown, 1976.
Translated from French by June P. Wilson, this is another biography of the Shah. The original French version has the title: L'irrésistible Ascension de Mohammad Reza, Shah d'Iran.

209 _____; _____; and _____. L'irrésistible Ascension de Mohammad Reza, Shah d'Iran. Paris: Plon, 1975.
Another biographical account of the Shah. Also translated into English under the title: The Imperial Shah: An Informal Biography.

II

POLITICAL CONDITIONS

POLITICAL PARTIES AND IDEOLOGIES

210 Abrahamian, Ervand. "Communism and Communalism in Iran: The Tudeh and the Firqah-i Dimukrat." International Journal of Middle East Studies. 1(4):291-316, 1970.
Examines the two major communist parties in Iran and factors leading to their development.

211 _____. "Factionalism in Iran: Political Groups in the 14th Parliament (1944-46)." Middle Eastern Studies. 14(1):22-55, 1978.
Uses the 14th Iranian Parliament as a case study to investigate the causes underlying the survival of the monarchy in an age of republicanism.

212 _____. "Kasravi: The Integrative Nationalist of Iran." Middle Eastern Studies. 9(3):271-295, 1973.
An account of life and ideas of Ahmad Kasravi, Iranian intellectual and writer. The main theme of this article is that Kasravi was a social reformist who hoped for "an integrated modern Iran."

213 _____. Social Bases of Iranian Politics: The Tudeh Party, 1941-1953. Ph.D. dissertation, Columbia University, 1969.
The Tudeh (masses) party's success during 1941-1953 and the reasons for its popularity are examined. Investigates the reasons behind failure of rival parties to gain popular support.

214 Alavi, Bozorg. "Der Iran in den Fängen des Neokolonialismus." Deutsche Aussenpolitik. 6:75-84, 1961.
Asserts that Iran has been trapped in neocolonialism. The author was a leftist Iranian professor and approaches his subject from that point of view.

215 _____. Kämpfendes Iran. Berlin, Dietz, 1955.
A leftist view of Iranian internal politics. The Tudeh party is emphasized and a critical view of Mossadeq's nationalization of oil is given.

216 _____. "Der Nationale Befreiungskampf in Iran." Wissenschaftliche Zeitschrift der Humboldt-Universität zu Berlin.

9(1/2):37-43, 1959/60.
Asserts that since 1953 foreign powers have used new methods to colonialize Iran and have concealed their imperialistic aspirations.

217 Ashrafi, Mehdi. Development and Transformation of Political Parties in Iran 1941-1975. Ph.D. dissertation, Claremont Graduate School, 1977.
Three political parties: The Tudeh party, the National Front, and the New Iran party are studied and their influence on party development in Iran is discussed. The transformation of a multiparty system to a single-party system (the National Resurgence party) is examined.

218 Banisadr, A.H.; Ghazanfarpour, A.; Ghazanfarpour, S.; and Vieille, P. "Les Elections et Leurs Fonctions en Iran." Revue Française de Science Politique. 27(1):34-63, 1977.
Discusses the functions of political elections in Iran and the foundation of a single-party system in 1975 and its implications.

219 Binder, Leonard. "Iranian Nationalism." In: Rivlin, Benjamin and Szyliowicz, Joseph S. (eds.), The Contemporary Middle East: Tradition and Innovation. New York: Random House, 1965. Pages 224-230.
"The varieties of nationalist feelings that characterize Iranian nationalism" are examined. The reasons behind failure of nationalism in Iran to serve as a mobilizing force are briefly analyzed.

220 Cottam, Richard. Nationalism in Iran: Updated through 1978. Pittsburgh: University of Pittsburgh Press, 1979.
The Iranian nationalism movement in the 1950's and Mossadeq's rise to power are discussed. Previously published in 1964 by the same publisher.

221 _____. "Political Party Development in Iran." Iranian Studies. 1(3):82-95, 1968.
Traces and analyzes the development of political parties in Iran from its intense activity after the abdication of Reza Shah in 1941 until August 1953 when it was suppressed. A brief discussion of the Iranian political party activity since 1953 is also given.

222 Courtois, V. "The Tudeh Party." Indo-Iranica. 7:14-22, 1954.
A discussion of the Communist party of Tudeh (masses) in Iran and its development.

223 D'Ermé, Giovanni. "I Partiti Politici in Persia dal 1941 al 1944." Oriente Moderno. 51:213-235, 1971.
Political events in Iran during World War II, including the formation of political parties, are discussed.

Political Conditions

224 Elwell-Sutton, L. P. "Nationalism and Neutralism in Iran."
Middle East Journal. 12(1):20-32, 1958.
The author argues that "more and more intellectuals are beginning to understand the value of traditional ways of life." The opposition of Iranians to Westernization is discussed.

225 _____. "Political Parties in Iran, 1941-1948." Middle East Journal. 3(1):45-62, 1949.
The political parties developed within this time period including the Tudeh party, the most organized and structured political party in Iran, are discussed.

226 Eskandari, Iradj and Bilen, I. "Anti-Communism Beating a Retreat." World Marxist Review. 17(8):116-122, 1974.
The anticommunist activities in Iran and Turkey are discussed and the Communist party's attempts to counter these activities are analyzed.

227 Helfgott, L. "Iran: Capitalist Formation on the Periphery."
RIPEH/The Review of Iranian Political Economy and History. 1(1):2-24, 1976.
A Marxist interpretation of Iranian history. The emphasis is on modern Iran.

228 Katouzian, Homayoun. "Nationalist Trends in Iran, 1921-1926."
International Journal of Middle East Studies. 10(4):533-551, 1979.
Examines nationalistic tendencies during early years of Reza Shah's regime.

229 Lenczowski, George. "The Communist Movement in Iran."
Middle East Journal. 1(1):29-45, 1947.
The significance of the Communist movement in Iran and the importance of the Tudeh (masses) party which was created on January 30, 1942 by a small group of leftist politicians are described in this article. Traces the origins of the party and examines its structure, evidence of Soviet support, its attacks on opposition, and its future.

230 Miller, William G. "Political Organization in Iran: From Dowreh to Political Party." Middle East Journal. 23(2/3):159-167, 343-350, 1969.
Dowreh (literally, cycle) is an Iranian tradition, usually among the urban upper and middle class, in which groups meet informally for social, cultural, recreational, intellectual, or political discussions. The members meet periodically, on a rotating basis, to discuss issues or ways to advance mutual welfare. This article discusses the significance of dowreh as a political organization.

231 Mozafari, Mehdi. L'Iran. Paris: Libraire générale de droit et de jurisprudence, 1978.

Contains useful information on political parties in Iran and their development.

232 Nabavi, J. "The Rastakhiz Party: A Year After Its Creation." Indian Political Science Review. 12(1):8-24, 1978.
In March 1975 Iran's bipartisan system came to an abrupt end when the Shah ordered a new political system under a single political party. This single party was named Iran National Resurgence party or Rastakhiz party. This article is an attempt to review the genesis, structure, and objectives of the Rastakhiz party. It also examines the possible consequences of this single-party system.

233 Nahavandi, H. "L'évolution du Parti Communiste Iranien, le Tudeh, de 1920 à 1981." Politique Etrangère. 46(3):651-668, 1981.
Traces the Iranian Communist party's (Tudeh) evolution since its foundation. Its link with the Soviet Union is emphasized.

234 Nikitine, Basile. "Democratie en Orient, un Point de Vue Persan." L'Afrique et l'Asie. 54:3-15, 1961.
The ideas of Mohammad Ali Islami, an Iranian intellectual, are examined.

235 Razi, G. H. "Genesis of Party in Iran: A Case Study of the Interaction Between the Political System and Political Parties." Iranian Studies. 3(2):58-90, 1970.

236 Rey, Lucien. "Persia in Perspective." New Left Review. Part I, 19:32-55, March-April 1963; Part II, 20:69-98, Summer 1963.
A leftist view of modern Iran.

237 Ricks, Thomas M. "Contemporary Iranian Economy and History: An Overview." RIPEH/The Review of Iranian Political Economy and History. 1(1):24-58, 1976.
A Marxist interpretation of Iran's economy and history since the nineteenth century with an emphasis on the Pahlavi era.

238 Ringer, B. B. and Sills, D. L. "Political Extremists in Iran: A Secondary Analysis of Communications Data." Public Opinion Quarterly. 16:689-701, 1952-53.
Various political groups in Iran are examined. The author contends that the extremists of the left and right share many common characteristics.

239 Ritter, Wolfgang. Der Iran unter der Diktatur des Schah-Regimes. Frankfurt am Main: Verlag Marxistische Blätter, 1979.
A leftist view of the Shah's regime in Iran. Includes the program of the Tudeh party, the Iranian Communist party.

240 Rouzbeh, Khosrov. Mein Herz Schlägt für Irans Zukunft. Berlin (GDR): Dietz Verlag, 1964.
The speeches delivered by the author before the military tribunal. This is a translation of a publication by Iran's Communist party, the Tudeh (masses) party under the title: Khosrov Rouzbeh Before the Military Tribunal. Rouzbeh was executed in 1958.

241 Sadeeg, Javad. Nationalities and Revolution in Iran. New York: Distributed by Pathfinder Press, 1974.
A Marxist view of contemporary Iranian history. The Azerbaijan crisis and the nationalization of oil are discussed within the Marxist framework.

242 Safari, H. "La Lutte Idéologique en Iran." Nouvelle Revue Internationale. 19(9):100-113, 1976.
A discussion of political ideologies in Iran. The development of the Tudeh party, the Iranian Communist party, is emphasized.

243 Ule, Wolfgang. "Entwicklung und Gegenwärtiges Parteiwesen im Iran." Vierteljahresberichte. 31:43-68, 1968.
Surveys the political parties developed in Iran since 1905.

244 Weinbaum, M. G. "Iran Finds a Party System: The Institutionalization of Iran Novin." Middle East Journal. 27(4):439-455, 1973.
Examines the structure and activities of the Iran Novin party based on measures of institutionalization suggested by Samuel Huntington.

245 Zabih, Sepehr. "Communism in Iran." Problems of Communism. 14:46-55, 1965.
The nature and influence of Communist ideology are examined. The Tudeh (masses) party, the most organized Communist party in Iran, is discussed.

246 _____. The Communist Movement in Iran. Berkeley: University of California Press, 1966.
A scholarly research of the Communist movement in Iran. Its history, basis for its mass appeal, and its place in Iranian political development are analyzed.

247 _____. The Dynamics of the Communist Movement in Iran, 1920-1962. Ph.D. dissertation, University of California, Berkeley, 1963.
Factors influencing the Communist movement in Iran are discussed. The Soviet Union's methods used to introduce Communism in Iran and the region are also examined.

INTERNAL POLITICS AND GOVERNMENTAL ADMINISTRATION

248 Abrahamian, Ervand. Iran Between Two Revolutions. Princeton: Princeton University Press, 1982.
   Analyzes the social bases of Iranian politics in an attempt to demonstrate the socioeconomic factors which have affected Iranian politics between the Constitutional Revolution of the late-nineteenth century to the Islamic revolution of 1979.

249 Afkhami, Gholamreza and Elahi, Cyrus. "Social Mobilization and Participation in Iran." In: Jacqz, Jane W. (ed.), Iran: Past, Present and Future. New York: Aspen Institute for Humanistic Studies, 1976. Pages 227-241.
   Analyzes the nature and necessity of political participation in Iran. The political system of Iran and the role of the Rastakhiz (resurgence) party are also examined.

250 Ashraf, Ahmad. Iran: Imperialism, Class and Modernization from Above. Ph.D. dissertation, New School for Social Research, 1971.

251 Avery, Peter. "Trends in Iran in the Past Five Years." World Today. 21(7):279-290, 1965.
   Reviews social and political events in Iran between 1960 to 1965. Elections for National Consultative Assembly in 1961, land reform and other reform measures, and opposition to modernization are among topics discussed.

252 Azadeh, Behrouze. "L'Iran Aujourd'hui." Temps Modernes. 27(298):2031-2066, 1971.
   Critical of Iranian politics and government of the Shah's period. Discusses lack of freedom and economic growth in Iran and attacks Iran's foreign policy of alliance with the West.

253 Banisadr, A.H.; Ghazanfarpour, A.; Ghazanfarpour, S.; and Vieille, Paul. "Iran, le Nouveau Contrat Social: Mythes et Réalités." Peuples Méditerranéen. 1:61-92, 1977.
   Criticizes the Iranian social and political structure under the ruling power. The consequences of Iran's economic power in the world market are analyzed.

254 Bill, James A. "The American Analysis of Iranian Politics." Iranian Studies. 10(3):164-195, 1977.
Problems involved in analyzing Iranian political process are examined.

255 _____. "The Patterns of Elite Politics in Iran." In: Lenczowski, George (ed.), Political Elites in the Middle East. Washington, D. C.: American Enterprise Institute for Public Policy Research, 1975. Pages 17-40.
Studies the role and characteristics of the political elite in Iran. The author views the Iranian system as essentially patrimonial.

256 _____. "The Plasticity in Informal Politics: The Case of Iran." Middle East Journal. 27(2):131-151, 1973.
Studies changes in the sociopolitical environment of modern Iran in light of its traditional system.

257 Binder, Leonard. "The Cabinet of Iran: A Case Study in Institutional Adaptation." Middle East Journal. 16(1): 29-47, 1962.
The author analyzes the roots and structure of the Iranian cabinet. Concludes that the Iranian cabinet has limited political and policy-making powers and therefore is not capable of achieving national goals.

258 _____. Iran: Political Development in a Changing Society. Berkeley: University of California Press, 1962.
Examines and analyzes the Iranian political system. The study is based on the author's research in Iran during the 1958-1959 period.

259 Carrère d'Encausse, H. "L'Iran en Quête d'un Equilibre." Revue Française de Science Politique. 17(2):213-236, 1967.
Analyzes the Iranian political system and its search for reaching an "equilibrium" in the region.

260 Davidian, Zaven. Iran in the Service of World Peace. Tehran: Davidian, 1971.
A public relations-type of document published on the occasion of the 2,500th anniversary celebration of the founding of the Iranian empire, which was celebrated on October 26, 1967.

261 Destrée, Annette. "La Politique Iranienne depuis 1945: Essai de Synthèse." Correspondance d'Orient. Etudes. 5-6:63-86, 1964.
Reviews the Iranian political scene since 1945. Both internal and external politics are discussed.

262 Fardanesh, Mohammad Ali. Foreign Relations and Internal Politics: A Developmental Analysis, Iran 1797-1963. Ph. D. dissertation, University of Colorado, 1972.

Two main approaches, analytical and historical/developmental, have been employed to discuss the interrelationships between internal political factors and foreign relations of Iran during the period covered.

263 Farmayan, Hafez F. "Politics During the Sixties: A Historical Analysis." In: Yar-Shater, Ehsan (ed.), Iran Faces the Seventies. New York: Praeger, 1971. Pages 88-116.
Reviews political events in Iran in the 1960's. The major events of this period include: passing of the Land Reform Act by the Parliament, rioting inspired by the opposition of landlords and Islamic clergy, proclamation by the Shah of six reform measures known as the White Revolution, and the assassination of Premier Hasan-Ali Mansur with the coming to power of Prime Minister Hoveyda.

264 Filippani-Ronconi, Pio. "The Tradition of Sacred Kingship in Iran." In: Lenczowski, George (ed.), Iran Under the Pahlavis. Stanford, California: Hoover Institution Press, 1978. Pages 51-83.
Traces the tradition, significance, and continuity of kingship in Iranian history from ancient times to the emergence of the Pahlavi dynasty.

265 Frescobadi, D. "L'Iran verso il Duemila." Affari Esteri. 26:268-282, 1975.
A survey of Iran's internal and external affairs. The roles of the Iran Novin party and the Shah in the political development of the country are examined.

266 Gable, Richard W. Government and Administration in Iran. Los Angeles: School of Public Administration, University of Southern California, 1959.

267 Giniewski, Paul. "L'Iran et ses Problèmes." Politique Etrangère. 25(3):285-292, 1960.
Iran's social and political problems are discussed. Relations with the U.S.S.R., Arab countries, and the Iraq-Iran dispute over the Shatt al-Arab are also examined.

268 Goodarzi, Manucher. The Significance and Problems of Civil Service Reform in a Developing Nation: The Experience of Iran. Ph.D. dissertation, University of Southern California, 1969.
This dissertation studies the problems involved in civil service reform in Iran. The conditions that must be changed to achieve an effective national development are discussed. Among these are the traditional management practices, traditional reliance upon favoritism, etc.

269 Graham, Robert. Iran: The Illusion of Power. London: Croom Helm, 1978.
Although this publication focuses on the economic con-

dition of Iran between 1973 and 1977 and especially the effects of the sudden increase in oil revenues on Iranian economy, it contains information on other aspects of Iranian politics and government. Chapter Four is entitled "Monarchy and the Pahlavi Dynasty" and Chapter Ten deals with the "Influence of the Military." A later revised edition of this book, published in 1980, includes a chapter on the Iranian revolution of 1978 which brought an end to the Pahlavi dynasty. The author was the Financial Times Middle East correspondent in Tehran from June 1975 to July 1977.

270 Gun, Nerin E. "Iran, Present and Future: An Interview with Prime Minister Abbas Hoveyda." Journal of Social and Political Affairs. 1(4):337-344, 1976.
Iran's policies regarding its present and future economic conditions, industrialization, oil pricing, and its position among the Third World nations are some of the topics discussed in this interview.

271 Hashemi, Fazlollah and Sadr, Anoushirvan. "Decentralization in Iran." In: CENTO Symposium on Decentralization of Government. Ankara: Office of U.S. Economic Coordinator for CENTO Affairs, 1968. Pages 78-83.
The authors outline the Iranian government's plans for decentralization. The plan covers decentralization on provincial, city, and village levels.

272 Housego, David. "Iran in the Ascendant: Economic Strengths, Political Weaknesses." Round Table. (London) 248:497-507, 1972.
The gap between Iran's economic progress and its lack of political development is discussed.

273 Hoveyda, Amir Abbas. "The Future of Iran." In: Jacqz, Jane W. (ed.), Iran: Past, Present and Future. New York: Aspen Institute for Humanistic Studies, 1976. Pages 447-456.
The former prime minister of Iran sketches that country's goals for the remaining years of the twentieth century and challenges facing the nation. Comments on a variety of issues including the political system, the economy, and education.

274 Inlow, Edgar Burke. Shahanshah: A Study of the Monarchy of Iran. Delhi: Motilal Banarsidass, 1979.
Despite its title which may imply another biography of the Shah, this book deals with the theoretical concept of "Shahanshah" in Iranian history. "This book is a study in political and legal theory. Its concern is with the power of the Shahanshah...."

275 Iran Financial and Commercial Service. Iran in Perspective, 1975: A Report. Reading: Paul R. Walter and Associates Inc., 1976.

A report on Iranian political and economic development in the year 1975. One major political development during this year was the rejection of the previous two-party system in favor of a single party--the Rastakhiz party.

276 Jandaghi, Ali. "The Present Situation in Iran." Monthly Review. 25(6):34-47, 1973.

Social classes, elites, and the military in Iran are reviewed in light of her twentieth-century political developments.

277 Kaviani, Bijan. Das Problem Demokratischer Wahlen im Iran. Tubingen, 1963.

A discussion of problems associated with democracy in Iran.

278 Keddie, Nikki R. "The Iranian Power Structure and Social Change, 1800-1969: An Overview." International Journal of Middle East Studies. 2(1):3-20, 1971.

An analytical study of changes in the Iranian power structure during the period indicated. The focus is on the mid-twentieth century. The author concludes that in general these changes have caused weakening of the power of certain groups and an overall strengthening of the central government.

279 Kingsley, R. "Premier Amini and Iran's Problems." Middle Eastern Affairs. 13(7):194-198, 1962.

Discusses problems facing Amini's government. Asserts that the main problem challenging his government lies in the resolution of the conflict between traditions of a feudal society and values of a more modern intelligentsia.

280 Kuklan, Hooshang. Theories and Practices of Technical Assistance and Administrative Reform, Iran: 1953-1973. Ph.D. dissertation, State University of New York at Albany, 1974.

Investigates the role of technical assistance provided by the U.S. and the United Nations in the administrative reform in developing countries. Iran is taken as a case study in this research.

281 Lenczowski, George. "Political Process and Institutions in Iran: The Second Pahlavi Kingship." In: Lenczowski, George, (ed.), Iran Under the Pahlavis. Stanford, California: Hoover Institution Press, 1978. Pages 432-475.

Discusses the role played by Majlis (the lower house of the Iranian Parliament) in political processes. The political parties and ideologies widespread during the Pahlavi dynasty, the concept and nature of the royal authority and the monarchy are also among subjects discussed. The priorities of each Pahlavi ruler dictated by the time and circumstances are compared.

282 Malek-Mahdavi, Ahmed. Le Parlement Iranien. Neuchâtel, 1954.

283 Mohammadi-Nejad, Hassan. "The Iranian Parliamentary Elections of 1975." International Journal of Middle East Studies. 8(1):103-116, 1977.
    Discusses and analyzes the election of Iranian Parliament in June 1975 and its results.

284 Nahavandi, H. "La Politique d'Indepéndance de l'Iran." Revue Iranienne des Relations Internationales/Iranian Review of International Relations. 7:5-18, 1976.
    A historical survey of Iran's quest for political independence. The emphasis is on the Pahlavi era.

285 Nakhai, M. L'évolution Politique de l'Iran. Brussels: Felix, 1938.
    A nationalist political history of contemporary Iran.

286 Pahlavi, Ashraf. Faces in a Mirror: Memoirs From Exile. Englewood Cliffs, New Jersey: Prentice-Hall, 1980.
    Autobiography of the Shah's twin sister. Useful for the study of Iran's internal politics as well as the royal family's involvement in political affairs of Iran.

287 Pahlavi, Mohammad Reza. Iran's Domestic and Foreign Policy: Excerpts from Speeches and Interviews of His Imperial Majesty, Mohammad Reza Pahlavi Aryamehr, Shahanshah of Iran. 1976.
    A compilation of quotations extracted from addresses, interviews, and public speeches of the Shah from October 1973 to July 1976. Compiled by Manoutchehr Ardalan, counselor at the Iranian Embassy in Washington, D.C.
    This is basically a public relations document containing the monarch's ideas related to foreign and internal policies of his regime. There are also his quotations on oil and defense policies during the period covered.

288 Rubio García, L. "Incertidumbre en el Irán." Cuadernos de Política Internacional. 13:73-85, 1953.
    Discusses the political instability in Iran and sees great obstacles for modernization and reforms.

289 Sadjady, Mohamed. Les Principes du Régime Parlementaire et leur Application en Perse. Paris: Editions Medicis, 1933.

290 Savory, Roger M. "The Principle of Homeostasis Considered in Relation to Political Events in Iran in the 1960's." International Journal of Middle East Studies. 3(3):282-302, 1972.
    Social change in Iranian society as well as the forces of opposition and their relationship to the Shah's reforms are analyzed.

291 Scarcia, B.M. "Die Weisse Reaktion des Schah." Wiener Tagebuch. 12:25-27, 1971.
Criticizes the Shah's White Revolution. Asserts that the rapid economic development in Iran has affected only the middle class and the bureaucracy and not the impoverished masses.

292 Scarcia, Gianroberto. "Interno alle Elezioni Persiane." Oriente Moderno. 40:537-552, 1960.
The Iranian national elections of 1960, which were annulled by the Shah because of social unrest in the country, are discussed.

293 Scarcia Amoretti, B. "Iran: Mistificazione o Società che Muta?" Politica Internazionale. 12:34-45, 1975.
Analyzes the political situation in Iran in 1975. The authoritarian regime of the Shah and its implications are studied.

294 Sedehi, Abolghassem. Constitution and Constitutionalism in Iran. Ph.D. dissertation, New York University, 1967.
The main objective of this dissertation is to describe the socioeconomic and political prerequisites for constitutionalism and democracy in Iran. The author believes that despite the existence of a constitution, constitutionalism has not existed in Iran.

295 _____ and Tabriztchi, S. "A Theory of Economic Growth and Political Development: The Case of Iran." International Studies. 13(3):424-440, 1974.
Attempts to discover the underlying causes of the gap between Iran's increasing economic growth and her lack of political development.

296 Spuler, Bertold. "Iran im Spiel der Weltmächte im 20. Jahrhundert." Die Welt als Geschichte. 14(2):119-131, 1954.
Reviews the interference of foreign powers in Iranian affairs in the twentieth century. The Russian, British and American rivalries in Iran are discussed up to the fall of Prime Minister Mossadeq in 1953.

297 Steinbach, Udo. "Irans Regionale und Internationale Rolle." Orient. (Opladen). 19(2):118-138, 1978.
Reviews Iran's regional and international policies. Her role in the Persian Gulf region is given special attention.

298 Tavallali, Djamchid. Le Parlement Iranien. Lausann: Impr. des Arts et Métiers, 1954.
A historical survey of the Iranian Parliament (the Majlis) since 1906 and its characteristics in the 1950's.

299 Vieille, Paul. "Etat et Féodalité en Iran." L'Homme et la Société. 17:255-279, 1970.

300 Weinbaum, M. G. "Dimensions of Elite Change in the Middle East." Comparative Political Studies. 12(2):123-150, 1979.
Examines political elites in several Middle Eastern countries including Iran and discusses political instability in these countries.

301 Westwood, A. F. "Elections and Politics in Iran." Middle East Journal. 15(2):153-164, 1961.
Discusses elections held in August and December of 1960.

302 _____. "Politics of Distrust in Iran." Annals of the American Academy of Political and Social Science. 358:123-135, 1965.
Discusses the political environment in Iran. Considers the lack of a stable majority coalition in the Majlis as one of the important factors in the instability of Iranian politics.

303 Wilber, Donald Newton. Iran: Oasis of Stability in Middle East? New York: Foreign Policy Association, 1959. (Headline series; no. 137)
After a historical background, the author discusses the political structure and goals of Iran. Most of the discussions are about events occurring in Iran during the 1950's. At the end, the author indicates that although the outlook is generally favorable, "the possibility of some form of violent upheavel in Iran" cannot be entirely discounted.

304 Young, T. C. "Iran in Continuing Crisis." Foreign Affairs. 40(2):275-292, 1962.
Iran's internal political problems are the focus of this study. The conflict between the Shah and the National Front, the lack of experienced and energetic politicians, and the people's mistrust of the Shah are among problems considered. However, the author maintains that at the root of the problems is the lack of responsible leadership without which the transition from a traditional to a modern society is extremely difficult if not impossible.

305 Zonis, Marvin. "Classes, Elites and Iranian Politics: The Exchange." Iranian Studies. 8(3):134-163, 1975.
A review of James Bill's The Politics of Iran: Groups, Classes and Modernization. (Columbus, Ohio: Charles E. Merrill, 1972.) See entry 935.

306 _____. The Political Elite of Iran. Princeton: Princeton University Press, 1971.
A detailed analysis of the relationship between the political processes and Iranian people. The values of Iranian political elites are examined.

307 _____. "The Political Elite of Iran: A Second Stratum?" In: Tachau, Frank (ed.), Political Elites and Political

Development in the Middle East. Cambridge, Massachusetts: Schenkman, 1975. Pages 193-216.
Analyzes the Iranian political elites, their values and priorities, and their relationship to the Shah as the center of power. Maintains that the political elites of Iran can be considered as a "second stratum" of the ruling class which is structurally located between the Shah and the nonelite.

308 _____. "Political Elites and Political Cynicism in Iran." Comparative Political Studies. 1(3):351-371, 1968.
Results of a research on interpersonal relations and psychocultural factors in Iran's political development. The values and role of the political elite are examined.

8

NATIONAL SECURITY AND ARMED FORCES

309 Bayne, E.A. and Collin, Richard O. Arms and Advisors: Views from Saudi Arabia and Iran. Hanover, New Hampshire: American Universities Field Staff, 1976.
The question of the sale of American arms and military technology to Iran and Saudi Arabia is approached and analyzed from various angles. The role of military advisors is discussed.

310 Burt, Richard. "Power and the Peacock Throne: Iran's Growing Military Strength." Round Table. (London) 260:349-356, 1975.
Analyzes the factors leading to Iran's military development. Fear of Soviet intervention, military expansion in neighboring Arab countries, balance of power in the Persian Gulf area, and tension with Saudi Arabia are considered among these factors.

311 Chubin, Shahram. "Iran's Defense and Foreign Policy." In: Amirie, Abbas and Twitchell, Hamilton A. (eds.), Iran in the 1980's. Tehran: Institute for International and Economic Studies, 1978. Pages 309-334.
Strategic significance and political as well as military aspects of Iran's security are discussed. Analyzes the country's defense and foreign policy perspectives.

312 _____. "Iran's Security in the 1980's." International Security. 2(3):51-80, 1978.
Iran's security on the regional level as well as in relation to the superpowers is analyzed. Asserts that considering Iran's strategic importance, she is underarmed.

313 Cottrell, Alvin J. "Iran's Armed Forces Under the Pahlavi Dynasty." In: Lenczowski, George (ed.), Iran Under the Pahlavis. Stanford, California: Hoover Institution Press, 1978. Pages 389-431.
Surveys development of Iran's armed forces since its beginning under Reza Shah, himself an officer in the Cossack Brigade. The emphasis is on post-1953 developments after Mossadeq's fall and when Iran's defense program stressed modernization of the ground forces. Iran's alli-

ance with the United States as well as a discussion of Imperial Iranian Ground Forces, Air Force and Navy are given. Includes a short section on "Iran and Nuclear Weapons."

314 _____ and Dougherty, James E. Iran's Quest for Security: U.S. Arms Transfers and the Nuclear Option. Cambridge, Massachusetts: Institute for Foreign Policy Analysis, 1977.
Studies the relationship between conventional arms transfers and the incentives and disincentives to nuclear proliferation in Iran. The adequacy of the Iranian conventional defense system is evaluated. Chapter Eight deals with "Arms Transfers and U.S. Domestic Constraints."

315 Croizat, Victor J. "Imperial Iranian Gendarmerie." Marine Corps Gazette. 59(10):28-31, 1975.
A brief report on the Imperial Iranian Gendarmerie and its improvement under the United States supervision since 1943.

316 Dupree, L. "Democracy and the Military Base of Power." Middle East Journal. 22(1):29-44, 1968.
Afghanistan and Pakistan as well as Iran are discussed.

317 Furlong, R. "Iran: A Power to Be Reckoned With." International Defense Review. (Geneva) 6(6):719-729, 1973.
A detailed study of Iran's military buildup. The purchase and manufacture of weapons are emphasized.

318 "A Glance at the Past and Present of the Imperial Iranian Air Force." Aerospace History. 19(4):184-187, 1973.
A historical survey of the Iranian air force from 1922 to 1968.

319 Green, Thomas F. "Building a Navy in a Hurry." U.S. Naval Institute Proceedings. 104(1):41-49, 1978.
Discusses the Imperial Iranian Navy (IIN), its growth and problems as well as the United States military aid and advisory personnel's involvement.

320 Grué, B. "Le Rôle Social de l'Armée en Iran." Orient. (Paris) 6(24):49-54, 1962.
Discusses the role of the army in national renovation of Iran and concludes that it plays an important role in uniting the nation.

321 Hollist, W. Ladd. "Alternative Explanation of Competitive Arms Processes: Tests on Four Pairs of Nations." American Journal of Political Science. 21(2):313-340, 1977.
Four pairs of countries: U.S.-U.S.S.R., Israel-Egypt, Iran-Iraq, and India-Pakistan are examined in an attempt to develop models which can predict a nation's military spending.

Political Conditions

322 Hurewitz, J. C. Middle East Politics: The Military Dimension. New York: Praeger, 1969.
  Chapter 15, entitled "An American Client: Iran," discusses the military politics of the Pahlavi regime with an emphasis on the role of the United States in Iranian military policies and programs.

323 Kazemzadeh, F. "The Origin and Early Development of the Persian Cossack Brigade." The American Slavic and East European Review. 15:351-363, 1956.
  Useful for the background study of the Iranian Armed Forces. Reza Shah himself was an officer in the Cossack Brigade when he engineered a coup d'etat in 1921.

324 Klare, Michael T. "The Political Economy of Arms Sales: United States-Saudi Arabia." Society. 11(6):41-49, 1974.
  The author argues that the United States policy of arms sales to allies in the Persian Gulf region may risk military rivalry between Iran and Saudi Arabia.

325 Martin, Laurence. "The Future Strategic Role of Iran." In: Amirsadeghi, Hossein (ed.), Twentieth-Century Iran. New York: Holmes & Meier, 1977. Pages 223-252.
  Iran's geopolitical position as well as her internal and external security are discussed in this essay.

326 Neuman, Stephanie. "Security, Military Expenditures and Socio-Economic Development: Reflections on Iran." Orbis. 22(3):569-594, 1978.
  Iran is taken as a case study to investigate the relationship between defense expenditure and development. The consequences of arms transfers are examined.

327 Parvin, Manoucher. "Military Expenditure in Iran: A Forgotten Question." Iranian Studies. 1(4):149-154, 1968.
  Inquires into the reasons for Iran's increasing military expenditure. Asserts that allocation of a larger portion of the national budget to economic growth is "more beneficial even from the viewpoint of 'national security'."

328 Pryor, Leslie M. "Arms and the Shah." Foreign Policy. 31: 56-71, 1978.
  Argues that unrestrained U.S. arms sales to Iran may endanger the stability in the area and damage U.S. interests in that country.

329 Quester, G. H. "The Shah and the Bomb." Policy Sciences. 8(1):21-32, 1977.
  The possibility of developing nuclear weapons by Iran is discussed.

330 Remick, William C. "The Case for Foreign Military Sales." U.S. Naval Institute Proceedings. 103(1/887):18-26, 1977.

The United States Foreign Military Sales Program, in general and with regard to Iran and Saudi Arabia, is discussed. The author argues that in the interest of regional security in the area, the United States should continue to respond favorably to the request for arms from these countries.

331 Rumney, Mason P. "The View from Iran." Military Review. 52(1):68-74, 1972.
Discusses Iran's role in developing peace and stability in the Middle East.

332 Schulz, Ann T. "Iran: The Descending Monarchy." Current History. 76:5, 33-34, 1979.
The Shah's military policies are criticized as being misdirected. The main goal of these policies was building a strong and loyal military against the Soviet intervention in Iran with advice and military cooperation from the United States. But the Shah's oppressive rule resulted in the 1978 revolution and his eventual overthrow.

333 Shah, S. A. The Political and Strategic Foundations of International Arms Transfer: A Case Study of American Arms Supplies to and Purchases by Iran and Saudi Arabia: 1968-76. Ph.D. dissertation, University of Virginia, 1977.
An analysis of political and strategic factors involved in American arms transfers to Iran and Saudi Arabia. The case of Iran and Saudi Arabia is utilized in order to find a general pattern in international arms transfers for all developing countries.

334 Shapiro, Walter. "Arming the Shah: Alms for the Rich." Washington Monthly. 6(12):28-32, 1975.
The changes in Iran's needs since 1947 are analyzed and their relation to American foreign policy are discussed. The author argues that the U.S. foreign and military policies need to be modified and adapted according to the changes in the international balance of power.

335 Sreedhar. "The Role of Armed Forces in Iranian Revolution." IDSA Journal (Institute for Defense Studies and Analyses, New Delhi). 12(2):121-142, 1979.
Factors contributing to the breakdown of the Iranian Armed Forces during the revolution of 1978/79 are analyzed.

336 United States. Congress. Senate. Committee on Foreign Relations. Subcommittee on Foreign Assistance. U.S. Military Sales to Iran: A Staff Report to the Subcommittee on Foreign Assistance of the Committee on Foreign Relations, United States Senate. Washington, D.C.: U.S. Government Printing Office, 1976.
The United States military program in Iran is studied.

Political Conditions   53

   Also contains substantial amount of information on Iranian Armed Forces. This report was written by Robert Mantel and Geoffrey Kemp.

FOREIGN POLICY AND GENERAL INTERNATIONAL RELATIONS

337 Amirie, Abbas. "Iran's View of International Issues." In: Amirie, Abbas and Twitchell, Hamilton A. (eds.), Iran in the 1980's. Tehran: Institute for International Political and Economic Studies, 1978. Pages 17-21.
A very brief discussion of three major international issues in the 1980's as viewed by Iran: The emergence of a multipolar system in international politics; the problem of the increasing gap between economically poor and wealthy nations; and the future of the energy problem.

338 Bahrampour, Firouz. Iran: Emergence of a Middle Eastern Power. Brooklyn: Theo. Gaus' Sons, 1970.
Contains information on Iran's foreign policy and relations. The author was the director of the International Relations Section, University of Tehran.

339 Bayne, Edward Ashley. Notes Toward a Study of Iranian Foreign Relations. New York: American Universities Field Staff, Reports Service, 1965.

340 Burrell, R. M. "Iranian Foreign Policy During the Last Decade." Asian Affairs. 61(1):7-15, 1974.
Explains the changes in Iranian foreign policy since 1962 and the reasons behind Iran's interest in strengthening her power in the Persian Gulf region.

341 _____. "Iranian Foreign Policy: Strategic Location, Economic Ambition, and Dynastic Determination." Journal of International Affairs. 29(2):129-138, 1975.
The Iranian foreign policy is analyzed in light of the Shah's vision to make Iran a major economic power.

342 Canat, Frédéric. "L'Iran sur la Brèche 1968-1978." Défense Nationale. 34(7):91-104, 1978.
Describes Iranian foreign policy and its extreme dependence on the United States.

343 Chubin, Shahram. Iran's Foreign Policy, 1958-1972: A Small State's Constraints and Choices. Ph.D. dissertation,

Columbia University, 1974.
Iranian diplomacy is studied as that of a small state, strategically located and of significance to the great power rivalry.

344 _____. "Iran's Foreign Policy 1960-1976: An Overview." In: Amirsadeghi, Hossein (ed.), Twentieth-Century Iran. New York: Holmes & Meier, 1977. Pages 197-222.
The bulk of the essay comprises treatment of Iran's foreign policy during the years 1973-1976 which the author maintains was a "period of dynamic initiative, wider security horizons and enhanced capabilities in a context more conductive to manoeuvre."

345 _____ and Zabih, Sepehr. The Foreign Relations of Iran: A Developing State in a Zone of Great-Power Conflict. Berkeley: University of California Press, 1974.
The authors analyze and discuss in detail the foreign policy of postwar Iran toward various countries. The book is divided into two parts. Part I discusses Iran's foreign relations on the international level. Relations with the Soviet Union and the United States are discussed. In this part Iran's foreign relations is approached as a "small power" and its relations with the superpowers is analyzed "in terms of opportunities provided it by the international context...." Part II is an analysis of Iran's relations on the regional level. Relations with Egypt, Iraq and the Persian Gulf region are examined.

346 Clark, Peter M. and Mowlana, Hamid. "Iran's Perception of Western Europe: A Study in National and Foreign Policy Articulation." International Interactions. 4(2):99-123, 1978.
The international edition of the Iranian newspaper Keyhan was analyzed as a source of elite perceptions of Western Europe. Discusses the correlations between these perceptions and national and foreign policy objectives.

347 Cottrell, Alvin J. "The Foreign Policy of the Shah." Strategic Review. 3(4):32-44, 1975.
The Shah's foreign policy is examined with an emphasis on policies since the Pakistan-India conflict in 1965. He decreased Iran's dependence for self-defense on CENTO after the U.S. failed to help Pakistan. His other foreign policies including his goal of securing the Persian Gulf area and the Indian Ocean region, his concern over Arab socialism, and his policies toward Iraq are also discussed.

348 Darvich-Kodjouri, Djamshid. Images and Perception in International Relations: A Case Study of Relationships Between Iran and the Great Powers. Ph.D. dissertation, Miami University, 1976.
This study concentrates on images of Iran held by Great Britain, the United States, and the Soviet Union.

349 Djalili, Mohammad Reza. "Les Relations Culturelles Internationales de l'Iran." Relations Internationales. (Téhéran) 2:107-126, 1974/75.
A systematic survey of the international cultural relations of Iran since the nineteenth century and up to the 1970's.

350 Elahi, Cyrus. Society and Foreign Policy in Iran. Ph.D. dissertation, the American University, 1970.
The societal influences on foreign policy in Iran are studied.

351 Ghoreyshi, Ahmad and Elahi, Cyrus. "Iran's International Position: An Interpretation." In: Jacqz, Jane W. (ed.), Iran: Past, Present and Future. New York: Aspen Institute for Humanistic Studies, 1976. Pages 369-386.
Security is considered to be a major concern in the Iranian foreign policy. The authors conclude that for the above reason, Iran is likely to continue increasing her military strength.

352 _____ and _____. "Irans Stellung in der Weltpolitik." Europa-Archiv. 31(12):385-395, 1976.
Surveys Iran's position in international politics. The authors contend that Iran's use of her oil revenues in order to achieve political independence and build a strong military has earned that country a growing credibility in international politics.

353 Gil Benumeya, R. "El Irán, Encrucijada Política Mundial." Revista de Política Internacional. 127:113-122, 1973.
Iran's growing international role is discussed.

354 Grifith, William E. "Iran's Foreign Policy in the Pahlavi Era." In: Lenczowski, George (ed.), Iran Under the Pahlavis. Stanford, California: Hoover Institution Press, 1978. Pages 365-388.
After a brief historical background, the foreign policy of Reza Shah and his successor Mohammad Reza Shah are discussed. The author maintains that Reza Shah's foreign policy was basically nationalistic in both economics and politics and foreshadowed that of the Shah in general and even in many details. Other topics covered include: "Foreign Policy Implications of the 1973 Oil Price Increase" and "The Iranian-Iraqi Rapprochement." Problems and prospects are also discussed.

355 Hurewitz, J.C. "Iran in World and Regional Affairs." In: Yar-Shater, Ehsan, Iran Faces the Seventies. New York: Praeger, 1971. Pages 117-142.
A review of Iranian diplomatic relations at the regional and international levels in the 1960's. These relations, which included winning the support of the Soviet Union

without jeopardizing her alliance with the U.S., are assessed as favorable in general by the author.

356 Khabiri, Cyrus. The Position of Iran in Contemporary Great Power Politics. Ph.D. dissertation, the American University, 1959.
Analyzes the political warfare aspects of the politics of the superpowers in Iran. It also examines the role each power has played to obstruct the others in gaining national and strategic interests.

357 Khadjenouri, M. "L'évolution des Relations Extérieures de l'Iran du Début du XIXe Siècle à la Deuxième Guerre Mondiale." Politique Etrangère. 41(2):127-148, 1976.
Surveys the history of Iranian foreign relations with Europe from the beginning of the nineteenth century to World War II. Altogether 140 years of the evolution of these relations are covered.

358 Khaleeli, Abbas. "Some Aspects of Iran's Foreign Relations." Pakistan Horizon. 21(1):14-20, 1968.
This is the author's address at the meeting of Pakistan Institute of International Affairs held on October 27, 1967 in Karachi.

359 Middle East Research & Information Project. Iranian Nationalism and the Great Powers, 1872-1954. Cambridge, Massachusetts: Middle East Research & Information Project, 1975. (MERIP Reports; no. 37)
Iran's struggle for independence in the presence of the rivalry between Great Britain and Russia is discussed. "The Reza Khan Era: 1921-1941); "American Penetration: 1941-1946"; "Sovereignty to Servitude: 1947-1954" are among topics covered.

360 Mozafari, M. "Les Nouvelles Dimensions de la Politique Etrangère de l'Iran." Politique Etrangère. 40(2):141-159, 1975.
Discusses Iran's foreign policy toward the superpowers as well as China and the European countries. Examines the influence of this policy on the Persian Gulf region. The author concludes that Iran might have achieved her long sought after "National Independence Politics."

361 Pahlavi, Mohammad Reza. Iran's Foreign Policy: A Compendium of the Writings and Statements of His Imperial Majesty Shahanshah Aryamehr. Teheran: Ministry of Foreign Affairs, Information & Press Dept., 1970(?)
Selected passages from the statements and writings of the Shah. They deal with various aspects of Iranian politics and government such as CENTO, the Bahrain dispute, the Persian Gulf area, etc.

362 _____. Twelve Speeches by His Imperial Majesty Mohammad Reza Pahlavi Aryamehr, Shahanshah of Iran, on Ideological Basis of Iran's National and International Policy. Tehran: Pahlavi Library, 1971.
This collection of the Shah's public addresses sheds light on Iranian foreign policy under his rule.

363 Park, Tong-Whan; Abolfathi, Farid; and Ward, Michael. "Resource Nationalism in the Foreign Policy Behavior of Oil Exporting Countries (1947-1974)." International Interactions. 2(4):247-262, 1976.
Five oil exporting countries--Algeria, Iran, Kuwait, Libya, and Saudi Arabia--are studied in order to examine the relationship between foreign policy behavior and resource nationalism.

364 Ramazani, Rouhollah K. "Emerging Patterns of Regional Relations in Iranian Foreign Policy." Orbis. 18(4):1043-1069, 1975.
Studies goals and objectives of Iran's regional policies and evaluates their implications for the United States foreign policy. Attempts to analyze underlying causes for Iran's growing influence in international politics.

365 _____. The Foreign Policy of Iran: A Developing Nation in World Affairs, 1500-1941. Charlottesville: University Press of Virginia, 1966.
Iran's foreign policy since its beginning is analyzed in detail. The emphasis is on the period beginning in 1905 and also on the period of the reign of Reza Shah until his abdication in favor of his son in 1941.

366 _____. "The Instrument of Iranian Foreign Policy." In: Jacqz, Jane W. (ed.), Iran: Past, Present and Future. New York: Aspen Institute for Humanistic Studies, 1976. Pages 387-396.
According to the author, Iran's main instruments of foreign policy include diplomacy, military force, and economy, especially oil. These instruments are discussed and examples are given.

367 _____. "Iran's Changing Foreign Policy: A Preliminary Discussion." Middle East Journal. 24(4):421-437, 1970.
Changes in Iranian foreign policy since the mid-1960's are explained. The increasing role played by Iran in international politics is discussed.

368 _____. Iran's Foreign Policy, 1941-1973: A Study of Foreign Policy in Modernizing Nations. Charlottesville: University Press of Virginia, 1975.
This is a comprehensive work which presents a view of American policy from an Iranian perspective. Supplements

the author's The Foreign Policy of Iran: A Developing Nation in World Affairs, 1500-1941 (See entry 365).

369 Shaoul, Eshagh Emran. Cultural Values and Foreign Policy Decision-Making in Iran: The Case of Iran's Recognition of Israel. Ph.D. dissertation, George Washington University, 1971.
Argues that in addition to international, regional, and local political factors, cultural factors had influenced Iran's decision to recognize Israel in March, 1950. Pre- and post-Islamic cultural values of Iran, the author claims, were in competition in the case under study.

370 Singh, K.R. "Iran: The Quest for Security: An Overview." India Quarterly. 30(2):125-132, 1974.
Surveys Iran's relations with the United States and the Soviet Union and her foreign policy toward these superpowers. Discusses Iran's relative independence and her decreasing dependence on the United States and relates this to the decline in threats to Iran from the north.

371 Steinbach, U. "Iran im Aussenpolitischen Aufbruch." Aussenpolitik. 25(3):315-328, 1974.
Discusses the increasing role played by Iran in international politics. Accumulation of oil wealth is considered as the main cause for this awakening.

372 Vassenhove, L. van. "La Politique Etrangère de la Perse." Revue Politique et Parlementaire. 145(433):419-433, 1930.
After presenting a historical background on Iran's foreign policy, this article emphasizes Reza Shah's policies and achievements in that arena.

373 Zabih, Sepehr. "Change and Continuity in Iran's Foreign Policy in Modern Times." World Politics. 23:522-543, 1971.
Reviews three books dealing with Iranian foreign policy.

374 _____. "Iran's International Posture: De facto Nonalignment Within a Pro-Western Alliance." Middle East Journal. 24(3):302-318, 1970.
Iran's foreign policy of "nonalignment" beginning after World War II is examined and its effect on the security of the region is discussed.

IRAN AND HER NEIGHBORS: AFGHANISTAN, PAKISTAN, IRAQ, AND TURKEY

375 Abidi, A. H. H. "Irano-Afghan Dispute Over the Helmand Waters." International Studies. 16(3):357-378, 1977.
Reviews the history of Iran and Afghanistan boundary dispute over the Helmand River. Analyzes the two countries' efforts for finding a political resolution which was finally achieved in June 1977.

376 Achoube-Amini, Rahmatollah. Le Conflit de Frontière Irako-Iranien. Paris: Société Anonyme l'Imprimeries Delalain, 1936.
A historical and political analysis of the Iraqi-Iranian frontier dispute written during the reign of Reza Shah.

377 Akhtar, Shameem. "The Iraqi-Iranian Dispute over the Shatt-el-Arab." Pakistan Horizon. 22(3):213-220, 1969.
Following a historical background on the dispute, the author proposes a peaceful resolution to the problem according to international law.

378 Amirie, Abbas. "Iran's Regional Foreign Policy Posture." India Quarterly. 34(4):457-470, 1978.
A discussion of the existing problems in the Middle East and the Iranian foreign policy toward her neighbors. The establishment of a regional détente with the Soviet Union, mediation between India and Pakistan, and between Pakistan and Afghanistan are given as examples of Iran's active/regional foreign policy role.

379 Choudhary, L. K. "Pakistan as a Factor in Indo-Iranian Relations." Indian Journal of Political Science. 35(4): 352-361, 1974.
The causes behind Iran's assistance to Pakistan during and after the 1965 Indo-Pakistan war are analyzed.

380 Dhanani, Gulshan. "The Shatt al-Arab Agreement: Legal Implications and Regional Consequences." Political Science Review. 14(3/4):80-92, 1975.
Through Algerian mediation, Iran and Iraq agreed to normalize their relations in March 1975 and signed a border

treaty three months later in Baghdad. This article analyzes the consequences of this agreement for both countries following a historical survey of the conflict.

381 Djalili, Mohammad Reza. "Le Rapprochement Irano-Irakien et Ses Conséquences." Politique Etrangère. 40(3):273-291, 1975.
The reconciliation signed on March 6, 1975 between Iran and Iraq and its consequences are discussed.

382 Dupree, L. "A Suggested Pakistan-Afghanistan-Iran Federation." Middle East Journal. 17(4):383-399, 1963.
The common background of Pakistan, Afghanistan, and Iran is reviewed and political and other obstacles toward a possible federation among these countries are analyzed. It is maintained that the United States and the Soviet Union would not be in favor of such a federation.

383 Edmonds, C.J. "The Iraqi-Persian Frontier: 1639-1938." Asian Affairs. 62(2):147-154, 1975.
The frontier conflicts between Iraq and Iran are surveyed. Various treaties between the two countries are discussed.

384 Ghadimipour, Fatemeh. "Les Relations Régionales de l'Iran avec les Pays Non-Arabes." Politique Etrangère. 41(2): 149-168, 1976.
The regional relationships of Iran with the non-Arab countries of Turkey, Afghanistan, and Pakistan are discussed.

385 Ghavami, Taghi. "Shatt-al-Arab (Arvand-Rud) Crisis." Naval War College Review. 27(2):58-64, 1974.
The boundary dispute between Iran and the neighboring Iraq over Shatt al-Arab is discussed. The author proposes a third-party mediation in order to resolve the conflict politically.

386 Iran. Vizarat-i Umur-i Kharijah. Some Facts Concerning the Dispute Between Iran and Iraq over the Shatt-al-Arab. Tehran: Ministry of Foreign Affairs, 1969.
The provisions of the 1937 treaty negotiated between Iran and Iraq under the British auspices regarding the Shatt al-Arab or Arvand Rud waterway have long been a source of contention between the two countries. This document discusses the Iranian point of view.

387 "Iran-Iraq: Documents on Abrogation of 1937 Treaty." International Legal Materials. 8(3):478-492, 1969.
Includes the 1937 boundry treaty between Iran and Iraq, abrogation statement by the Iranian government (April 19, 1969), and the two governments' correspondence with the United Nations Security Council regarding this matter.

388 al-Izzi, Khalid Yahya.   The Shatt al-Arab River Dispute, in
      Terms of Law.   Baghdad, Iraq: Ministry of Information,
      al-Huriyah Printing House, 1972.
         A historical and legal investigation of the Shatt al-Arab
      River dispute between Iran and Iraq based on Iranian as
      well as Iraqi sources. This publication has two parts. In
      Part One, the history, the author traces the roots of the
      conflict back to the rivalry between the Old Ottoman Empire
      and the Persian Empire. He then presents a historical back-
      ground of the conflict during the world wars and after the
      Second World War. In Part Two, the author provides some
      facts about the river and proceeds to consider the legal as-
      pects of the conflict examining in detail the arguments for
      redrawing the boundary line on Shatt al-Arab along the thal-
      weg line. Several appendices provide various texts of trea-
      ties and other documents.

389 Jain, H.M.   "Legal Aspects of the Shatt al-Arab Dispute."
      Indian Journal of Politics.   8(1-2):91-108, 1974.
         The treaties between Iran and Iraq regarding the Shatt al-
      Arab River are surveyed and their legal implications are dis-
      cussed.

390 Koszinowski, T.   "Der Irakisch-Iranische Konflikt und Seine
      Beilegung." Orient.   (Opladen) 17(1):72-86, 1976.
         The border conflict between Iran and Iraq is discussed
      and the future consequences of the reconciliation of March
      1975 between the two countries are mentioned.

391 Lauterpacht, E.   "Rivers Boundaries: Legal Aspects of the
      Shatt al-Arab Frontier."   International and Comparative
      Law Quarterly.   9(2):208-236, 1960.
         Answers some of the legal questions regarding the bound-
      ary dispute between Iran and Iraq.

392 Melamid, Alexander.   "The Shatt al-Arab Boundary Dispute."
      Middle East Journal.   22(3):351-357, 1968.
         Asserts that the intensity of the Shatt al-Arab River dis-
      pute between Iran and Iraq has been decreased because of
      relocation of oil and dry cargo activities from that river.

393 Mohammadally, Safia S.   "Pakistan-Iran Relations (1947-1979)."
      Pakistan Horizon.   32(4):51-63, 1979.
         Surveys the relations between Pakistan and Iran during
      the Shah's regime.

394 Peretz, Don.   "The Middle East."   Freedom at Issue.   34:25-
      27, 1976.
         The events in the Middle East in 1975 are reviewed. It
      includes a discussion of Iran-Iraq boundary dispute.

395 Rossi, Pierre.   "Le Litige Frontalier entre l'Irak et l'Iran."
      Orient.   (Paris) 12:19-26, 1959.

Political Conditions   63

Reviews legal aspects of the Shatt al-Arab River dispute between Iran and Iraq and examines arguments offered by the two governments in connection with this conflict.

396 Scarcia, Gianoroberto. "La Controversia tra Persia e Iraq per lo Shatt el-Arab (Dicembre 1959-Gennaio 1960)." Oriente Moderno. 40:77-93, 1960.
Discusses the controversy over the frontier conflict between Iran and Iraq. Focuses on the period between 1959 and 1960.

397 Sevian, Vahe J. "The Evolution of the Boundary Between Iraq and Iran." In: Fisher, Charles A. (ed.), Essays in Political Geography. New York: Barnes and Noble, 1968. Pages 211-223.
Rich in providing factual information on the political as well as geographical factors contributing to the evolution of Iran-Iraq boundary.

398 Tahir-Kheli, Shirin. "Iran and Pakistan: Cooperation in an Area of Conflict." Asian Survey. 17(5):474-490, 1977.
Iran-Pakistan relations on the local, regional, and international levels are discussed since 1947 when Pakistan became independent. Cooperation between the two countries is emphasized.

399 Tomasek, R.D. "The Resolution of Major Controversies Between Iran and Iraq." World Affairs. 139:206-230, 1976-77.
The March 1975 agreement between Iran and Iraq, in which provisions for resolution of the Shatt al-Arab River dispute, the Kurdish problem, and other boundary problems were made, is discussed and analyzed.

400 Yusuf, Kaniz Fatima. Economic and Political Cooperation of Pakistan, Iran, and Afghanistan. Ph.D. dissertation, Clark University, 1959.
The author maintains that the possibility of economic and political cooperation among the three countries is a product of the strains to which these nations are subjected by the international power rivalries.

RELATIONS WITH THE PERSIAN GULF AND THE INDIAN OCEAN REGIONS

401 Adamiyat, Fereydoun. Bahrein Islands: A Legal and Diplomatic Study of the British-Iranian Controversy. New York: Praeger, 1955.

Attempts to study the British and Iranian diplomacy regarding the Persian Gulf region, especially the Bahrain Islands, historically as well as from the viewpoint of international law. The last chapter, "Legal Interpretation," is an analysis of the Iranian and the British cases. The validity of the two countries' claims to these islands is examined.

402 Alaolmolki, Nozar. Emergence of Regional Hegemonical Power: Iran as a Case Study in the Region of Persian Gulf. Ph.D. dissertation, Miami University, 1977.

Discusses the causes which have motivated Iran to strengthen her role in the Persian Gulf region. Evaluates Iran's achievements in that regard.

403 Amirie, Abbas. "Iran als Regionalmacht: Persischer Golf und Indischer Ozean als Wirkungsfeld einer Unabhängigen Aussenpolitik." Europa-Archiv. 33(2):43-52, 1978.

Discusses how Iran became a regional power in the Persian Gulf and the Indian Ocean regions after the British withdrawal from these areas.

404 ———— (ed.). The Persian Gulf and Indian Ocean in International Politics. Tehran: Institute for International Political and Economic Studies, 1975.

Contains papers presented at an international conference on the Persian Gulf and the Indian Ocean held in Tehran on March 25-27, 1975. A variety of topics were discussed, ranging from American and Soviet naval buildups to policies of Iran in the Persian Gulf region. The latter was presented by Amir Taheri of Iran.

405 al-Baharna, H. "The Fact-Finding Mission of the United Nations Secretary General and the Settlement of the Bahrain-Iran Dispute, May 1970." International and Comparative Law Quarterly. 22(3):541-552, 1973.

The United Nations' involvement in the Bahrain-Iran dispute is examined.

406 Braun, Ursula. "Wachsende Polarisierung in der Region des
     Arabischen Golfes." Europa Archiv. 28(17):603-612, 1973.
         Discusses the destabilization of the Persian Gulf region
     as a result of British withdrawal from that area.

407 Brewer, William D. "Yesterday and Tomorrow in the Persian
     Gulf." Middle East Journal. 23(2):149-158, 1969.
         The consequences of the British withdrawal from the
     Persian Gulf region for the littoral states are examined.
     It is maintained that the withdrawal facilitated the develop-
     ment of a cordial and strong relationship between Iran,
     Saudi Arabia, and Kuwait.

408 Cottrell, Alvin J. "Iran, the Arabs and the Persian Gulf."
     Orbis. 17(3):978-988, 1973.
         Iran's foreign, economic, and military policies are re-
     viewed in light of her position in the Persian Gulf area sub-
     sequent to the British withdrawal from that region.

409 _____. "A New Persian Hegemony?" Interplay. 3(12):
     9-15, 1970.
         Discusses the political situation in the Persian Gulf after
     British withdrawal and filling of the power vacuum by Iran.

410 Croizat, Victor J. "Stability in the Persian Gulf." U.S. Naval
     Institute Proceedings. 99(7):48-59, 1973.
         After a brief historical background of the Persian Gulf
     area, the political consequences of the British withdrawal
     from that region is discussed. Iran is considered the best
     choice to succeed the British in that area.

411 Djalili, Mohammad Reza "Evolution de la Politique Iranienne
     de l'Océan Indien." Revue Iranienne des Relations Inter-
     nationales/Iranian Review of International Relations. 8:185-
     198, 1976.
         Discusses the development of Iranian foreign policy toward
     the Indian Ocean region since 1960.

412 _____. "The Indian Ocean: Seen from Iran." IDSA Jour-
     nal. (Institute for Defense Studies and Analyses, New Del-
     hi). 9(2):107-115, 1976.
         Iran's interest in the Indian Ocean is discussed and her
     policy toward that region examined. Iran's objective is con-
     sidered to be establishing peace in the area.

413 Esmaili, Malek. Le Golfe Persique et les Iles de Bahrein.
     Paris: Domat-Montchrestien, 1936.
         Discusses the dispute over the Bahrain Islands during
     Reza Shah's reign.

414 Faroughy, Abbas. The Bahrein Islands (750-1951): A Contribu-
     tion to the Study of Power Politics in the Persian Gulf;
     an Historical, Economic, and Geographical Survey. New

York: Verry, Fisher, 1951.
This book is divided into two parts: "General Description" and "History. " The last section of Part II deals briefly with the twentieth-century Bahrain.

415 Fawzi, Abd al-Sattar. The Persian Claim to Bahrain. Baghdad: Ministry of Information, 1970.
The British government's announcement of its intention to withdraw from the Persian Gulf region was received with alarm in Iran. In order to be able to safeguard her interests in that area, and clear the way for a favorable regional environment, Iran in 1970 relinquished her historic claim to Bahrain. This book briefly discusses the situation from Iraq's vantage point.

416 Gil Benumeya, R. "El Imperio del Irán, Corazón del Oriente. " Revista de Política Internacional. 117:123-130, 1971.
Discusses the importance of Iran in the Middle East and her role after the British left the Persian Gulf.

417 Gordon, Edward. "Resolution of the Bahrain Dispute. " American Journal of International Law. 65(3):560-568, 1971.
Discusses the role of the U.S. in bringing about a peaceful settlement of the dispute between Iran and Great Britain over the status of Bahrain in 1968-70.

418 Halliday, Fred. "Iran and the Gulf. " Middle East International. 77:10-11, 1977.
Examines relations of Iran and the Arab states in regard to the Persian Gulf.

419 Holden, David. "The Persian Gulf: After the British Raj. " Foreign Affairs. 49:721-735, 1971.
Claims that there is a possibility of unrest following the British withdrawal from the Gulf and examines the Saudi-Iranian competition to dominate the region.

420 Imhoff, Christoph von. "Iran als Makler am Persischen Golf. " Aussenpolitik. 22(9):563-572, 1971.
Iran's new leading position in the Persian Gulf following the British withdrawal from that region is examined.

421 _____. "Vom Persischen Golf zum Indischen Ozean. " Aussenpolitik. 26(1):40-55, 1975.
Iran's foreign policy toward Persian Gulf and the Indian Ocean regions is discussed.

422 Kelly, J.B. "The Persian Claim to Bahrain. " International Affairs. 33:51-71, 1957.
Political history of the Islands of Bahrain is presented. and Iran's claim to the Islands is considered to be illegitimate.

423 Kennedy, Edward M. "The Persian Gulf: Arms Race or Arms Control?" Foreign Affairs. 54:14-35, 1975.
Discusses the competition between Iran and Saudi Arabia for control of the Persian Gulf and the American arms flow to that area.

424 Labrousse, H. "Petrole et Tensions Autour du Golfe." Défense Nationale. 35(8-9):57-68, 1979.
The effects of worldwide energy crisis and changes in Iranian politics on political tensions in the Persian Gulf area are examined.

425 Lateef, Abdul. Iran, Emerging Gulf Power. Lahore: Progressive Publishers, 1977.
This brief monograph attempts to examine the modernization and the political and economic development of Iran under the Pahlavi dynasty. Iran's growing power in the Persian Gulf area is briefly analyzed.

426 Lindt, A. R. "Politics in the Persian Gulf." Journal of the Royal Central Asian Society. 26:619-633, 1939.
Lecture given to the Royal Central Asian Society on July 26, 1939. The lecturer, a Swiss citizen, throws some light on the Reza Shah's policies regarding the Persian Gulf which are, for example, Iran's claim to the possession of the Bahrain Islands.

427 Long, D. E. The Persian Gulf: An Introduction to Its Peoples, Politics and Economics. Boulder, Colorado: Westview Press, 1976.
Contains useful information regarding Iran's foreign policy in this area. For example, in Chapter 3, "Regional Politics of the Gulf" and Chapter 6, "Economic Prospects in the Gulf," Iran's position is discussed in detail.

428 MacLeod, A. "Shah of the Indian Ocean?" Pacific Community. 7(3):423-432, 1976.
A background history of Iran's quest for power in the Indian Ocean region is presented. The consequences of her influence in the area are examined.

429 Marlowe, John. The Persian Gulf in the Twentieth Century. New York: Praeger, 1962.
Iran's position regarding the Persian Gulf region under the Shah's regime is examined (Chapters IX and XII).

430 Martín de la Escalera, C. "Irán y el Predominio en el Golfo Pérsico." Revista de Política Internacional. 119:159-176, 1972.
After a sympathetic discussion of the Shah's achievements in the areas of agrarian reform, economic development, etc., this article examines Iran's increasing

role in the Persian Gulf area which the author maintains will ensure the stability of the region.

431 Marwah, Onkar. "Iran as a Regional Power: Flexibility and Constraints." In: Mughisuddin, M. (ed.), Conflict and Cooperation in the Persian Gulf. New York: Praeger, 1977. Pages 29-45.
Assesses Iranian foreign policy toward the Persian Gulf region especially since 1973. Analyzes Iran's objectives in regard to that region and asserts that since 1973 Iran has succeeded in becoming a powerful force in the area.

432 Moghtader, Hushang. "The Settlement of the Bahrain Question: A Study in Anglo-Iranian-United Nations Diplomacy." Pakistan Horizon. 26(2):16-29, 1973.
Following a historical survey, changes in Iranian policy regarding the Bahrain Islands are analyzed. The peaceful settlement of the dispute over these islands through cooperation among Iran, Great Britain, and the U.N. is discussed.

433 Owen, R.P. "The British Withdrawal from the Persian Gulf." World Today. 28(2):75-81, 1972.
Discusses the consequences of the British withdrawal from the Persian Gulf area. The rivalry between the Arab states and Iran in filling the vacuum is discussed.

434 Paolini, M. "Iran: Ambizioni di Potenza nell'Area del Golfo." Politica Internazionale. 12:57-66, 1975.
Iran's role in the Persian Gulf area is studied.

435 Ramazani, Rouhollah K. "Iran's Search for Regional Cooperation." Middle East Journal. 30(2):173-186, 1976.
Relations between Iran and the Arab states of the Persian Gulf region are examined. After the withdrawal of the British from the region, Iran has initiated an even more active diplomacy which has resulted in improved relationships with the various governments of the Gulf region.

436 _____. The Persian Gulf: Iran's Role. Charlottesville: University Press of Virginia, 1972.
This study examines Iran's role in the Persian Gulf following the British withdrawal from that area in 1971.

437 Reinhard, George M. Strategic Problems of the Indian Ocean Area: The Iran-Afghanistan-Pakistan Sector of the International Frontier. Ph.D. dissertation, the Catholic University, 1968.
Analyzes the strategies of the Great Powers in regard to the Indian Ocean area.

438 Rondot, Philippe. "La Compétition pour la Maîtrise du Golfe." Défense Nationale. 33(7):103-114, 1977.

Discusses the competition between Iran and Saudi Arabia for the control of the Persian Gulf.

439 Rondot, Pierre. "L'Iran Face à l'Arabisme sur le Golfe Persique." Revue de Défense Nationale. 24(6/7):1047-1061, 1968.
The involvement of Iran in the Persian Gulf area is discussed and a comparison is made between the politics of the Arab countries and Iran.

440 Schulz, Ann T. "A Leadership Role for Iran in the Persian Gulf." Current History. 62:25-30, 1972.
Iran's role in the Persian Gulf region after the British retreat is examined.

441 Singh, K. R. "Conflict and Cooperation in the Gulf." International Studies. 15(4):487-508, 1976.
Iran's emergence as the guardian of the Persian Gulf after the British withdrawal is discussed. The future consequences are analyzed.

442 Steinbach, U. "Irans Rolle im Arabischen Nahen Osten und Indischen Ozean." Orient. (Opladen) 17(2):88-114, 1976.
Focuses on Iran's foreign policy toward the Persian Gulf region. However, relations with Israel and India are also examined.

443 Thoman, Roy E. "Iraq and the Persian Gulf Region." Current History. 64:21-38, 1973.
Iraq's competition with Iran and Kuwait for dominance in the Persian Gulf area following the power vacuum left in the region as a consequence of the British retreat is studied.

444 _____. "The Persian Gulf Region." Current History. 60:38-45, 1971.
Examining primary sources, the author discusses the situation in the Persian Gulf region after the British withdrawal. Iran's position along with other regional states is analyzed.

445 Towliat, Mohsen. Iran as a Regional Power in the Persian Gulf. Ph.D. dissertation, Claremont Graduate School, 1978.
An appraisal of Iran's military and economic capabilities in safeguarding the Persian Gulf region.

446 "United Nations Security Council. Resolution 287 (1970): Adopted by the Security Council at its 1536th Meeting on 11 May 1970." Middle East Journal. 24(3):373-380, 1970.
Presents the text of the resolution which deals with Iran and Great Britain decisions regarding the Bahrain Islands.

447 Wright, Denis. "The Changed Balance of Power in the Persian Gulf." Asian Affairs. 60(3):255-262, 1973.

Discusses the change in balance of power after the British withdrawal from the Persian Gulf area. The role of Iran as a dominant power in the area and its consequences for the industrialized nations are analyzed.

448 Zabih, Sepehr. "Iran's Policy Toward the Persian Gulf." International Journal of Middle East Studies. 7(3):345-358, 1976.

Iran's foreign policy toward the Persian Gulf region is analyzed. The author asserts that this policy, in which Iran continues to strengthen her position in the region, is an indication of a shift from a rigid pro-Western foreign policy.

449 Zampa, Leone. "Gli Stati Minori del Golfo Persico." Affari Esteri. 7(26):317-337, 1975.

Surveys the Arab states of the Persian Gulf area. Their conflicts with Iraq and Iran are discussed.

IRAN AND THE SOVIET UNION

450 Agabekov, G. OGPU: The Russian Secret Terror. New York: Brentano's, 1931.
Soviet subservice activities in Iran during the Reza Shah era are described in this memoir. See also entry 1.

451 Bala, Mirza. "Die Aspiration der Sowjets auf Südaserbeidschan." Sowjet Studien. 1:75-81, 1956.
A discussion of the Soviet Union's agitations to prevent political and economic cooperation between Southern Azerbaijan and the Iranian government.

452 Beloff, Max. The Foreign Policy of Soviet Russia. London; New York: Oxford University Press, 1947, 1948.
This two-volume work is an in-depth description of the Soviet Union's policy toward Iran during the periods between the wars. (Volume I, 1929-1936; volume II, 1936-1941.)

453 Benab, Younes P. The Soviet Union and Britain in Iran, 1917-1927: A Case Study of the Domestic Impact of East-West Rivalry. Ph.D. dissertation, the Catholic University of America, 1974.
The Anglo-Russian rivlary during 1917-1927 and its impact on social, economic, political, and ideological changes in Iran are analyzed. The influence of the Bolshevic Revolution in Iran during this period is also examined.

454 Berner, Wolfgang. "Der Aufsteig des Iran zur Wirtschaftsmacht und die Entwicklung der Iranisch-Sowjetischen Beziehungen." Politik und Zeitgeschichte. 12:16-31, 1975.
The economic development of Iran as well as the evolution of Iran-U.S.S.R. relations are the focus of this study. The effects on political defense of Iran because of the Soviet Union's economic relations with Iran are examined. The consequences of this situation on Russo-German relations are also considered.

455 ———. Die Iranisch-Sowjetische Zusammenarbeit im Wirtschaftlich-Technischen Bereich: Erfahrungsbericht über eine Informationsreise in den Iran im Zeitraum 6-28. Mai 1974. Köln: Bundesinstitut für Ostwissenschaftliche und Inter-

nationale Studien, 1974.
A brief discussion of Irano-Soviet collaboration in economic and technical areas.

456 Berry, John A. "Oil and Soviet Policy in the Middle East." Middle East Journal. 26(2):149-160, 1972.
Traces the involvement and interest of the Soviet Union in Middle Eastern oil. A brief discussion of an agreement between Iran and the Soviet Union regarding purchase of natural gas from Iran and the consequences of this agreement on Irano-Soviet relationship is also given.

457 Borzoui, Farzin. Das Wirken des Staatsmannes Ahmad Quwam in der Iranischen Politik unter Besonderer Berücksichtigung Seines Vertragswerkes mit der Sowjetunion. Heidelberg, 1975.
Surveys political activities of Ahmad Qavam, Iranian Prime Minister during the post-World War II Azerbaijan crisis. Emphasizes his agreement with the Soviet government regarding resolution of the crisis.

458 Conolly, Violet. Soviet Economic Policy in the East: Turkey, Persia, Afghanistan, Mongolia and Tana Tuva, Sin Kiang. London: Oxford University Press, 1933.
Chapter III, "Soviet Economic Relations with Persia," contains some useful information on the subject for the Reza Shah period. Reprinted in 1981 by Hyperion Press.

459 Davenport, Robert Wesley. Soviet Economic Relations with Iran, 1917-1930. Ph.D. dissertation, Columbia University, 1953.
Major economic issues arising in Soviet-Iranian relations during the period 1917-1930 are discussed. This is an attempt to investigate the objectives of the Soviet economic policy in Iran and their effects.

460 Fatemi, Faramarz. The U.S.S.R. in Iran: The Irano-Soviet Dispute and the Pattern of Azerbaijan Revolution, 1941-1947. Ph.D. dissertation, New School of Social Research, 1976.
The Soviet Union's motives for occupying Northern Iran after WW II are analyzed.

461 Fischer, Louis. The Soviets in World Affairs: A History of the Relations Between the Soviet Union and the Rest of the World. London: Jonathan Cape, 1930.
Useful for the study of the Soviet Union's foreign policy toward Iran.

462 Geyer, Dietrich. Die Sowjetunion und Iran: Eine Untersuchung zur Aussenpolitik der UdSSR im Nahen Osten, 1917-1954. Tübingen: Böhlau-Verlag Köln, 1955.
The Soviet-Iranian relations during the period 1917-1954

Political Conditions   73

are discussed in detail. The last chapter deals with the
Soviet Union's foreign policy toward the Middle East as
well as Iran.

463 Ghoreichi, Ahmad. Soviet Foreign Policy in Iran 1917-1960.
Ph. D. dissertation, University of Colorado, 1965.
Traces the Soviet policies in Iran from the Bolshevic
Revolution to 1960. The author maintains that policy in
Iran was basically the continuation of Czarist policy with
the addition of the communist ideology.

464 Hensel, Howard M. Soviet Policy in the Persian Gulf, 1965-
1975. Ph. D. dissertation, University of Virginia, 1976.
Examines the Soviet Union's efforts to fill the vacuum
brought on by Britain's withdrawal from the Gulf in 1971.
Since Iran filled that vacuum soon thereafter, this study
presents an insight into the temporary power imbalance
in the area.

465 Imhoff, Christoph von. "Iran und Sein Sowjetischer Nachbar."
Aussenpolitik. 22(1):28-37, 1971.
Iran's political and economic relations with the Soviet
Union are discussed and analyzed.

466 Kutuzov, V. "USSR-Iran: Expansion and Deepening of Trade
and Economic Relations." Foreign Trade. 12:21-24, 1977.
A historical sketch of the Soviet-Iranian trade relations
since 1927 and their effect on the political relations between
the two countries.

467 Lacoste, Raymond. La Russie Soviétique et la Question d'Orient.
La Poussée Soviétique vers les Mers Chaudes, Méditerranée
et Golfe Persique. Paris: Les Editions Internationales,
1946.
This general source on postwar Soviet policy contains
references to Iran during that period, especially pages 131-
233, "La Russie et la Perse."

468 Laqueur, Walter. "Russlands Durchbruch." Monat. (West
Germany). 22(260):51-61, 1970.
The Soviet Union's penetration in the Middle Eastern
countries including Iran is examined. In Iran, U.S.S.R.'s
tool has been trade rather than Communism.

469 Laurent, François. "La Politique Actuelle de l'U.R.S.S. en
Iran." Orient. (Paris) 5:47-58, 1958.
The Soviet Union's political, cultural, and economic ac-
tivities in Iran are discussed. Dissatisfaction with the
American policy motivated the Soviets to increase their ac-
tivities in Iran.

470 Lenczowski, George. Russia and the West in Iran, 1918-1948:
A Study in Big Power Rivalry. New York: Greenwood

Press, 1968.
This is a reprint of the author's work of the same title published in 1949 by Cornell University Press. The political developments in Iran since World War I are reviewed. The origin of Communism in Iran is discussed. Considered one of the best sources on the subject, this book also contains several appendices on political parties and treaties of Iran.

471 Mehnert, K. "Asien am Eisernen Vorhang, III: Iran und die Sowjetunion." Osteuropa. 10(4):217-224, 1960.
Discusses Iran's relationship with the Soviet Union after the fall of Mossadeq in 1953.

472 _____. "Iran und UdSSR 1942-1953." Osteuropa. 3(5): 374-381, 1953.
Discusses the relationship between Iran and the Soviet Union during the period 1942-1953.

473 Meister, Irene W. Soviet Policy in Iran, 1917-1950: A Study in Techniques. Ph.D. dissertation, Fletcher School of Law and Diplomacy, 1954.
A detailed analysis of Russo-Iranian relations from 1917 to 1950 with an emphasis on the relations between 1941 to 1950. Examines the methods used by the Soviet Union to achieve her goal of complete Sovietization of Iran including the use of radio propaganda techniques.

474 Menon, Rajan. "Soviet Policy in the Indian Ocean Region." Current History. 76:176-179, 186, 192, 1979.
Examines the Soviet Union's policy in the Indian Ocean in light of its relations with Iran, Afghanistan, India, Pakistan, and Bangladesh.

475 Meyer-Ranke, Peter. "Irans Neue Rolle: Ordnungsmacht im Mittelost." Aussenpolitik. 19(5):298-306, 1968.
The reasons underlying the rapprochement between the Soviet Union and Iran are examined.

476 Müller, Kurt. "Der Iran: Ein Brückenkopf in der Neuen Strategie der Osteuropäischen Länder im CENTO-Pakt-Raum." Vierteljahresberichte. 38:381-397, 1969.
Studies the assistance given to Iran by the Soviet Union and the Eastern European countries. Neutralization of Iran is considered to be one of the motives behind these relations.

477 Navai, M. Les Relations Economiques Irano-Russes. Paris: Les Editions Domat-Montchrestien, 1935.
Discusses the economic relations between Iran and Russia before World War II.

478 Nollau, Günther and Wiehe, Hans Jürgen. Russia's South Flank: Soviet Operations in Iran, Turkey, and Afghanistan. New York: Praeger, 1963.

An attempt to assess the Soviet threat to Iran, Turkey, and Afghanistan on the basis of available historical documents and personal observation. The first chapter is devoted entirely to Iran. Translated by Victor Andersen.

479 Noorani, A. G. "Soviet Ambitions in South Asia." International Security. 4(3):31-59, 1979-80.
Examines the Soviet Union's policies in Iran, Afghanistan, and Pakistan. It is maintained that these policies were aimed at increasing the security of Russia's Asian borders.

480 Parvin, Manoucher. "Political Economy of Soviet-Iranian Trade: An Overview of Theory and Practice." Middle East Journal. 31(1):31-43, 1977.
Analyzes the causes and consequences of the Irano-Soviet trade. Surveys historical and theoretical patterns of economic trade between the two countries.

481 Pirayech, Purandocht. Persisch-Russiche Beziehungen Zwischen den Beiden Weltkriegen. München: Mikrokopie München, 1964.
The Soviet-Iranian relations during the period between the two world wars are discussed.

482 Rashidi, Ramezan Ali. Iran's Economic Relations with the Soviet Union 1917-1968. Ph.D. dissertation, University of Pennsylvania, 1968.
Irano-Soviet economic contacts during this period are described in detail. The study is divided into three periods: 1917-1941; 1941-1954; and 1954-1968.

483 Scarcia, Gianroberto. "Aspetti Giuridici e Politici della Recente Polemica fra Persia e Unione Sovietica." Oriente Moderno. 39:499-513, 1959.
The author argues that the Soviet Union has shifted her policy of nonintervention in Iranian internal affairs to one of intervention.

484 Tekiner, Suleiman. "Soviet-Iranian Relations over the Last Half Century." Studies on the Soviet Union. 8(4):36-44, 1969.
Soviet Union's relations with Iran, her interest in that country, as well as her efforts in converting Iran into a Soviet sattelite are discussed. The author indicates that the USSR's efforts in Sovietization of Iran came to an end in 1953 when Mossadeq's government was overthrown.

485 Wasserberg, Arlyn B. Politics of Soviet Interference: Soviet Foreign Policy Towards Iran. Ph.D. dissertation, City University of New York, 1979.
Examines the Soviet Union's foreign policy in Iran during 1920-1921 and 1945-1946. The author maintains that one of the most important factors for the Soviet interference in

Iran was probably the lack of a third country to protect Iran and her interests. Methods used by the Soviets in their foreign policy toward Iran are also discussed.

486 Weaver, Paul E. Soviet Interference in Iran 1945-1946. Master's thesis, Georgetown University, 1951.

The occupation of Northern Iran in 1941 by the Soviet Union and the subsequent interferences of that country in Iranian affairs immediately following World War II are discussed. The last chapter deals with the "Soviet and Iran actions at the United Nations" regarding these interferences.

487 _____. Soviet Strategy in Iran: 1941-1957. Ph.D. dissertation, the American University, 1958.

Political, economic, and military activities of the Soviet Union in Iran during World War II and the postwar period are studied. This research demonstrates a flexible strategy used by the Soviet Union in Iran rather than a rigid "master plan."

488 Young, T.C. "The Race Between Russia and Reform in Iran." Foreign Affairs. 28(2):278-289, 1950.

Discusses Iran's struggle for reform and the involvement of the U.S. and the Soviet Union in Iranian politics.

13

RELATIONS WITH EUROPE

489 Ansari, Hormoz. Deutsch-Iranische Beziehungen nach dem Zweiten Weltkrieg. 1967.
A discussion of German-Iranian relationships after World War II.

490 Beladíez, E. "España e Irán." Revista de Política Internacional. 62-63:271-276, 1962.
A brief review of the relationship between Iran and Spain.

491 Boisen, Ingolf. Iran and Denmark Through the Ages. Copenhagen: Kampsax, 1965.
The bulk of material in this publication deals with the Dano-Iranian cultural relationship during the pre-Pahlavi Iranian history. The last two chapters, however, briefly discuss the relationship during the Pahlavi dynasty, including the role of Danish engineers in the construction of the Trans-Iranian Railway during Reza Shah's reign. The contract regarding this project was signed in Tehran on April 22, 1933. This publication is translated into English by David Hohnen.

492 Chahidzadeh, Hossien. Les Relations Politiques entre l'Iran et la Suisse. Tehran, 1958.
Discusses political relations between Iran and Switzerland.

493 "Development of Czechoslovak-Iranian Economic Relations." Czechoslovac Foreign Trade. 18:16-17, 1978.
Traces the Czechoslovac-Iranian trade relationship back to 1929. Czechoslovakia was a purchaser of natural gas and crude oil from Iran.

494 Fleury, Antoine. "La Pénétration Economique de l'Allemagne en Turquie et en Iran après la Première Guerre Mondiale: L'impact de l'Evolution des Structures Economiques sur les Echanges Commerciaux." Relations Internationales. (Paris) 1:155-171, 1974.
The economic interests of Germany in Iran and Turkey after World War I are examined. These interests increased significantly during the Nazi period.

495 Hesse, Fritz. "Zur Abschaffung der Kapitulationen in Persien."

Europäische Gespräche. 7(7):358-373, 1929.
Describes the agreements between Germany and Persia in
February 1929 which provided for diplomatic and economic
relations and removal of capitulations.

496 Hirschfeld, Yair P. "German Policy Towards Iran: Continuity
and Change from Weimar to Hitler, 1919-1939." Jahrbuch
des Institut für Deutsche Geschichte. 1:117-141, 1975.
Discusses German-Iranian relations during the Weimar
and Nazi periods. The author maintains that Germany's
economic and political influence in Iran was greater during
the Weimar period.

497 Hoeppner, R. R. "Iran-Deutschland-Europäische Gemeinschaft."
Aussenpolitik. 26(3):334-349, 1975.
The relationship among Iran, Germany, and the European
Economic Community (EEC) is examined.

498 Hueber, Reinhard. Deutschland und der Wirtschaftsaufbau des
Vorderen Orients. Stuttgart: Ferdinand Enke Verlag, 1938.
Contains information on commercial relations between Iran
and Germany before World War II.

499 Kappeler, D. "Future Prospects for European Integration and
Their Implications for the Third World and Iran." Revue
Iranienne des Relations Internationales/Iranian Review of
International Relations. 7:61-87, 1976.
Increase in European integration is considered beneficial
for the Third World countries, including Iran.

500 Kochwasser, Friedrich. Iran und Wir: Geschichte der Deutsch-
Iranischen Handels- und Wirtschaftsbeziehungen. Herrenalb/
Schwarzwald: H. Erdmann, 1961.
A historical survey of German-Iranian trade and economic
relations from the late Middle Ages to the present. Empha-
sis is on the development since 1945.

501 Maczynski, Michal. "Polish-Iranian Economic Cooperation."
Polish Foreign Trade. 8:7-10, 1978.
Surveys Polish-Iranian economic relations since the 1970's.

502 Mahrad, Ahmad. Die Deutsch-Persischen Beziehungen von 1918-
1933. Bern: Herbert Lang, 1974.
An in-depth discussion of Irano-German relations during
Reza Shah's reign.

503 _____. Dokumentation über die Persisch-Deutschen Beziehungen von 1918-1933. Bern: Herbert Lang; Frankfurt/
Main: Peter Lang, 1975.
Supplements the author's Die Deutsch-Persischen Beziehungen von 1918-1933, which deals with Irano-German relations during Reza Shah's rule.

504 _____. Die Wirtschafts- und Handelsbeziehungen Zwischen Iran und dem Nationalsozialistischen Deutschen Reich. Anzali: Gilan-Publikation, 1979.
Originally presented as the author's Habilitationsschrift, Universität Hannover, 1978. A useful study of economic and foreign relations between Iran and Germany during Reza Shah. Contains reproductions of original documents.

505 Nava, Santi. "L'Italia e le altre Potenze in Persia." Vita Italiana. 18(202):74-81, 1930.
Outlines the relations of different countries with Iran and claims that the influence of Great Britain and the United States is declining.

506 Sohrab, Siawusch. Die Deutsch-Persischen Wirtschaftsbeziehungen vor dem Ersten Weltkrieg. Frankfurt/Main: Peter Lang; Bern: Herbert Lang, 1976.
A study of Irano-German foreign economic relations.

507 Studiengesellschaft für Wirtschaftliche Entwicklung. Iran als Entwicklungsland. Frankfurt/Main: Metzner, 1959.
Reviews the report of a German economic delegation to Iran following a brief discussion of Iran's foreign economic policy. The subject of the report was the possibilities of cooperation between Iran and West Germany.

508 Vasiu, Alex. "Les Relations Roumano-Iraniennes: Example de Coexistence et de Cooperation entre Etats à Différents Systèmes Socio-Politiques." Revue Roumaine d'Etudes Internationales. 5(13):47-67, 1971.
Surveys the diplomatic and cultural relations between Iran and Romania during the Shah's regime.

509 Zadé, Sultan. "La Perse et l'Impérialisme Britanique." Correspondance d'Orient. Etudes. 23(405):125-129, 1931.
Written during Reza Shah's reign, this article describes Anglo-Iranian relations and asserts that Iran is still fearful of British imperialism.

14

IRAN AND THE UNITED STATES

510 Alexander, Yonah and Nanes, Allan (eds.). The United States and Iran: A Documentary History. Frederick, Maryland: Aletheia Books, 1980.
A valuable compilation of documents tracing the history of U.S.-Iran relations from 1856 to 1979.

511 Ali, Mehrunnisa. "Iran's Relations with the United States and USSR." Pakistan Horizon. 26(3):45-68, 1973.
Examines the foreign policies of the United States and the Soviet Union toward Iran since 1945. Iran's response to these countries is analyzed.

512 Amuzegar, Jahangir. The Role of the United States Technical Assistance in the Development of Underdeveloped Countries with Special Reference to Iran. Ph.D. dissertation, University of California, Los Angeles, 1955.
The effectiveness of the Point Four Program in Iran is discussed and its long-range impact on Iranian economy is evaluated.

513 _____. Technical Assistance in Theory and Practice: The Case of Iran. New York: Praeger, 1966.
Assesses foreign technical assistance and its role in socioeconomic growth of developing countries. The American Point Four Program in Iran is examined as a case study.

514 Arcilesi, Salvatore Alfred. Development of United States Foreign Policy in Iran, 1949-1960. Ph.D. dissertation, University of Virginia, 1965.
The author asserts that the United States policy in Iran has achieved its goal of creating economic and political stability.

515 Bryson, Thomas A. American Diplomatic Relations with the Middle East, 1784-1975: A Survey. Metuchen, New Jersey: Scarecrow Press, 1977.
A general work on U.S.-Middle East relations, this document contains important materials on Iran-U.S. relations.

516 Cottam, Richard. *Competitive Interference and Twentieth Century Diplomacy.* Pittsburgh: University of Pittsburgh Press, 1967.
Chapter Four, "The United States and Iran," is devoted to American foreign policy toward Iran.

517 Decker, Donald James. *U.S. Policy Regarding the Baghdad Pact.* Ph.D. dissertation, the American University, 1975.
Studies the factors leading to the foundation of the Baghdad Pact and the role of Secretary Dulles in its formation. Analyzes the U.S. policy regarding the pact.

518 Eisenhower, Dwight D. *Waging Peace, 1956-1961: The White House Years.* New York: Doubleday, 1965.
This interesting memoir contains information which sheds light on the American role in the creation of the Baghdad Pact.

519 Firoozi, Fereydoon. *The United States Economic Aid to Iran, 1950-1960.* Ph.D. dissertation, Dropsie University, 1966.

520 _____. "The United States Economic Interest in Iran." *International Studies.* 15(1):29-43, 1976.
A historical survey of economic relations between Iran and the United States since the beginning. Iran's primary motive in seeking relations with the U.S. was protection against Russian and British ambitions. The two countries sought even closer relations after 1953.

521 Fishburne, Charles Carroll. *United States Policy Toward Iran, 1959-1963.* Ph.D. dissertation, Florida State University, 1964.
A critical study and evaluation of the American foreign policy toward Iran. The overall result is considered a very successful American policy during this period.

522 Foroughi, Mahmoud. "Iran's Policy Towards the United States." In: Amirie, Abbas and Twitchell, Hamilton A. (eds.), *Iran in the 1980's.* Tehran: Institute for International Political and Economic Studies, 1978. Pages 335-352.
Following a general discussion of Iranian foreign policy, this essay briefly reviews major trends in the development of Iran's foreign policy toward the United States since 1851.

523 Fort, Raymond. *A Study of the Development of the American Technical Assistance Program in Iran.* Ph.D. dissertation, Cornell University, 1961.
Analyzes reasons underlying the United States technical assistance to Iran and political as well as economic factors involved in that undertaking. The United States used the programs already underway in Europe as models for this assistance.

524 Gardner, Lloyd C. Architects of Illusion: Men and Ideas in American Foreign Policy, 1941-1949. Chicago: Quadrangle, 1970.
   In this study, the author presents his New Left position regarding the United States foreign policy toward Iran during World War II. He maintains that the United States policy was motivated by economic gain in Iranian oil rather than by consideration of defense.

525 Gold, Fern R. and Conant, Melvin A. Access to Oil: The United States Relationship with Saudi Arabia and Iran. Washington, D.C.: U.S. Government Printing Office, 1977.
   Examines the U.S. relations with Saudi Arabia and Iran in regard to oil. Part IV is devoted to Iran. In addition, a discussion of the Franco-Algerian relationship, 1962-73, is included as an example of a similar relationship.

526 Harbutt, Fraser J. The Fulton Speech and the Iran Crisis of 1946: A Turning Point in American Foreign Policy. Ph.D. dissertation, University of California, Berkeley, 1976.
   Investigates the relationship between Winston Churchill's Fulton Speech and the American foreign policy toward Iran and the Soviet Union. Argues that the speech was more decisive than the Truman Doctrine.

527 Harris, F.S. "The Beginnings of Point IV Work in Iran." Middle East Journal. 7(2):222-228, 1953.
   Reviews the U.S. aid to Iran through the Point Four Program and improvements brought about in education, health and agriculture.

528 Hekmat, Hormoz. Iran's Response to Soviet-American Rivalry, 1951-1962: A Comparative Study. Ph.D. dissertation, Columbia University, 1974.
   Analyzes and compares Iran's neutralist stance in the cold war during Mossadeq's regime (1951-53) to its pro-Western position under the Shah's direction (1953-62).

529 Hendershot, Clarence. Politics, Polemics and Pedagogs: A Study of United States Technical Assistance in Education to Iran, Including Negotiations, Political Considerations in Iran and the United States, Programming, Methods, Problems, Results, and Evaluation. New York: Vantage Press, 1975.
   An in-depth analysis of the U.S. aid to Iran over a sixteen-year span. Although the focus of the study is on education, it examines economic, political and social aspects of the United States technical assistance in education in Iran. The author was involved in the program and gives a first-hand account of the activities.

530 Heravi, Mehdi. Iranian-American Diplomacy. Brooklyn, N.Y.: T. Gaus' Sons, 1969.

Studies the development of Iranian-American relations from the establishment of the American legation in Tehran in 1883 until the end of the Second World War. Attempts to "study the historical factors and evaluate the foreign policy of the U.S. in regard to Iran."

531 Hoskins, Halford L. Middle East Oil in United States Foreign Policy. Washington, 1950.
Discusses the United States policies regarding oil in the Middle East. The effect of Middle Eastern as well as Iranian oil on the U.S. security is examined.

532 _____. The Middle East: Problem Area in World Politics. New York: Macmillan, 1957.
Argues that United States foreign policy toward Iran did not always follow British initiative.

533 Hull, Cordell. The Memoirs of Cordell Hull. New York: Macmillan, 1948.
The second volume of this memoir contains useful information regarding the U.S. policy toward the Middle East in World War II. The U.S. policy was an aggressive one and attempted to secure oil in Iran and Saudi Arabia.

534 Irani, Ghobad. American Diplomacy: An Option Analysis for the Azerbaijan Crisis, 1945-1946. Hyattsville, Maryland: Institute of Middle Eastern and North African Affairs, 1978.
Utilizing American diplomatic and United Nations documentary materials, the author analyzes the United States foreign policy toward the Soviet military and political intervention in Northern Iran at the close of World War II.

535 _____. "American Diplomacy in Iran: A Review of Literature." Revue Iranienne des Relations Internationales/Iranian Review of International Relations. 4:169-172, 1975.
Reviews major works concerning U.S. policy in Iran.

536 _____. "U.S. Strategic Interests in Iran and Saudi Arabia." Parameters. 7(4):21-34, 1977.
The strategic importance of Iran and Saudi Arabia in the Middle East and the United States foreign policy toward these two countries, the author maintains, will result in decreasing the Soviet influence throughout the Middle East.

537 Just, A.W. "Iran Zwischen den Mächten." Aussenpolitik. 1(3):202-208, 1950.
Discusses the strategic importance of Iran and the political interest which the Soviet Union and the United States take in this country. The growing dominant role of the U.S. in Iran after World War II replacing the British interest is examined.

538 Kazemian, Gholam H. The Impact of U.S. Technical Aid on the Rural Development of Iran. Brooklyn: Gaus, 1968.
Evaluates the impact of American aid programs such as Point Four, AID, Near East Foundation, etc. on the rural development in Iran.

539 Kermani, Taghi. The United States Participation in the Economic Development of the Middle East, with Special Reference to Iran, Iraq, and Jordan. Ph.D. dissertation, University of Nebraska, 1959.
American foreign aid to Iran, whose aim was creating political and economic stability, is discussed and analyzed.

540 Kerwin, Harry Wayne. An Analysis and Evaluation of the Program of Technical Assistance to Education Conducted in Iran by the Government of the United States from 1952-1962. Ph.D. dissertation, American University, 1964.

541 Kolko, Gabriel. The Politics of War: The World and United States Foreign Policy, 1943-1945. New York: Random House, 1968.
Argues that the reason for the Soviet Union's move to achieve access to oil in Iran was an aggressive American policy to secure oil in the Middle East.

542 Kolko, Joyce and Kolko, Gabriel. The Limits of Power: The World and United States Foreign Policy, 1945-1954. New York: Harper & Row, 1972.
Contains materials on U.S. policy in postwar Iran. Claims that U.S. policy was motivated by securing new sources of oil and not by defending the country from the Soviet Union.

543 Ledeen, Michael and Lewis, William. Debacle: The American Failure in Iran. New York: Alfred A. Knopf, 1981.
Discusses the failure of American foreign policy in Iran during the 1978/79 crisis. Chapter Three, "Carter and Iran," is a critical account of the policies of the Carter administration in regard to Iran.

544 Lenczowski, George. The Middle East in World Affairs. Ithaca: Cornell University Press, 1952.
Argues that American foreign policy in Iran during World War II was independent and frequently at odds with Great Britain's.

545 _____. "U.S. Policy Towards Iran." In: Amirie, Abbas and Twitchell, Hamilton A. (eds.), Iran in the 1980's. Tehran: Institute for International Political and Economic Studies, 1978. Pages 353-389.
Following a historical review of the United States policy toward Iran 1945-1975, the author focuses on developments in the 1970's and the issues which are likely to persist into the 1980's.

546 _____. "United States' Support for Iran's Independence and Integrity, 1945-1959." Annals of the American Academy of Political and Social Science. 401:45-55, 1972.
Surveys and analyzes the post-World War II U.S.-Iran relationship. Concludes that the American policy of containment of international communism has proven successful in Iran and achieved its objectives.

547 Magnus, Ralph H. Documents on the Middle East. Washington, D.C.: American Enterprise Institute for Public Policy Research, 1969.
A collection of documents for the purpose of illustrating the development of the U.S. policies in the Middle East. Chapter IV, entitled "United States Relations with the Northern Tier States," includes five documents from December 1943 to July 1965. One of the documents is a message from President Eisenhower to Prime Minister Mossadeq, June 29, 1953 on the impossibility of increasing U.S. economic aid pending a settlement of the Anglo-Iranian oil crisis.

548 Middle East Research & Information Project. America's Shah, Shahanshah's Iran. Washington: Middle East Research & Information Project, 1975. (MERIP Reports; no. 40.)
Concentrates on the Shah's regime and its dependence on the United States. Among other topics covered are: "Playing at Democracy: Mardom vs. Melliyun"; "The Pahlavi Foundation"; "The National Front: Brief Resurgence and Final Defeat"; and "The White Revolution: Kulaks to the Rescue."

549 Millspaugh, Arthur C. The American Task in Persia. New York: Arno Press, 1973.
Reprint of the 1925 edition of the same title published by Century Co., this is the author's survey of the first American Financial Mission in Iran. The author, who was administrator general of the finances of Persia, reviews the developments in Iran after World War I including Reza Shah's early years as ruler of Iran.

550 _____. Americans in Persia. New York: Da Capo Press, 1976, 1946.
First published in 1946 by the Brookings Institution, this is a "personal report" of Dr. Millspaugh's experiences and observations as administrator general of the finances of Persia (1922-1927 and 1943-1945). The policies of the Iranian government are severely criticized. Chapter 11 is a discussion of American principles, policies and practices in Iran.

551 Mojdehi, Hassan. Arthur C. Millspaugh's Two Missions to Iran and Their Impact on American-Iranian Relations. Ph.D.

dissertation, Ball State University, 1975.
Studies Millspaugh's role in Iranian affairs during his two missions from 1922 to 1927 and from 1943 to 1945. The United States position regarding these missions is examined.

552 O'Neill, Bard E. and Viotti, Paul R. "Iran and American Security Policy in the Middle East." Naval War College Review. 27(4):54-65, 1975.
The author believes a strong relationship between Iran and the U.S. is necessary to safeguard the American interests in the Middle East.

553 Partin, Michael Wayne. United States-Iranian Relations, 1945-47. Ph.D. dissertation, North Texas State University, 1977.
Analyzes the U.S.-Iran relations during the critical period of the cold war.

554 Pfau, Richard. "Containment in Iran, 1946: The Shift to an Active Policy." Diplomatic History. 1(4):359-372, 1977.
The active policy of the United States toward Iran in regard with bringing an end to the Soviet influence in Iran after World War II is examined.

555 _____. "The Legal Status of American Forces in Iran." Middle East Journal. 28(2):141-153, 1974.
United States' right to extraterritoriality for its armed forces in Iran is examines from a legal standpoint.

556 _____. The United States and Iran, 1941-1947: Origins of Partnership. Ph.D. dissertation, University of Virginia, 1975.
The evolutionary process of American foreign policy in Iran is examined. Discusses the American interest in Iranian oil.

557 Ramazani, Rouhollah K. "Iran and the United States: An Experiment in Enduring Friendship." Middle East Journal. 30(3):322-334, 1976.
A survey of the Iran-U.S. relations with a brief discussion of the reasons underlying the friendship between the two countries. Other topics discussed include the influence of the American educational system on Iranian schools and universities and the American interests in Iranian oil.

558 Roosevelt, Kermit. Countercoup: The Struggle for the Control of Iran. New York: McGraw-Hill, 1979.
See entry 158.

559 Rubin, Barry. Paved with Good Intentions: The American Experience and Iran. New York: Oxford University Press, 1980.
Traces the Iran-U.S. relations since the turn of the

century. The focus is on the relations after 1953 when the U.S. helped the Shah to remain in power. The main theme of the book is that American policies in Iran seemed in theory directed toward rationally formulated goals but failed mainly because of the mutual ignorance of the two countries as well as the lack of sensitivity to Iranian internal political tensions on the United States' side.

560 Sale, Richard. "Carter and Iran: From Idealism to Disaster." Washington Quarterly. 3(4):75-87, 1980.
Reviews the opinions of the critics of the Carter administration's policy toward the Shah and Iran during the Iranian crisis of 1978/79. Asserts that extreme repression dictated by the Shah was the main cause of his fall.

561 Saleh, Ali Pasha. Cultural Ties Between Iran and the United States. Tehran (?), 1976.
Published as a contribution to the American Revolution Bicentennial, this monograph contains chapters on various Iran-U.S. relations. Chapter Five is devoted to the origin of diplomatic relations between the two countries; Chapter Seven deals with the Universal Welfare Legion, and Chapter Eleven is devoted to Peace Corps. Contains many portraits and illustrations.

562 Sheehan, Michael Kahl. Iran: The Impact of United States Interests and Policies, 1941-1954. Brooklyn, New York: T. Gaus' Sons, 1968.
Outlines the American policies and interests regarding Iran during 1941-1954 and analyzes the impact of these policies on Iranian economy, military, and politics. The author attempts to show that, contrary to established belief, the U.S. did have a policy toward Iran earlier than 1947.

563 Sober, Sidney. "The U.S. and Iran: An Increasing Partnership." In: Amirie, Abbas and Twitchell, Hamilton A. (eds.), Iran in the 1980's. Tehran: Institute for International Political and Economic Studies, 1978. Pages 391-395.
Outlines the future of Iran-United States relationship.

564 Speiser, E. A. United States and the Near East. Cambridge, Massachusetts: Harvard United University Press, 1947.
Discusses the development of the United States foreign policy interests in the Middle Eastern countries including Iran after World War II. A revised edition of this book was published in 1971 by Greenwood Press.

565 Sullivan, William H. Mission to Iran. New York: W. W. Norton & Co., 1981.
The author, who was the U.S. ambassador to Iran from June 1977 to April 1979, describes his experience as well

as the United States foreign policy toward Iran during that period, which included the civil unrest and revolution in Iran. He criticizes Carter's administration and especially the reaction of the Department of State to the events in Iran during the 1978/79 revolution.

566 Tabari, Keyvan. Iran's Policies Toward the United States During the Anglo-Russian Occupation, 1941-1946. Ph.D. dissertation, Columbia University, 1967.
  A systematic investigation of Iranian-American relations during the Anglo-Russian wartime occupation of Iran. The major Iranian policies toward the United States were: The "third power" policy; the alignment and counteralignment; and the negative and positive equilibria policies.

567 Thomas, Lewis V. and Frye, Richard N. The United States and Turkey and Iran. Cambridge: Harvard University Press, 1951.
  A brief chapter is devoted to the relations between Iran and the U.S. This work concentrates mainly on the history and culture of Iran and Turkey and discusses the rise of nationalism and Westernization in these countries.

568 Thorpe, J.A. The Mission of Arthur C. Millspaugh to Iran. 1943-1945. Ph.D. dissertation, University of Wisconsin-Madison, 1973.
  Investigates Millspaugh's missions to Iran as an instrument of American policy in that country. Attributes the missions' failures to the defects of the State Department's adviser plan rather than to Millspaugh's leadership and personality.

569 United States. Congress. House. Permanent Select Committee on Intelligence. Subcommittee on Evaluation. Iran: Evaluation of U.S. Intelligence Performance Prior to November 1978: Staff Report. Washington, D.C.: U.S. Government Printing Office, 1979.
  Briefly evaluates the reasons behind the failure of the U.S. intelligence services to provide adequate warning in regard to the fall of the Shah in 1978/79.

570 United States. Congress. Senate. Committee on Foreign Relations. Activities of the Development and Resources Corporation in Iran. Hearing before Committee on Foreign Relations, United States Senate, eighty-seventh congress, second session. March 20, 1962. Washington: U.S. Government Printing Office, 1962.

571 United States. Department of State. Human Rights and U.S. Policy: Argentina, Haiti, Indonesia, Iran, Peru, and the Philippines. Washington, D.C.: U.S. Government Printing Office, 1976.
  "Reports submitted to the Committee on International

Relations, U.S. House of Representatives by the Department of State, pursuant to section 502B(c) of the International Security assistance and arms export control act of 1976."
A compilation of six declassified State Department's reports on the human rights situation in these countries and the impact on U.S. foreign policy.

572 United States. Department of State. Agency for International Development. Technical Cooperation with Iran: A Case Study of Opportunities and Policy Implications for the United States. Washington, D.C.: Agency for International Development, 1972.
Surveys the cooperation between Iran and the United States regarding technical activities in the past. However, the main purpose of the study is to take Iran as a case study in investigating the priorities for technical assistance to countries not eligible for concessional assistance.

573 Waltman, Jerry. "American-Iranian Relations, 1972-1976: A Search for Explanations." Southeastern Political Review. 9(2):2-33, 1981.
An attempt to create theoretical models in order to study the American-Iranian relations during the time period under investigation.

574 Warne, William E. Mission for Peace: Point 4 in Iran. New York: Bobbs-Merrill, 1956.
Studies Point Four Program in Iran and concludes that the program achieved its objectives and succeeded.

RELATIONS WITH OTHER COUNTRIES

575 Ali, Mehrunnisa. "The Changing Pattern of India-Iran Relations." Pakistan Horizon. 28(4):53-66, 1975.
Discusses the shift of the balance of power in India's favor after the India-Pakistan war of 1971 and its effect on Indo-Iranian relations.

576 Ayoob, Mohammed. "Indo-Iranian Relations: Strategic, Political, and Economic Dimensions." India Quarterly. 33(1):1-18, 1977.
Surveys Indo-Iranian relations. The conflicts between the two countries during the Bangladesh war and India's position regarding Iran's role in the Persian Gulf region are examined. Some of the obstacles in the way of more collaboration between the two countries such as Iran's dependence on the U.S. and India's link with the Soviet Union are considered.

577 Chubin, Shahram. "Iran: Between the Arab West and the Asian East." Survival. 16(4):172-182, 1974.
Discusses the increasing strategic importance of Iran in the area and analyzes the issues related to the Persian Gulf, Indian subcontinent, and the Arab-Israel zone in light of this importance.

578 Entessar, Nader. "The People's Republic of China and Iran: An Overview of Their Relationship." Asia Quarterly. 1:79-88, 1978.
Examines the development of relations between China and Iran with an emphasis on this relationship regarding the Indian Ocean and the Persian Gulf areas.

579 Foot, Rosemary. "China's New Relationships with Iran." Contemporary Review. 226(1309):100-104, 1975.
The relationship between Iran and China is examined from 1950-1973. The effect of Sino-Soviet conflict on this relationship is also discussed.

580 "Iran Recalls Its Ancient Origins." External Affairs. (Canada) 23(10):397-399, 1971.
Briefly reviews Iranian history and relations with Canada.

581 Nabavi, J. "A Commentary on the Relations Between Iran and the People's Republic of China." International Relations. 2:127-136, 1974/75.
Discusses Iran's recognition of China and relations with this country. A background history is provided.

582 "New Development in Sino-Iranian Friendly Relations." Peking Review. 21:5-10, 1978.
Examines the relationship between China and Iran in light of Chairman Hua's visit to Iran in 1978.

583 Puri, Rakshat. "The South Asian Cockpit." China Report. (India) 9(2):10-19, 1973.
Discusses the relations among South Asian countries of Iran, India, Pakistan, Iraq, and Bangladesh. The influence of China and the Soviet Union on these countries between 1964 and 1972 is examined.

584 Ramazani, Rouhollah K. "Iran and the Arab-Israeli Conflict." Middle East Journal. 32(4):413-428, 1978.
Discusses Iran-Israel relations and their consequences for the Arab-Israeli conflict.

585 Reppa, Robert B. Israel and Iran: Bilateral Relationships and Effect on the Indian Ocean Basin. New York: Praeger, 1974.
Discusses the relationship between Iran and Israel, especially in regard to the Indian Ocean Basin. Following a background history and general information about each country, Iran-Israel common interests and divisive factors are examined. The last chapter entitled, "The Outlook," gives a brief account of the future of Iran-Israel interrelationship. An extensive bibliography follows the text.

586 _____. Israel and Iran: Their Development, Interrelationship, and Effect on the Indian Ocean Basin. Ph.D. dissertation, University of Maryland, 1973.
Examines developments, interests, and differences between Iran and Israel in the context of the relationship of the two countries with each other as well as with the Soviet Union, the United States, China, Japan, major European countries, and the Indian Ocean region. The focus of the study is on the rivalry for the control of the Indian Ocean Basin.

587 Stevens, Willy. "L'Iran et le Monde Arabe." Chronique de Politique Etrangère. 20(2):119-131, 1967.
Iran-Arab relations especially regarding the Persian Gulf area are discussed.

588 Weinbaum, M. G. "Iran and Israel: The Discreet Entente." Orbis. 18(4):1070-1087, 1975.
Discusses the foreign policy of Iran toward Israel.

589 Wriggins, Howard. "Changing Power Relations Between the Middle East and South Asia." Orbis. 20(3):785-803, 1976.

Iran's economic power in the 1970's and its consequences are analyzed. The significant shift which this economic power has caused in the relations between Iran and the Arab states and between India and Pakistan is discussed.

590 Young, Richard. "Equitable Solutions for Offshore Boundries: The 1968 Saudi Arabia-Iran Agreement: Notes and Comments." American Journal of International Law. 64(1): 152-157, 1970.

Studies the agreement of October 24, 1968 between Saudi Arabia and Iran in regard to offshore areas in the Persian Gulf and compares it with a similar case.

RELATIONS WITH REGIONAL AND
INTERNATIONAL ORGANIZATIONS

591 Abidi, A. A. H. "R. C. D. : The Formative Phase. " Indian Journal of Politics. 11(2):131-146, 1977.
 A discussion of the Regional Cooperation for Development (RCD), formed in July 1964 by Iran, Turkey, and Pakistan in order to promote economic, trade, and cultural relations.

592 Akrami, Reza. Zuzammenarbeit Zwischen den Staaten des Cento-Pakts auf Politischem, Wirtschaftlichem und Kulturellem Gebiet und deren Schwierigkeiten in der Jüngsten Vergangenheit. Bonn: Rheinische Friedrich-Wilhelms-Universität, 1970.
 Originally presented as the author's dissertation, this detailed study traces the origins of CENTO since its creation as the Baghdad Pact. The activities of CENTO members are discussed in detail.

593 Alavi, Bozorg. "Der Bagdad-Pakt. " Deutsche Aussenpolitik. 3:375-384, 1958.
 Discusses the 1958 meeting of the Baghdad Pact held in Ankara, Turkey. Appraises the outcome from a Communist point of view.

594 Asopa, Sheel K. Military Alliance and Regional Cooperation in West Asia: A Study of the Politics of the Northern Tier. Meerut: Meenakshi Prakashan, 1971.
 Inquires into the political and military reasons which motivated Iran, Turkey, and Pakistan to form an alliance with the Western powers. The impact of this alliance on regional and international affairs is evaluated. The formation of the Baghdad Pact, the Central Treaty Organization (CENTO), and the Regional Cooperation for Development (RCD) is discussed in detail.

595 Chowdhury, A. H. M. Nuruddin. Regional Cooperation for Development: Its Nature and Significance. Karachi: Pakistan Institute of Development Economics, 1965.
 Formed in July 1964 among Iran, Turkey, and Pakistan, RCD was charged with promotion of economic, cultural

relations, and trade among the members. This brief publication attempts to examine RCD's development.

596 Fartash, Manoutchehr. "The 'Disarmament Club' at Work." Bulletin of the Atomic Scientists. 33(1):57-62, 1977.
　　The author, Iran's representative to the United Nations' Conference of the Committee on Disarmament, describes his views on disarmament. He also makes suggestions as to how to increase the effectiveness of the efforts made by the committee regarding disarmament.

597 Fleury, Antoine. "La Constitution d'un 'Bloc Oriental': Le Pacte de Saadabad Comme Contribution à la Sécurité Collective dans les Annés Trente." Revue d'Histoire de la Deuxième Guerre Mondiale. 27(106):1-18, 1977.
　　Analyzes the creation and roots of the Saadabad Pact, signed by representatives of Iran, Iraq, Afghanistan, and Turkey on July 8, 1937. This treaty of mutual friendship, according to the author, was originated by the four members themselves rather than the usual opinion that it was initiated by Great Britain or the Soviet Union.

598 George, Patrick Cyril. The United States and the Central Treaty Organization. Ph.D. dissertation, University of Virginia, 1968.
　　American role in CENTO is examined and its use as a defense structure in the Middle East is analyzed.

599 Hadley, Guy. CENTO, the Forgotten Alliance: A Study of the Central Treaty Organization. Brighton: Institute for the Study of International Organization, 1971.
　　Studies the development of the Central Treaty Organization (CENTO), a treaty consisting of eight articles whereby the contracting parties--Turkey, Iran, Pakistan, and Great Britain--agreed to cooperate for mutual security and defense. Iran joined CENTO on October 12, 1955.

600 Hale, W.M. and Bharier, Julian. "CENTO, R.C.D., and the Northern Tier: A Political and Economic Appraisal." Middle Eastern Studies. 8(2):217-226, 1972.
　　Evaluates performance of Regional Cooperation for Development (RCD), an organization formed in 1964 by the Northern Tier of the Central Treaty Organization (CENTO). The overall performance of RCD is rated as low and reasons for this weakness are presented.

601 Hashmi, Zia H. The Dynamics of Contemporary Regional Integration: The Growth of Regionalism Among Iran, Pakistan, and Turkey. Ph.D. dissertation, University of Southern California, 1970.
　　Using the experience of Western Europe as a case study, the author examines the process of developing RCD (Regional

Cooperation for Development) among Iran, Pakistan, and Turkey.

602 _____. "Regional Cooperation Among Pakistan, Iran, and Turkey." GPSA Journal. (Georgia Political Science Association.) 1(1):33-58, 1973.
Studies the importance of RCD (Regional Cooperation for Development) established in July 1964 among Iran, Turkey, and Pakistan. Considers these countries pioneers among Asian nations to have formed such a cooperative agreement.

603 Hetrick, Kenneth Lee. The United Nations as a National Foreign Policy Instrument: The Iranian Case of 1946. Ph.D. dissertation, Rutgers University, 1979.
Studies the influence of the United Nations on the resolution of the 1946 dispute and on Great Power relations.

604 Kaiser, Karl. "Iran and the Europe of the Nine: A Relationship of Growing Independence." World Today. 32(6):251-259, 1976.
English version of same article which appeared in German in Europa-Archiv, 31(12):407-416, 1976. See next entry.

605 _____. "Iran und das Europa der Neun: Probleme und Zukunftsaufgaben eines Wachsenden Interdependenzverhältnisses." Europa-Archiv. 31(12):407-416, 1976.
Discusses the relationship of Iran and the European Economic Community (EEC).

606 Kazemzadeh, Hossein. Iran and Post-War Political Issues: Policy Reflections in the United Nations. Ph.D. dissertation, Princeton University, 1954.
Contains examples of Iran-United Nations relationship in resolving international political conflicts affecting Iran. See also entry 116.

607 Khalatbary, Abbas. L'Iran et le Pacte Oriental. Paris: A. Pedone, 1938.
A study of the background and provisions of the Saadabad Pact, formed July 1937.

608 Matthews, Michael. "The Growth and Development of the Organization of Petroleum Exporting Countries 1959-1976." Humboldt Journal of Social Relations. 3(2):17-24, 1976.
Outlines the fifteen-year history and development of OPEC.

609 Meshah Zadeh, Mostafa. La Politique de l'Iran dans la Société des Nations. Paris: A. Pedone, 1936.
Iran's participation in the League of Nations is discussed.

610 Pfeffer, Karl Heinz. "Zur Regionalplanung Pakistans, Irans, und der Türkei." Orient. (Hamburg) 7(1):3-10, 1966.

A study of history and organization of Regional Cooperation for Development (RCD) formed in 1964 among Iran, Pakistan, and Turkey.

611 Ramazani, Rouhollah K. The Northern Tier: Afghanistan, Iran, and Turkey. Princeton, New Jersey: Van Nostrand, 1966.
The possibility of the "fusion" of Iran, Turkey, and Afghanistan is discussed using the concept of the Northern Tier. The numerous factors which act as obstacles toward that union are considered.

612 Remba, Oded. "The Bagdad Pact: Economic Aspects." Middle Eastern Affairs. 9:131-140, 1958.
A discussion of the economic committee of the Baghdad Pact as a "planning body" of the pact.

613 Watt, D. C. "The Sa'dabad Pact of July 8, 1937." Journal of the Royal Central Asian Society. 49:296-306, 1962.
Studies the origins and significance of the pact between Iran, Iraq, Turkey, and Afghanistan.

614 Wilber, Donald Newton. "Prospects for Federation in the Northern Tier." Middle East Journal. 12 (4):385-394, 1958.
The potential possibilities and advantages of regional federation among Turkey, Iran, Afghanistan, and Pakistan are sketched.

615 Wymar, Benno. Regional Cooperation for Development: Iran, Pakistan, and Turkey. Ph.D. dissertation, University of Nebraska-Lincoln, 1973.
An analysis and assessment of the Regional Cooperation for Development (RCD) which was established in July 1964 in Istanbul, Turkey.

III

ECONOMIC CONDITIONS

ECONOMIC PLANNING AND DEVELOPMENT

616 Akhavan, Soheil. Economic Planning in Iran, the Fifth and Sixth National Development Plans. Ph.D. dissertation, Florida State University, 1977.
An analytical study of economic planning in Iran with an emphasis on the fifth and the sixth plans.

617 Amuzegar, Jahangir. "Administrative Barriers to Economic Development in Iran." Middle East Economic Papers. 1-21, 1958.
Criticizes the structure of the government and the civil service system as the major obstacles against economic planning and development.

618 _____. "Capital Formation and Development Finance." In: Yar-Shater, Ehsan (ed.), Iran Faces the Seventies. New York: Praeger, 1971. Pages 66-87.
Iran's postwar capital formation is analyzed in this essay. Various development plans are examined with a focus on the characteristics of the Third (1962-1968) and Fourth (1968-1972) Plans.

619 _____ and Fekrat, M. Ali. Iran: Economic Development under Dualistic Conditions. Chicago: University of Chicago Press, 1971.
This study has two objectives according to the authors: 1. to explore the interaction between the foreign-oriented and all-important oil sector and the other sectors of the Iranian economy; and 2. to use the Iranian experience as a basis for a more generalized model for elsewhere.

620 Baldwin, George B. Planning and Development in Iran. Baltimore: John Hopkins Press, 1967.
Analyzes the development plans of 1949-1955 and 1955-1962. Political and social problems as well as manpower shortage were among causes of less than optimal planning.

621 Bharier, Julian. Economic Development in Iran, 1900-1970. London, New York: Oxford University Press, 1971.
A detailed study of Iran's economic development. All aspects of economy including government policy, manpower,

and money are dealt with, but political aspect is not sufficiently emphasized.

622 Bonnell, Helen Marie. Foreign Economic Relations in the Development of Iran. Ph.D. dissertation, the American University, 1957.
Various factors in the field of international economic relations are studied in order to determine contemporary Iranian economic development. Foreign trades, balance of payments, and financial control are among issues analyzed.

623 Bruton, Henry J. "Notes on Development in Iran." Economic Development and Cultural Change. 9:625-640, 1961.
Iran's second Seven-Year Plan is criticized.

624 Clapp, Gordon R. "Iran: A TVA for the Khuzestan Region." Middle East Journal. 11(1):1-11, 1957.
Discusses the negotiations leading to an agreement between Iran and Development and Resources Corporation, a private American company, to develop the Khuzestan province. The author was chairman of the board of directors of the Tennessee Valley Authority (TVA) from 1946 to 1954.

625 Conference on Development Planning. Teheran(?): Central Treaty Organization, 1962 or 1963.
Report of a CENTO conference in which Iran, Turkey, Pakistan, the United States, and the United Kingdom participated. The conference was held in Tehran, Iran in May 1962.

626 Daftary, Farhad. "Development Planning In Iran: A Historical Survey." Iranian Studies. 6(4):176-228, 1973.
After a brief review of Iran's first efforts at planning, the author examines the various development plans and analyzes the nature and characteristics of each plan.

627 Elm, Mostafa M. Governmental Economic Planning in Iran. Ph.D. dissertation, Syracuse University, 1959.
A critical survey of Iran's second Seven-Year Plan and a study of that country's economic resources and problems. The study makes recommendations for changes in economic planning and development.

628 Farahmand, Sohrab. Der Wirtschaftsaufbau des Iran, unter Besonderer Berücksichtigung der Tätigkeit der Planbehörde. Basel: Kyklos-Verlag, 1965.
The economic structure of Iran is examined in detail. The role of the Plan Organization in Iranian economy is also discussed.

629 Fartash, Manoutchehr. "Le Developpement Economique et le Problème Politique du Moyen-Orient." Politique Etrangère.

18:23-34, 1953.
Discusses economic development in Iran under the first Seven-Year Plan and its interruption because of the oil crisis.

630 Fekrat, Ali. "Economic Growth and Development in Iran." In: Jacqz, Jane W. (ed.), Iran: Past, Present and Future. New York: Aspen Institute for Humanistic Studies, 1976. Pages 73-81.
Outlines Iran's economic growth in various sectors: The oil sector, manufacturing and services, which the author calls the "modern sector," and the agricultural sector.

631 Ganji, Manouchehr and Milani, Abbas. "Iran: Development During the Last 50 Years." In: Jacqz, Jane W. (ed.), Iran: Past, Present and Future. New York: Aspen Institute for Humanistic Studies, 1976. Pages 33-55.
A general discussion of Iranian economic, social, and educational development during the reign of the two rulers of the Pahlavi dynasty and comparison with pre-Pahlavi periods. Contains several statistical tables.

632 Hammeed, Kamal A. and Bennett, Margaret N. "Iran's Future Economy." Middle East Journal. 29(4):418-432, 1975.
Some of the problems in planning and their effect on Iran's economic growth are discussed. The emphasis is on the foreign trade sector.

633 The Imperial Government of Iran. Plan Organization. Fourth National Development Plan, 1968-1972. Tehran, 1968.
Describes Iran's fourth National Development Plan. The plan emphasized industrial and technological growth.

634 Issawi, Charles. "The Iranian Economy 1925-1975: Fifty Years of Economic Development." In: Lenczowski, George (ed.), Iran Under the Pahlavis. Stanford, California: Hoover Institution Press, 1978. Pages 129-166.
An overview of Iranian economy during the Pahlavi era. After summarizing the economic condition of pre-Pahlavi period, this essay discusses economic development in various sectors including the oil industry, agriculture, transportation, etc. The performance of the Iranian economy is then evaluated. Contains several statistical tables.

635 Looney, Robert E. A Development Strategy for Iran through the 1980's. New York: Praeger, 1977.
"Attempts to provide a long-term overview of Iran's development efforts and accomplishments." The evolutionary patterns in economic, social, and political areas are discussed and future problems facing Iran are identified.

636 _____. The Economic Development of Iran, 1959-1981. New York: Praeger, 1973.

Surveys the economic and demographic developments since the late 1950's. An assessment of long-term prospects is also presented.

637 Mehner, Harald. "Development and Planning in Iran After World War II." In: Lenczowski, George (ed.), Iran Under the Pahlavis. Stanford University: Hoover Institution Press, 1978. Pages 167-199.
An overview of economic planning in Iran. Discusses five economic plans implemented in Iran since 1949. Aims and objectives of planning, financing the plans, problems in implementation, and finally an evaluation of the results of planning in Iran are discussed.

638 Minai, Ahmad. Economic Development of Iran Under the Reign of Reza Shah (1926-1941). Ph.D. dissertation, the American University, 1961.
Surveys the economic progress in Iran under the reign of Reza Shah. No special attention is given to the sociopolitical issues. The study shows that in spite of the economic progress during this period, the lack of sufficient attention to the agricultural sector and failure to develop human resources negatively affected the industrialization program and decreased the rate of economic development.

639 Moarefi, Ali. The Iranian Seven-Year Plan and its Monetary Effects. Ph.D. dissertation, Georgetown University, 1950.
A detailed study of the plan with an emphasis on the problems of financing it.

640 Moghtader, Hushang. "Irans Erdöleinkünfte und Wirtschaftspläne." Aussenpolitik. 28(4):424-436, 1977.
Discusses the tremendous increase in oil revenues for Iran which resulted from the OPEC countries' decision to increase oil prices and Iranian government's plans to utilize these gains to achieve economic and other goals.

641 Molavi, M.A. "Les Blocages du Développement en Iran." Tiers-Monde. 8(30):349-370, 1967.
Iranian economic growth is discussed and an attempt is made to discover the underlying social and economic causes which block a more rapid development.

642 Müller, Wilhelm. Die Wirtschaftlichen Entwicklungsprobleme Irans. Wien: Verlag Notring, 1971.
Provides information on Iran's economy and natural resources. The problems involving economic development are examined. An assessment of Iran's four development plans is given.

643 Müllers, Horst. "Zur Entwicklung des Iranischen Verkehrs- und Verbindungswesens." Orient. (Hamburg) 7(6):195-201, 1966.

Iran's transportation system and improvement program envisioned in the third Development Plan are discussed.

644 Overseas Consultants, Inc., New York. Report on Seven Year Development Plan for the Plan Organization of the Imperial Government of Iran. New York: Overseas Consultants Inc., 1949.

This five-volume work is the report of the Overseas Consultants mission who arrived in Iran from the United States to advise on the Seven-Year National Development Plan in January 1949. The volumes are rich in providing information on all aspects of the Iranian economy of that period ranging from agriculture, transportation, industry, and mining to water resources, housing, and public health. The first volume is devoted to "Summary and General Conclusion."

645 Sadri, Amir. L'état et le Financement du Développement Economique sur l'Example Iranien. Teheran, 1965.

Takes Iran as a case study to examine the subject of financing development projects. The role of the state in economic policy is analyzed.

646 Sazman-i Barnamah. Fourth National Development Plan, 1968-1972. Tehran: Plan Organization, 1968.

The fourth Development Plan (1968-1972) increased the pace of economic growth. A number of large projects were under construction during this plan including a gas pipeline leading to the Soviet border. This document discusses the nature of the fourth plan.

647 _____. Iran Plans for the Future: A Summary of Activities. Tehran: Public Bureau, Plan Organization, 1960.

The Plan Organization (later renamed the Plan and Budget Organization) was formed in 1947. Development plans were formulated through guidelines provided by the high economic officials of the government working for the organization. This document outlines some of the activities of the Plan Organization.

648 _____. Review of the Second Seven-Year Plan Program of Iran. Tehran: Division of Economic Affairs, Plan Organization, 1960.

Evaluates the performance of the second Seven-Year Plan (1955-1962) in order to monitor its progress.

649 _____. 3rd Development Plan, 1341-1346: Final Report. Tehran: Plan Organization of Iran, 1970.

In the third Development Plan (1962-1968) the primary objective was to raise real GNP by an average of at least six percent a year. This document reports the achievements of the third plan.

650 Scharlau, K. "Iran als Entwicklungsland. Als Beispiel der Problematik der Entwicklungsländer Überhaupt." Zeitschrift für Politik. 7(4):371-381, 1960.

Taking Iran as a case study of a country struggling for development, this essay discusses the problems and obstacles and generalizes the Iranian case into an example for all underdeveloped countries.

651 Shafaq, Rezazadeh and Lotz, J. D. "The Iranian Seven-Year Development Plan." Middle East Journal. 4(1):100-105, 1950.

In 1949, the first systematic attempt at planning a coordinated development program in Iran was made and the Seven-Year Economic Development Plan was adopted. Background and organization of the plan and the problems facing it are discussed in this article.

652 Sykes, Edward. "Some Economic Problems of Persia." Journal of the Royal Central Asian Society. 37:262-272, 1950.

Outlines problems facing Iran in agricultural and industrial areas, inflation, and deteriorating living standards. Examines the Iranian Seven-Year Plan and the reasons Iran chose an American firm, Overseas Consultants Inc., to assist the government with the plan.

653 Wright, George Ernest. Regional Inequality in the Economic Development of Iran 1962-1970. Ph.D. dissertation, the University of Michigan, 1977.

Studies the relationship between Iran's economic growth and changes in the regional distribution of the gains from the economic growth.

654 Zarbafian, Shamseddin. Technology Transfer and Economic Development in Iran, 1962-77. Ph.D. dissertation, Colorado State University, 1979.

Investigates the impact of imported technology on the Iranian economy and its productivity during the period under study.

655 Zelli, M. Manoutchehr. "The Economic Progress of Iran." Journal of the Royal Central Asian Society. 53:43-49, 1966.

A survey of Iranian economic development. Developments in industry as well as agriculture and natural resources are discussed.

18

MONETARY AND FISCAL POLICIES

656 Afshar, Kamran. A Monetary Estimate of Iran's GNP, 1900-1975. Ph.D. dissertation, Florida State University, 1977.
Investigates the possibility of estimating Iran's GNP for the period 1900-1975.

657 Ashrafi, Jamshid. An Analysis of the Effects of Investment Expenditures on the Balance of Payments of Iran, 1955-1962. Ph.D. dissertation, University of Southern California, 1963.
This study investigates the nature of the balance of payments' disequilibrium and indicates major factors responsible for the external imbalance of Iran. It suggests possibilities of economic development in Iran without quantitative restriction of imports and balance of payment difficulties.

658 Bank Markazi Iran. National Income of Iran, 1338-1344. (1959-1965). Tehran: Central Bank of Iran, Economic Research Dept., 1968.
Contains the Gross National Product (GNP) and expenditure for 1959-1965.

659 Benedick, Richard Elliot. Industrial Finance in Iran. Boston: Grad. Sch. of Bus. Admin., Harvard University, 1964.
A useful study of the financial sector of the developing economy of Iran.

660 Chidfar, Z.M. Le Réforme Monétaire et l'Etalon Or en Iran. Paris: Domat-Montchrestien, 1935.

661 Clawson, Patrick. "The Internationalization of Capital and Capital Accumulation in Iran and Iraq." The Insurgent Sociologist. 7(2):64-73, 1977.
Studies the effect of internationalization of the capitalist mode of production on industrialization in Iran and Iraq.

662 Cumming-Bruce, N. "Billion-Dollar Credit Needs May Make Lenders More Cautious." Middle East Economic Digest. 21:3, December 1977.
Extensive credit needed to finance ambitious future

projects in Iran and its effect on her ability to obtain loan are discussed.

663 _____. "Plans Need More Private Funds, But Confidence Is Lacking." Middle East Economic Digest. 22:7-8, July 1978.

The lack of investor confidence in Iran's political future due to social unrest and opposition to the Shah's regime is briefly examined.

664 Daftary, Farhad. "The Balance of Payments Deficit and the Problem of Inflation in Iran, 1955-1962." Iranian Studies. 5(1):2-25, 1972.

Reviews the economic difficulties of Iran during the 1955-1962 period and their major underlying causes.

665 Farmanfarma, Ali-Naghi. Budgetary Administration and Procedure in Iran. Ph.D. dissertation, University of Southern California, 1959.

Budget administration and procedure as practiced by the Iranian government are analyzed.

666 Fesharaki, Fereidun. "Iran's Petrodollars: Surplus or Deficit? -- An Examination of Alternative Iranian Policies." In: Jacqz, Jane W. (ed.), Iran: Past, Present and Future. New York: Aspen Institute for Humanistic Studies, 1976. Pages 301-327.

Iran's position regarding petrodollar in 1974-1975 is examined and options available to Iran in modifying her expenditure policy in the face of declining oil revenues are discussed.

667 Firoozi, Fereydoon. "Income Distribution and Taxation Laws of Iran." International Journal of Middle East Studies. 9(1):73-87, 1978.

Legislation and taxation laws of Iran from 1925 to 1974 are examined to demonstrate the Iranian government's policy to improve income distribution through taxation.

668 _____. "The Iranian Budgets: 1964-1970." International Journal of Middle East Studies. 5(3):328-343, 1974.

Studies the fiscal policies of the Iranian government.

669 Kiani, Manutschehr. "Irans Wahrungs- und Bankwesen." Orient. (Hamburg) 10(4):123-127, 1969.

Surveys the banking situation in Iran.

670 Looney, Robert E. Income Distribution Policies and Economic Growth in Semiindustrialized Countries: A Comparative Study of Iran, Mexico, Brazil, and South Korea. New York: Praeger, 1975.

Seven chapters discuss various aspects of income distribution ranging from credit and capital market to effect of education on income distribution. In each chapter Iran has been treated separately and compared with the other three countries.

671 Millspaugh, Arthur C. Financial and Economic Situation of Persia, 1926. New York: Published by the Imperial Persian Government and distributed under the auspices of The Persia Society, 1926.
  This brief publication is the official report of Millspaugh, administrator general of the finances of Persia, and marks the beginning of gradual economic development in Iran of the Reza Shah period.

672 Mochaver, Fazlollah. L'évolution des Finances Iraniennes. Paris: Librairie Technique et Economique, 1938.
  A detailed history of the development of finance in Iran. The last section deals with the Reza Shah's period.

673 Nowshirvani, Vahid F. and Bildner, Robert. "Direct Foreign Investment in the Non-Oil Sectors of the Iranian Economy." Iranian Studies. 6(2-3):66-109, 1973.
  Iran's foreign investment policies and its pattern, particularly in the period after 1955, are examined. Reviews possible impacts of foreign investment on the Iranian economy.

674 Pesaran, M. H. "Income Distribution and Its Major Determinants in Iran." In: Jacqz, Jane W. (ed.), Iran: Past, Present and Future. New York: Aspen Institute for Humanistic Studies, 1976. Pages 267-286.
  The importance of equitable distribution of income to political and economic stability is discussed. The relationship between economic growth and distribution in Iran is studied.

675 Pour Homayoun, Ali Asghar. La Banque Nationale de l'Iran et Son Rôle dans le Développement Economique du Pays. Paris: Domat-Montchrestien, 1937.
  Surveys the history of banking development in Iran. The emergence of Bank Melli Iran as a leading bank of the country and its role in Iranian economy are discussed.

676 Shahid, Hushang. Economic Growth and Distribution of Income in Iran. Ph.D. dissertation, Colorado State University, 1977.
  Investigates the effect of economic growth on income distribution. The findings show that the growth in Iranian economy has not contributed to greater equality of income.

677 Shoraka, Jalil. "Opportunities for Investment in Iran." In: Amirie, Abbas and Twitchell, Hamilton A. (eds.), Iran in the 1980's. Tehran: Institute for International Political and Economic Studies, 1978. Pages 195-230.
  The purpose of this study "is to offer a descriptive

evaluation of the fundamental prerequisites for effective mobilization of investment resources." Investment opportunities in various sectors of the economy are explored.

678 Yaganegi, Esfandiar B. <u>Recent Financial and Monetary History of Persia.</u> New York, 1934.
Discusses finance and trade during Reza Shah's rule as well as a historical summary of the European political and economic influences in Iran.

ENERGY, NATURAL RESOURCES, AND INDUSTRIALIZATION

679 Amuzegar, Jahangir. Iran. Newark: Center for the Study of Marine Policy, College of Marine Studies, University of Delaware, 1975.
The fifth in the series "Energy Policies of the World," this book discusses, in detail, Iran's energy policy. The book is divided into three parts. In Part I the author discusses the historical development of individual policies regarding oil, gas, electricity, and nuclear energy. Part II is entitled "National Energy Policy: The 1970's and Beyond." Part III is devoted to institutional arrangements.

680 Askari, Hossein and Majin, Shohreh. "Recent Economic Growth in Iran." Middle Eastern Studies. 12(3):105-123, 1976.
Iran's industrial growth as a result of increased oil exports; shortage of manpower; and lack of agricultural growth are among topics discussed.

681 Badii, Rabi. "L'Iran en Mutation Industrielle." Cahiers de Géographie de Québec. 8(44):379-389, 1974.
Discusses Iran's transition from an agrarian society into an industrial one.

682 Banisadr, A. H. and Vieille, Paul. "L'Iran et les Multinationales." Esprit. 11:105-111, 1977.
Iran's efforts to industrialize and its objectives are analyzed.

683 Beaumont, Peter. "Water Resource Development in Iran." Geographical Journal. 140(3):418-431, 1974.
Discusses the multipurpose water resource projects initiated during the second Seven-Year Plan which were continued in the succeeding plans. A survey of Iran's water resource development in the past is also given.

684 Carey, J. P. C. and Carey, Andrew G. "Industrial Growth and Development Planning in Iran." Middle East Journal. 29(1):1-15, 1975.
Iran's determination to industrialize is discussed.

685 Ebrahimzadeh, Cyrus. "The Economics of Hydro-Electric Power in Iran." Tahqiqat-e Eqtesadi. 6(15,16):54-79, 1969.
Production in the hydroelectric power stations is analyzed. The supply/demand and other economic factors in this area are examined.

686 Fallah, Reza "Iran's Energy Policies and Perspectives." In: Amirie, Abbas and Twitchell, Hamilton A. (eds.), Iran in the 1980's. Tehran: Institute for International Political and Economic Studies, 1978. Pages 233-249.
Explores patterns of Iran's primary energy consumption and outlines that country's energy policies over the next two decades.

687 Grunwald, K. "L'industrializzamento della Persia." Oriente Moderno. 18:102-108, 1938.

688 Kia, Abbas Chamseddine. Essai sur l'Histoire Industrielle de l'Iran. Paris: M. Lavergne, imprimeur, 1939.
Originally presented as the author's thesis, University of Paris. Traces the history of industrial development in Iran. The emphasis is on the Reza Shah period.

689 Korby, Wilfried. Probleme der Industriellen Entwicklung und Konzentration in Iran. Wiesbaden: Reichert, 1977.
Originally presented as the author's thesis, this publication is a discussion of industrialization in Iran and problems associated with it. Contains summaries in English and Persian.

690 Martini, Aldo. Iran: Analisi de Mercato: Assetto Industriale e Dinamica di Sviluppo: Prospettive e Guida per gli Imprenditori. Torino: Stamperia Artistica Nazionale, 1976(?)

691 Mojtahedi, Ahmad. "Non-Oil Mining in Iran." Pakistan Horizon. 31(4):94-99, 1978.
Policies of the Iranian government with regard to mining of non-oil resources from the 1920's to the 1970's are described.

692 Najmabadi, F. "Strategies of Industrial Development in Iran." In: Jacqz, Jane W. (ed.), Iran: Past, Present and Future. New York: Aspen Institute for Humanistic Studies, 1976. Pages 105-121.
Traces the history of industrialization in Iran since pre-World War II and during Reza Shah's reign when a number of light industries were developed. Policies and strategies which contributed to Iran's industrial development are explored. The future of industrialization in Iran is briefly discussed.

693 Pirnia, Hossein. An Economic Report on the Conservation and Utilization of the Natural Resources of Iran with Reference

to the Iranian Seven-Year-Plan for Reconstruction and Development. Tehran: Bank Melli Iran Press, 1949.

A brief report on the various natural resources of Iran prepared on the basis of information available in the late 1940's. The resources are discussed in six categories: soil; water; forest and pasture lands; mineral resources; coal, oil and other sources of energy; and fisheries. The author, who was a member of the committee which drew up the Iranian Seven-Year Plan, also summarizes goals and objectives of this development plan. This report was submitted to the United Nations Organization Scientific Conference on the Conservation and Utilization of Natural Resources. Outdated, but useful and informative.

694 Sabeti, Houshang. "The Growth of Iranian Industry." In: Amirie, Abbas and Twitchell, Hamilton A. (eds.), Iran in the 1980's. Tehran: Institute for International Political and Economic Studies, 1978. Pages 151-175.

Iran's effort to industrialize in the past economic plans is reviewed and the future of industries in the 1980's surveyed.

695 Samadi, Hadi. Die Bedeutung der Industrialisierung für die Wirtschaftliche Entwicklung des Iran. Köln, 1971.

The significance of industrialization for economic development of Iran is examined.

696 Schulz, Ann T. "Iran's New Industrial State." Current History. 72:15-18, 38, 1977.

The Shah's policies regarding oil production, agriculture, industrialization, economic planning, and foreign investment since 1953 are discussed.

697 Soheily, Hossein. Essai sur l'Industrialisation de l'Iran. Montreux (Suisse), 1950.

Deals with economic questions and industrialization of Iran during Reza Shah's regime.

698 Turner, Louis and Bedore, James M. Middle East Industrialisation: A Study of Saudi and Iranian Downstream Investments. New York: Praeger, 1979.

Published soon after the fall of the Shah, it contains information on the Shah's industrial ambitions in the post-1973 era. Chapter 3 is entitled, "The Iranian Projects."

699 _____ and _____. "The Trade Politics of Middle Eastern Industrialization." Foreign Affairs. 57(2):306-322, 1978/79.

The effects of industrialization in countries like Iran and Saudi Arabia on other countries are studied. The authors maintain that entrance of such countries into the industrial market will raise many difficult political problems.

OIL INDUSTRY AND POLITICS OF OIL

700 Ahrari, Mohammed E. The Dynamics of Oil Diplomacy: Conflict and Consensus. Ph. D. dissertation, Southern Illinois University, 1976.
Studies the conflicts between the oil companies and the "host countries" including Iran. Attempts to show that these conflicts played a major role in the creation of the Organization of Petroleum Exporting Countries (OPEC).

701 Amiralai, Chamseddine. Le Pétrole et l'Indépendance de l'Iran. Aix-en-Provence: La Pensée Universitaire, 1961.

702 _____. Les Régimes Politiques et le Consortium du Pétrole en Iran, 1953-1962. Aix-en-Provence: La Pensée Universitaire, 1963.

703 Amuzegar, Jahangir. "Ölpreis und Weltwirtschaftliches Gleichgewicht: Die Vorschläge des Schahs von Iran für eine Internationale Entwicklungs- und Hilfsorganisation." Europa-Archiv. 29(9):277-284, 1974.
Discusses the significance and international role of oil and the Shah's views on establishing an international organization for cooperation between the oil exporting and importing countries in order to solve some of the problems associated with this issue.

704 Anglo-Iranian Oil Company, Ltd. 50 Years of Oil: A Survey of the World-Wide Activities of the Anglo-Iranian Oil Company. London, 1952.
A history and outline of activities of the company.

705 _____. Our Industry. London: AIOC Central Planning Dept., 1947.
Surveys the development of oil industry in Iran.

706 _____. A Short History of the Anglo-Iranian Oil Company. London: AIOC, 1948.
A very brief account of the company's background and the development of oil industry in Iran.

707 Anjuman-i Naft-i Iran. Oil Industry in Iran. Tehran: Iranian

Economic Conditions 113

Petroleum Institute, 1963.
The purpose of this book is "to introduce the development, varied activities and goals of the Iranian oil industry to the members of the 6th World Petroleum Congress." Contains many illustrations as well as tables and charts.

708 Asrari, Reza. The Contribution of the Oil Industry to the Economic Development and Social Progress of Iran. Ph.D. dissertation, University of Northern Colorado, 1973.

709 Azami-Zangueneh, Abd al-Hamid. Le Pétrole en Perse. Paris: F. Loviton, 1933.
A useful source for the background study of the Iranian oil dispute of the 1950's.

710 Beck, Peter J. "The Anglo-Persian Oil Dispute 1932-33." Journal of Contemporary History. 9(4):123-151, 1974.
Surveys the history of the dispute between Iran and Great Britain over the Anglo-Persian Oil Company (APOC) and its resolution by the League of Nations. The events which later led to nationalization of oil in Iran are also discussed.

711 Bhattacharya, Anindya K. The Myth of Petropower. Lexington, Massachusetts: Lexington Books, 1977.
"The purpose of this book is to analyze the financial aspects of OPEC oil revenues in terms of both their utilization in domestic development plans and the disposition of OPEC financial surplus abroad." Part II is devoted to Iran.

712 Brooks, Michael. Oil and Foreign Policy. London: Lawrence & Wishart, 1949.
A study of the relationship between oil and politics. Chapter II contains information on Iran. Most of the data is outdated.

713 Bryan, William. The Economics of the Anglo-Iranian Oil Dispute. Ph.D. dissertation, the University of Wisconsin, 1957.
Explores the social and economic impacts of the Anglo-Iranian Oil Company. A Background history of the company and its activities in Iran are presented.

714 Campbell, John C. "Oil Power in the Middle East." Foreign Affairs. 56(1):89-110, 1977.
Major oil powers in the Middle East especially Iran and Saudi Arabia are examined and the effects that these countries may have on the United States and the West in general are discussed.

715 Carey, J.P.C. "Iran and Control of Its Oil Resources." Political Science Quarterly. 89(1):147-174, 1974.
Studies the significance of oil in Iranian economy and

that country's efforts to control this valuable source of energy. The increasing importance of natural gas both as an exporting commodity and for local use is also discussed.

716 _____ and Carey, Andrew G. "Oil and Economic Development in Iran." Political Science Quarterly. 75(1):66-86, 1960.
Examines the advantages of the Consortium of companies operating the oil industry in Iran over the former Anglo-Iranian Oil Company (AIOC). Discusses the role of oil revenues in financing the Seven-Year Plan, an economic development plan administered by the Plan Organization.

717 Chandler, Geoffrey. "The Innocence of Oil Companies." Foreign Policy. 27:52-71, 1977.
The author argues that the belief that major oil companies are extremely powerful and influential is not true. Several reasons for the apparent power of the oil companies are given including the response of the companies and the West to the nationalization of oil in Iran and Mossadeq's era.

718 Cooper, A. R. C. "A Visit to the Anglo-Persian Oil-Fields." Journal of the Royal Central Asian Society. 13:148-161, 1926.
Describes the oil fields and refineries located in Southwest Iran with their headquarters at Mohammereh and Abadan. A useful study of the Iranian oil industry during Reza Shah's reign.

719 Duclos, L. J. "L'Episode de Téhéran." Revue Française de Science Politique. 22(6):1237-1255, 1972.
A discussion of the Tehran oil agreements of 1972.

720 Elwell-Sutton, L. P. Persian Oil: A Study in Power Politics. Westport, Connecticut: Greenwood Press, 1975.
Traces the relations between the Anglo-Iranian Oil Company and the Iranian government since the turn of the century. A reprint of the 1955 edition.

721 Engler, Robert. The Politics of Oil: A Study of Private Power and Democratic Directions. New York: Macmillan, 1961.
See entry 127.

722 Fallah, R. "Economics of Oil." In: Jacqz, Jane W. (ed.), Iran: Past, Present and Future. New York: Aspen Institute for Humanistic Studies, 1976. Pages 291-300.
Following a historical background, discusses the pricing of oil and the role of OPEC, Organization of Petroleum Exporting Countries, in the economics of oil.

723 Farmanfarmaian, Khodadad. "The Oil Industry and Native Enterprise in Iran." Middle Eastern Affairs. 8:333-341,

1957.
The impact of the oil industry on Iranian economy is examined.

724 Ferrier, Ronald. "The Development of the Iranian Oil Industry." In: Amirsadeghi, Hossein (ed.), Twentieth-Century Iran. New York: Holmes & Meier, 1977. Pages 93-128.
Topics covered in this essay are: The concessionary period of oil industry; the postconcession period, after oil was nationalized; the roles of National Iranian Oil Co. (NIOC) and the consortium; the role played by the international politics; and the place of oil in the Iranian economy.

725 Fesharaki, Fereidun. Development of the Iranian Oil Industry: International and Domestic Aspects. New York: Praeger, 1976.
This book is an outgrowth of the author's doctoral dissertation at the University of Surrey in England. Although its focus is on Iran, "the discussions are kept within the context of the economics and politics of the oil industry in the region as a whole."

726 Grossi, Gianaldo. Iran: Petrolio, Violenza, Potere. Milano: G. Mazzotta, 1975.

727 Gupta, Raj Narain. Oil in the Modern World. Allahabad: Kitab Mahal, 1949.
A reprint of this book was published in 1976 by Hyperion Press. Chapter Five deals with production and transportation of oil in Iran.

728 Hesse, Fritz. "Zur Geschichte und Bedeutung der Anglo-Persian Oil Co." Zeitschrift für Geopolitik. 6(9):805-812, 1929.
Discusses the history and importance of the Anglo-Persian Oil Company (APOC). The economic significance of the Company for Iran and its political influence by forestalling the Soviet move in the country are emphasized.

729 Hoeppner, Rolf-Roger. Zur Entwicklung der Erdölwirtschaft Irans von 1954-1973: Einführung und Dokumentation. Hamburg: Deutsches Orient-Institut, 1973.
A documentary treatment of the development of oil economy in Iran. Includes texts of various agreements in English.

730 International Labour Office. Labour Conditions in the Oil Industry in Iran: Report of a Mission of the International Labour Office (January-February 1950). Geneva, 1950.
Contains useful statistics and discusses many of the problems that faced employers and labor throughout Iran during the period covered. Prepared for the Petroleum Committee of the International Labour Organisation.

731 The International Petroleum Cartel, the Iranian Consortium, and U.S. National Security. Prepared for the use of Subcommittee on Multinational Corporations of the Committee on Foreign Relations, United States Senate. Washington, D.C.: U.S. Government Printing Office, 1974.
This U.S. Government publication contains certain secret documents which were declassified in 1974 and made public from the files of the National Security Council, the Department of State and the Department of Justice. "... These documents explain and relate two conflicting policies of the United States Government in the field of international oil. These policies were 1. Prosecution of the International Petroleum Cartel Case, and 2. Creation of the Iranian Consortium."

732 Jones J.H. "My Visit to the Persian Oilfields." Journal of the Royal Central Asian Society. 34:56-68, 1947.
The author was a member of a delegation sent to Iran by the British Government to investigate the political agitation and labor unrest in the oil fields of the Anglo-Iranian Oil Company. This article is a report of the author's observations and recommendations to improve the situation.

733 Kuschiar, Amir Hossein. Der Einfluss der Erdölindustrie auf die Politische Gestaltung des Irans. Köln, 1959.
A discussion of the effects of oil on politics in Iran.

734 Magnus, Ralph. "Middle East Oil and the OPEC Nations." Current History. 70:22-26, 1976.
Discusses problems the OPEC nations face in maintaining a solid front against the Western industrial nations.

735 Majidi, Abdol-Majid. "Iran, 1980-85: Problems and Challenges of Development." World Today. 33(7):267-274, 1977.
The emphasis is on the risks involved in benefits derived from oil revenues for an oil exporting country such as Iran.

736 Massudi-Toiserkan, Schapur. Historische Entwicklung des Persischen Erdölproblems. Bonn, 1960.
A historical study of Iran's oil industry and its problems.

737 Melamid, Alexander. "Petroleum Product Distribution and the Evolution of Economic Regions in Iran." Geographical Review. 65(4):510-525, 1975.
Analyzes Iran's petroleum production regions and surveys their evolution since the 1860's.

738 Moghari, Mohammad. Impact of the Oil Technology on Iran, 1901-1951. Iowa: Iowa State University (?), 1975.
The first two chapters are devoted to a background study of the influence of the West on Iran (Chapter 1) and a historical survey of the Iranian oil industry (Chapter 2). In the remaining three chapters the author discusses the political,

economic and social impacts of the oil industry on Iran in the first half of this century. The study was sponsored by the Committee on Technology and Social Change in Foreign Cultures, Iowa State University.

739 Moran, Theodore H. "Why Oil Prices Go Up: The Future: OPEC Wants Them." Foreign Policy. 25:58-77, 1976/1977.
Analyzes the trend in international oil prices by studying two major oil-producing countries, Iran and Saudi Arabia. Possible United States responses to escalating oil prices are examined.

740 Nakhai, M. Le Pétrole en Iran. Bruxelles: J. Félix, 1938.
A history of oil development in Northern and Southern Iran. Contains the texts of concessions given to Anglo-Iranian Oil Company (AIOC) and Amirian Oil Company.

741 Nazari, Hassan. Der Ökonomische und Politische Kampf um das Iranische Erdöl. Köln: Pahl-Rugenstein, 1971.
Examines the economic and political aspects of Iranian oil industry.

742 Oppenheim, V. H. "Why Oil Prices Go Up: The Past: We Pushed Them." Foreign Policy. 25:24-57, 1976/77.
Examines the United States policy regarding the international oil market and attempts to find the reasons behind the increase in oil prices since 1971. Maintains that the U.S. encouraged the Middle East oil producing countries to raise oil prices.

743 Pahlavi, Mohammad Reza. Shahanshah of Iran on Oil: Tehran Agreement: Background & Perspectives. London: Transorient, 1971.
A compilation of five public statements of the Shah and important documents relevant to the Tehran Oil Agreement (February 15, 1971).

744 Panahi, Bahram. Erdöl, Gegenwart und Zukunft des Iran: Die Entwicklungstendenzen des Iran: Erdölpotentials seit der Nationalisierung. Köln; Wien: Böhlau, 1975.
A study of Iranian oil since its nationalization in 1951.

745 Perroux, François. "The Anglo-Iranian Co. et les Effets de Domination." Economies et Sociétés. 2(9):1725-1743, 1968.
This article was first published in Economie Appliquée in January-March 1952. The effects of the company's influence over the oil market are analyzed.

746 Persia-Consortium Agreement. Tehran, 1954.
English and Persian texts of the oil agreement between Iran and the oil consortium signed in 1954.

747 Regard, J. L'Iran et les Pétrodollars. Paris: Documentation Française, 1975.

748 Rosenberg, Robert L. "Qum-1956: A Misadventure in Iranian Oil." Business History Review. 49(1):81-104, 1975.
   The unsuccessful story of an international consortium formed to exploit new oil discoveries in Iran in 1956. Milton Reynolds and Charles Allen, Jr. are mentioned as key leaders of that misadventure.

749 Rouhani, Fuad. A History of O.P.E.C. New York: Praeger, 1971.
   Attempts to present a comprehensive history of OPEC, its genesis, achievements and future. Contains a country profile of all OPEC members including Iran.

750 Rowland, John and Cadman, Basil Cadman. Ambassador for Oil: The Life of John, First Baron Cadman. London: H. Jenkins, 1960.
   The official biography of John, First Baron Cadman of Silverdale (1877-1941). Contains important information about the Anglo-Persian Oil Company. John Cadman was technical advisor to the company and in 1923 he became director and later chairman. Chapter XI is entitled: "Anglo-Persian Developments."

751 Scharlau, K. "Erdöl und Politik in Iran." Zeitschrift für Politik. 7(3):295-307, 1960.
   A historical survey of the relationship between oil and politics in Iran. Foreign interference in Iranian affairs for the control of oil resources is among subjects discussed.

752 Stobaugh, Robert B. "The Evolution of Iranian Oil Policy, 1925-1975." In: Lenczowski, George (ed.), Iran Under the Pahlavis. Stanford, California: Hoover Institution Press, 1978. Pages 201-252.
   The goals sought in formulating Iranian oil policies: 1. Seeking independence from domination by foreign companies and 2. Obtaining higher revenues, are discussed. Contains several statistical charts and graphs.

753 United States. Petroleum Administration for War. Petroleum in War and Peace. Washington, D.C., 1945.
   Papers presented by the Petroleum Administration for War before the U.S. Senate. The impact of oil on the economy of the United States is examined. Includes information on oil production in Iran.

754 Veccia Vaglieri, Laura. "Storia del Petrolio di Persia." Comunità Internazionale. 11(4):595-619, 1956.
   Reviews the history of oil industry in Iran and the role of the Anglo-Iranian Oil Company (AIOC).

755 Williamson, John W. In a Persian Oil Field: A Study in Scientific and Industrial Development. London: E. Benn limited, 1927.
A survey of the development of the oil industry in Iran.

FOREIGN ECONOMIC POLICY AND
OTHER ASPECTS OF THE ECONOMY

756 Adli, Abolfazl. Aussenhandel und Aussenwirtschaftspolitik des Iran. Berlin: Dunker und Humblot, 1960.
A historical survey of Iranian foreign trade and foreign economic policy since 1931.

757 Agah, Manouchehr. "An Overview of Iran's Economic Aims." In: Amirie, Abbas and Twitchell, Hamilton A. (eds.), Iran in the 1980's. Tehran: Institute for International Political and Economic Studies, 1978. Pages 93-98.
Attempts to outline some of the future goals of the Iranian economy. Various issues such as oil resources and their use, manpower, development of economic infrastructure, and foreign investment are briefly explored.

758 Amini, Ali. L'institution du Monopole du Commerce Extérieur en Perse. Paris: Rousseau & Cie, 1932.

759 Amuzegar, Jahangir. Iran: An Economic Profile. Washington, D.C.: Middle East Institute, 1977.
"This study is intended to serve as a basic source of reference on the Iranian economy--its infrastructure, policies and performance." It is divided into four parts: Part I, Economic Structure and Forces; Part II, Production and Distribution Patterns; Part III, Economic Plans and Policies; and Part IV, Performance and Prospects.

760 _____. "On the Road to a Great Civilization." In: Amirie, Abbas and Twitchell, Hamilton A. (eds.), Iran in the 1980's. Tehran: Institute for International Political and Economic Studies, 1978. Pages 99-107.
A somewhat optimistic and laudatory view of Iran and her economic future.

761 Artzt, P. Wirtschaft und Verkehr Persiens. Vienna: Dissertation, Hochschule für Welthandel, 1934.
This study focuses on the economic developments of Iran during the reign of Reza Shah.

762 Asia Development Corporation. Iran. New York: Chase World

Information Corp., 1976.
Designed to inform corporate executives interested in business opportunities in Iran, this publication provides information on a variety of subjects geared to individuals in the business world. The subjects covered range from general facts about Iran, its economy, labor, and industry to living conditions and transportation. Contains numerous maps and statistical tables. Asia Development Corporation is a privately owned company headquartered in Oakland, California. This book was prepared by this company and Chase World Information Corporation.

763 Askari, Hossein; Richter, Gunter; and Cummings, John T. "Efficiency of LDC Trading Patterns: The Case of Iran." American Economic Review. 69(2):191-195, 1979.
Iran is studied as a typical Less Developed Country (LDC) in order to investigate the reasons behind her inefficient trading patterns, for example her overpayment for imports in the 1970's.

764 Confederazione Generale dell'Industria Italiana. Missione Economica Italiana in Iran, 23 Novembre-2 Dicembre 1957. Roma: Confederazione Generale dell'Industria Italiana, 1958(?).
This three-volume work is a report of an Italian economic mission to Iran in 1957.

765 Connell, John. "Economic Change in an Iranian Village." Middle East Journal. 28(3):309-314, 1974.
The economic conditions of a small village in the Gilan province from 1962-1970's are examined. The changes in the agricultural production and other economic conditions in this village as a result of the Empress Farah Dam are discussed.

766 Djazaeri, Chams-ed-Dine. La Crise Economique Mondiale et Ses Répercussions en Iran. Paris: Librairie Technique et Economique, 1938.
Studies the world economic depression of 1929 and its effects on Iran.

767 Djourabtchi, Hassan. La Structure Economique de l'Iran. Genève: E. Droz, 1955.
Studies the economic potential and resources of Iran, other than oil and carpets.

768 Doeval, Hans. Persiens Auswärtige Wirtschaftsbeziehungen. Hamburg: Friedrichsen, 1933.
A useful treatment of Iranian foreign trade before and during the world depression.

769 Fardi, Mohsen A. "Iran's International Economic Outlook." In: Jacqz, Jane W. (ed.), Iran: Past, Present and Future.

New York: Aspen Institute for Humanistic Studies, 1976. Pages 347-365.
The purpose of this article is to evaluate the performance of Iran's foreign trade in the past and to explore its future prospects.

770 Fateh, Moustafa Khan. The Economic Position of Persia. London: P. S. King and Son, 1926.
A brief survey of resources, economic activities, and possibilities for development in Iran during the Reza Shah period.

771 Fucito, Guido. L'Iran: Situazione Economica e Scambi Commerciali con l'Estero. Roma: Istituto Poligrafico dello Stato, 1948.

772 Furon, Raymond. L'Iran: Perse et Afghanistan. Paris: Payot, 1951.
The economic condition of Iran is examined in Chapter XII of this work.

773 Gray, F. A. G. Report on the Economic and Commercial Conditions in Iran During 1937-38. London: Department of Overseas Trade, 1939(?).
One of the periodic reports published by the British Department of Overseas Trade dealing with the economic situation during Reza Shah's period.

774 Gupta, Raj Narain. Iran: An Economic Study. New Delhi: Indian Institute of International Affairs, 1947.
Post-World War II Iranian economic conditions are the subject of this study.

775 Halliday, Fred. "Iran: The Economic Contradictions." Middle East Research and Information Project. 8:9+, 1978.
Discusses problems and contradictions in Iranian economy in various areas such as oil, agriculture, etc. Anticipates serious economic crisis for Iran and asserts that there is a potential social revolution ahead.

776 International Chamber of Commerce. Iranian Committee. Iran Shows the Way. Tehran: Iranian National Committee, International Chamber of Commerce, 1976.
Contains useful information on the Iranian economy and effects of modernization on the country.

777 Iran in the 1970's: Opportunities in a Dynamic, Developing Economy. Tehran: Iran Chamber of Commerce, Industries & Mines, 1971.
The first part provides background information on the economy, society, and history of Iran. The remaining parts include chapters on the economic aspects of the White Revolution, oil and related industries, and the

778 Issawi, Charles. "The Economy: An Assessment of Performance." In: Yar-Shater, Ehsan (ed.), Iran Faces the Seventies. New York: Praeger, 1971. Pages 44-65.
The performance of Iranian economy in the 1960's is evaluated on the basis of growth, stability, structural development, international balance, and social justice. The author concludes that the overall performance has proved satisfactory and this trend is likely to be continued provided the country remains politically stable.

779 _____. Iran's Economic Upsurge." Middle East Journal. 21(4):447-461, 1967.
Iran's economic growth and its underlying causes are discussed.

780 Katouzian, Homa. The Political Economy of Modern Iran: Despotism and Pseudo-Modernism, 1926-1979. New York: New York University Press, 1981.
In a historical setting, attempts to analyze social and economic changes in Iran of the twentieth century. It includes an assessment of contemporary political and economic developments.

781 Kazemi, Parviz. Le Commerce Extérieur de la Perse: Comment et Assurer le Développement. Paris: Rousseau et Cie, 1930.
Deals with the economic situation in Iran during the reign of Reza Shah.

782 Looney, Robert E. Iran at the End of the Century: A Hegelian Forecast. Lexington, Massachusetts: Lexington Books, 1977.
The goal of this book as indicated in its Preface is "to make a long-run forecast for the Iranian economy by integrating the modern analytical tools of economics with the theory of historical changes stemming from the work of Hegel."

783 McLachlan, Keith. "The Iranian Economy, 1960-1976." In: Amirsadeghi, Hossein (ed.), Twentieth-Century Iran. New York: Holmes & Meier, 1977. Pages 129-169.
A survey of economic conditions of Iran between 1960-1976. The pattern of change in the structure of Iranian economy due to land reform and increase in oil revenues is followed and problems facing the economy in the future are outlined.

784 Malekpur, Abdollah. Die Wirtschaftsverfassung Irans. Berlin: Buchdruckerei Frickert, 1935.

Useful for the study of economic conditions under Reza Shah.

785 Mehran, Hassan Ali. "Iran in the World Economic Setting. " In: Jacqz, Jane W. (ed.), Iran: Past, Present and Future. New York: Aspen Institute for Humanistic Studies, 1976. Pages 339-345.
A survey of Iran's international economic and trade relations up to 1975.

786 Moghadam, Gholam Reza. Iran's Foreign Trade Policy and Economic Development in the Interwar Period. Ph. D. dissertation, Stanford University, 1956.
Attempts to analyze and assess Iran's foreign trade policy and its impact on the country's economic development.

787 Moghtader, Hushang. "Irans Aussenwirtschaftliche Beziehungen. " Aussenpolitik. Part I, 29(1):98-117, 1978; Part II, 29(2): 209-226, 1978.
The first part of this article is a discussion of Iran's economic growth due to tremendous increase in oil revenues and her expansion of economic development programs on local as well as international levels. The second part deals with Iran's economic relations with socialistic and Third World countries.

788 Nikitine, R. "La Structure Economique de la Perse. " Revue Economique Internationale. 23(3):591-625, 1931.
A study of economic conditions in Iran during Reza Shah's regime. Agriculture, transportation, finance, and foreign trade are examined.

789 La Persia e il Piano di Sviluppo Economicò. Milano-Varese: Istituto Editoriale Cisalpino, 1969.
Report of a meeting held in Pavia in March 1968. The speakers discussed various aspects of the Iranian economy.

790 Pesaran, M. H. World Economic Prospects and the Iranian Economy. Tehran: Institute for International Political and Economic Studies, 1976.
This study analyzes "Iran's shifting trade patterns and their relation with the world economy. "

791 Pirnia, Hossein. A Short Survey of the Economic Conditions of Iran. Tehran: Published for the Economic Information Bureau, 1945.
A very brief but useful study of Iran's economic situation for the period under study, with a Preface by Arthur C. Millspaugh.

792 Plan Organization. Statistical Centre of Iran. Statistical Yearbook 1968. Teheran: Statistical Centre of Iran, 1971.

793 Rad-Serecht, Farhad. "Intégration au Système Economique Mondial et Degré d'Autonomie Nationale: Le Cas de l'Iran." Politique Etrangère. 43(4):429-437, 1978.

794 Rajput, A. B. Iran To-day. Lahore: Lion Press, 1953.
Contains a post-World War II economic survey of Iran.

795 Salvadori, Massimo. "Aspetti della Politica Economica Persiana." L'Oltremare. 5(9):336-359, 1931.
Studies Iran's economic policies during Reza Shah's regime. Monetary reform, foreign commerce, and communications are among subjects treated in this article.

796 Simmonds, S. Economic Conditions in Iran (Persia), July 1935. London: Department of Overseas Trade, 1935.
One of the periodic reports issued by the British Department of Overseas Trade dealing with economic conditions in Iran during the reign of Reza Shah.

797 Stauffer, Thomas R. "Economics of Nomadism in Iran." Middle East Journal. 19(3):284-302, 1965.
Inquires into the contributions of the nomadic tribes of Iran to that country's economy. The tribal resettlement issue is also discussed.

798 Tofigh, Firouz. "Development of Iran: A Statistical Note." In: Jacqz, Jane W. (ed.), Iran: Past, Present and Future. New York: Aspen Institute for Humanistic Studies, 1976. Pages 57-70.
Provides statistical information on population, urbanization, labor force, national income, industry, agriculture, and foreign trade.

799 Vakil, Firouz. "Iran's Basic Macroeconomic Problems: A 20-Year Horizon." In: Jacqz, Jane W. (ed.), Iran: Past, Present and Future. New York: Aspen Institute for Humanistic Studies, 1976. Pages 83-104.
Focuses on analyzing major economic problems facing Iran in the areas of oil industry, inflation, urban-rural income gap, and the promotion of non-oil exports. Includes statistical tables. Also published in: Economic Development and Cultural Change. 25(4):713-729, 1977.

800 _____. "Some Macro-Economic Considerations." In: Amirie, Abbas and Twitchell, Hamilton A. (eds.), Iran in the 1980's. Tehran: Institute for International Political and Economic Studies, 1978. Pages 111-149.
Examines Iran's long-term economic problems and a

Contains statistical information on various aspects of the Iranian economy. This is the second volume in this series appearing in English. The first volume of this yearbook was for the year 1966. No volume was published for 1967.

strategy for development. The fifth Development Plan is assessed and future plans are analyzed. Major problems in the macroeconomic area which are likely to appear in the 1980's are explored.

AGRICULTURE AND LAND REFORM

801 Ajami, Ismail. "Agriculture and Rural Development in Iran." In: Jacqz, Jane W. (ed.), Iran: Past, Present and Future. New York: Aspen Institute for Humanistic Studies, 1976. Pages 131-156.
Presents a theoretical framework for agricultural development and attempts to analyze the traditional Iranian agricultural structure. A discussion of the implementation of the land reform program of 1962 covering its social, political, and economic effects, follows.

802 Ajdari, Ahmad. "Les Conditions de la Réforme Agraire en Iran." Développement et Civilisations. 22:37-46, 1965.
Iranian agrarian reform is discussed. Political and social conditions underlying the reform are examined.

803 Arfa, Hassan. "Land Reform in Iran." Journal of the Royal Central Asian Society. 50:132-137, 1963.
A general discussion of the land reform which began in 1962.

804 Bagley, F. R. C. "A Bright Future After Oil: Dams and Agro-Industry in Khuzistan." Middle East Journal. 30(1):25-35, 1976.
The five agro-industrial units developed in the Iranian province of Khuzistan are described.

805 Brun, Thierry A. and Dumont, René. "Iran: Imperial Pretentions and Agricultural Dependence." Middle East Research and Information Project. 71:15-20, 1978.
See next entry.

806 _____ and _____. "Des Prétentions Impériales à la Dépendance Alimentaire: Remarques sur le Développement du Secteur Agro-Alimentaire en Iran." Peuples Mediterranéens. 2:3-24, 1978.
The decrease in agricultural production and failure of the land reform are discussed. The future consequences are outlined.

807 Carey, J.P.C. and Carey, Andrew G. "Iranian Agriculture and Its Development: 1952-1973." International Journal of Middle East Studies. 7(3):359-382, 1976.
Traces Iran's agricultural development. The author demonstrates that Iranian agriculture, unlike other sections of the economy, failed to reach its expected goals.

808 Craig, Daniel. "The Impact of Land Reform on an Iranian Village." Middle East Journal. 32(2):141-154, 1978.
The adverse impact of land reform on a village called Nasrin is assessed and reasons for its failure examined.

809 Delavallé, J.P. "La Réforme Agraire en Iran." Orient. (Paris) 28:37-54, 1963.
Presents a background history of the Iranian land reform.

810 Denman, D.R. The King's Vista: A Land Reform Which Has Changed the Face of Persia. Berkhamstead: Geographical Publications, 1973.
The purpose of this study is to describe the Iranian land reform from the point of view of individuals responsible for it. Explores the peculiarities of the agrarian reform in Iran.

811 _____. "Land Reforms of Shah and People." In: Lenczowski, George (ed.), Iran Under the Pahlavis. Stanford, California: Hoover Institution Press, 1978. Pages 253-301.
A history and analysis of the land reform in Iran. The three phases of the land reform policy are examined. Issues related to this project such as the Literacy Corps, Health Corps, and Extension and Development Corps are also discussed.

812 Doroudian, R. "Modernization of Rural Economy in Iran." In: Jacqz, Jane W. (Ed.), Iran: Past, Present and Future. New York: Aspen Institute for Humanistic Studies, 1976. Pages 157-168.
The programs undertaken to modernize the agricultural sector in Iran after the land reform are discussed. Four models adopted to solve problems associated with agriculture: Rural Cooperative Societies; Agribusiness; Farm Corporations; and Production Cooperatives are explored and evaluated.

813 Fisher, C.B. "The Feudal System in Persia." Journal of Farm Economics. 13(4):621-629, 1931.
Describes the feudal system of land management, its problems, and deficiencies in Iran during the early 1930's.

814 Freivalds, John. "Farm Corporations in Iran: An Alternative to Traditional Agriculture." Middle East Journal. 26(2):185-193, 1972.

The organization, work strategy, distribution of dividends, and other issues related to farm cooperatives in Iran are described. Farm cooperatives and the Israeli kibbutz are compared.

815 Gittinger, James Price. Planning for Agricultural Development: The Iranian Experiences. Washington, D.C.: National Planning Association (Center for Development Planning), 1965.
Describes the planning process for the agricultural section of the third Development Plan (1962-1968) and how it was prepared.

816 Greussing, Kurt. "Politische Ökonomie des Dorfes im Iran: Zum Verhältnis von Dörflicher Klassenentwicklung und Landreform." Mardom Nameh. 1:26-65, 1975.
A study in political economy of the Iranian village. The interrelationship of rural class development and the Iranian land reform is examined.

817 Hadary, Gideon. "The Agrarian Reform Problem in Iran." Middle East Journal. 5(2):181-196, 1951.
The economic status of Iranian farmers and problems facing the agricultural sector of Iran's economy are described. Efforts at improvement and reform in this area are outlined.

818 Hayden, Lyle J. "Living Standards in Rural Iran: A Case Study." Middle East Journal. 3(2):140-150, 1949.
The economic status of the Iranian peasant is described by studying a typical village, Aliabad, located in the central plateau of Iran. System of ownership and production, health conditions, and some improvement projects undertaken by the government are examined.

819 Hobbs, John A. "Land Reform in Iran: A Revolution from Above." Orbis. 7(3):617-630, 1963.
Iran's land reform and its strength and weaknesses are examined. The problems facing Iranian farmers as a result of land reform implementation "from above" are discussed.

820 Hooglund, Eric J. The Effects of Land Reform Program on Rural Iran, 1962-72. Ph.D. dissertation, Johns Hopkins University, 1975.
Asserts that the main effect of the Iranian land reform has increased governmental control of the rural areas.

821 _____. "The Khwushnishin Population of Iran." Iranian Studies. 6(4):229-241, 1973.
A study of the landless farmers of Iran and the problems confronting them.

822 _____. Land and Revolution in Iran, 1960-1980. Austin, Texas: University of Texas Press, 1982.
Following a background study of the land reform in Iran since 1962, the book analyzes and assesses its social, economic, and political impacts on rural Iran. The last chapter is devoted to the study of the role of rural population in the revolution of 1978/79.

823 Katouzian, M. A. "Land Reform in Iran: A Case Study in the Political Economy of Social Engineering." Journal of Peasant Studies. 1(2):220-239, 1974.
Studies the Iranian land reform between 1962 and 1972. Following an examination of its development, concludes that it has not improved the socioeconomic status of Iran's peasantry.

824 _____. "Oil Versus Agriculture: A Cast Study of Dual Resource Depletion in Iran." Journal of Peasant Studies. 5 (3):347-369, 1978.
Demonstrates that the failure of Iran's agriculture is the result of increase in oil revenues and misguided public expenditure policies because of this increase.

825 Keddie, Nikki R. "The Iranian Village Before and After Land Reform." Journal of Contemporary History. 3(3):69-91, 1968.
Analyzes the impact of Iran's land reform on rural life. Concludes that the condition of the farmers has not changed substantially.

826 Khamsi, Farhad. "Land Reform in Iran." Monthly Review. 21(2):20-28, 1969.
An Iranian student's criticism of the land reform. The author argues that the real beneficiaries of this reform are the landlords and not the poor farmers.

827 Khosrovi, K. "Les Paysans Sans Terre en Iran: Les Khochnechin." Sociologia Ruralis. 13(3-4):289-293, 1973.
The situation of the Khoshneshin, the landless peasants of Iran, is discussed. It is argued that agrarian reform has worsened the condition of this group.

828 _____. "La Réforme Agraire et l'Apparition d'une Nouvelle Classe en Iran." Etudes Rurales. 34:122-126, 1969.
The results of land reform in Iran and the appearance of a new "rural middle class" are discussed.

829 Kristjanson, Baldur H. "The Agrarian-Based Development of Iran." Land Economics. 36:1-13, 1960.
Discusses the land tenure situation in Iran and examines the program of the Crown lands distribution and problems associated with it.

830 Lambton, A. K. S. "Land Reform and Rural Co-operative Societies in Persia." Journal of the Royal Central Asian Society. 56:142-155; 245-258, 1969.
Reviews the provisions of the Land Reform Law of 1962 and evaluates the results of the land reform program and rural cooperative societies. Outlines the problems associated with them.

831 _____. Landlord and Peasant in Persia: A Study of Land Tenure and Land Revenue Administration. New York: Oxford University Press, 1953.
This is a scholarly and an in-depth work on the Iranian land tenure system. Problems associated with the peasant class are analyzed and possible solutions for increase in productivity are recommended. Legislative measures taken during Reza Shah's reign in regard to land tenure and related issues are also discussed. Reprinted in 1969.

832 _____. The Persian Land Reform, 1962-1966. Oxford: Clarendon Press, 1969.
The laws and their implications are examined in order to survey the Iranian land reform program. The role of the cooperative societies in achieving the goals of the reform is also discussed.

833 _____. "Some Reflections on the Question of Rural Development and Land Reform in Iran." Tahqiqat-e Eqtesadi. 3 (9-10):3-9, 1965.
The author emphasizes the relationship between rural development with development in other sectors of the Iranian society. She asserts that unless this connection is understood, the land reform cannot be carried out satisfactorily.

834 Mahdavy, Hossein. "The Coming Crisis in Iran." Foreign Affairs. 44(1):134-146, October 1965.
The problems associated with the land reform are discussed. The author who is a former deputy director in Iran's Plan Organization, asserts that the Iranian land reform is basically a political measure that the government has used in order to offset the opposition in urban areas.

835 Malek, Hossein. "Après la Réforme Agraire Iranienne." Annales de Géographie. 75(409):268-713, 1966.
Iran's agrarian reform is examined from various angles. The author emphasizes that the reform's success depends on certain social foundations which are lacking in Iranian society.

836 Miller, William Green. "Hosseinabad: A Persian Village." Middle East Journal. 18(4):483-498, 1964.
Social and economic impacts of Iran's land reform on this village are examined.

837 Moghaddam, Reza. "Land Reform and Rural Development in Iran." Land Economics. 48:162-168, 1972.
Discusses factors leading to the success of land reform in Iran.

838 Nikgohar, Abdolhossein. "Quelques Observations sur la Réforme Agraire Iranienne." Revue Française de Sociologie. 16: 685-703, 1975.
Some observations on the Iranian land reform and the activities of the Incorporated Land Company (ILC), an Iranian institution set up during the 1962 land reform.

839 Quintana Pali, Santiago. "Políticas de Reforma Agraria en Egipto e Irán: Una Comparación entre dos Casos de Desarrollo Capitalista." Estudios de Asia y Africa. 14(3):405-465, 1979.
Attempts to compare the Iranian and Egyptian land reforms and outlines the similarities.

840 Salzman, P. C. "Persian Land Reform and the Shah: A Critical Comment on Lambton's View." Muslim World. 62(3): 241-246, 1972.
Argues that it was the Shah and not Hassan Arsanjani, the minister of agriculture of Iran, who played the major role in Iranian land reform of the 1960's.

841 Sandjabi, Karim. Essai sur l'Economie Rurale et le Régime Agraire de la Perse. Paris: Domat-Montchrestien, 1934.

842 Scarcia, Gianroberto. "Governo, Riforma Agraria e Opposizione in Persia." Oriente Moderno. 42:731-801, 1962.
A detailed study of the agrarian reform in Iran. Iran's internal problems in the early 1960's are also examined.

843 Schirazi, Ali. "Iranische Landreform unter der Perspektive Oppositioneller Gruppen." Mardom Nameh. 2:41-54, 1976.
A discussion of the Iranian land reform from the viewpoint of the oppositional groups. Includes a review of Persian literature by the oppositional groups on the political impact and consequences of the land reform.

844 "Second Bill on Increasing the Farmer's Share and the Agricultural Development Organization." Middle East Journal. 7(1):81-87, 1953.
Text of the bill is printed as translated from Etelaat, a major Iranian newspaper.

845 Shoko, Okazaki. "Shirang-Sofla: The Economics of a Northeast Iranian Village." Developing Economies. 7(3):261-283, 1969.
An analysis of agricultural economy of the village of Shirang-Sofla located in the Gorgan region. Labor

Economic Conditions

situation, land ownership, and class stratification are among subjects studied.

846 Simonet, Pierre A. "Féodalisme et Liberalisme Economique en Iran." Développement et Civilisations. 11:37-54, 1962.
The agrarian structure and feudalism in Iran are studied. The shortcomings of a liberal development program in such a structure are discussed.

847 Sternberg-Sarel, Benno. "Tradition et Développement en Iran: Les Villages de la Plaine de Ghazvin." Etudes Rurales. 206-218, 1966.
Discusses the results of a study of four Iranian villages and the impact of the land reform on them.

848 Tardow. "Die Agrarverhältnisse Persiens." Agrar-Probleme. 3(1-2):186-204, 1930.
Describes the agricultural and feudal system of land management during Reza Shah's regime.

849 Tripet, François. "Les Bouleversements de l'Univers Rural en Iran." L'Afrique et l'Asie. 95/96:27-40, 1971.
Studies the impact of agrarian reform on Iran. The role of the Teaching Corps in the rural areas is also discussed.

850 Tuma, Elias H. "Agrarian Reform in Historical Perspective Revisited." Comparative Studies in Society and History. 21(1):3-29, 1979.
Agrarian reform programs in eight countries including Iran are analyzed and the results are discussed. One of the results, according to the author, is that except for Cuba and China the reforms have had little impact on improving the living conditions of the farmers.

851 Vahidi, Iraj. "A Profile of Iranian Agriculture." In: Amirie, Abbas and Twitchell, Hamilton A. (eds.), Iran in the 1980's. Tehran: Institute for International Political and Economic Studies, 1978. Pages 177-193.
The contribution of agriculture to the Iranian economy is explored and its future forecasted. Problems related to agricultural development are also examined.

852 Vieille, Paul. "Les Coopératives Agricoles en Iran." Archives Internationales de Sociologie de la Coopération et du Développement. 32:45-60, 1972.
Discusses the agricultural cooperatives established as a result of the Iranian land reform laws of 1962-63.

853 _____. "Les Paysans, la Petite Bourgeoisie Rurale, et l'Etat après la Réforme Agraire en Iran." Annales. Economies, Sociétés, Civilisations. 27(2);347-372, 1972.
Studies the impact of the Iranian land reform for the Gilan region.

854 Ward, Gordon H. "Farmers Cooperatives Under Land Reform in Iran." Indian Cooperative Review. 3(2):865-872, 1966.

855 Weinbaum, M. G. "Agricultural Policy and Development Politics in Iran." Middle East Journal. 31(4):434-450, 1977.
Critical of the agricultural policy in Iran after the White Revolution. Maintains that the lack of a coherent policy is due to the bureaucracy's inflexibility in adopting more constructive measures.

IV

SOCIAL CONDITIONS

THE SOCIETY AND GENERAL SOCIAL CONDITIONS

856 Abrahamian, Ervand. "The Crowd in Iranian Politics 1905-
1953." Past and Present. 41:184-210, 1968.
Analyzes the role of the crowd in Iranian history. Examines the structure of the crowd in the preindustrial era (1905-1925) and the semi-industrial period (1941-1953).

857 Adibi, Hossein. "Rural-Urban Migration in Iran." The Australian and New Zealand Journal of Sociology. 13(2): 175-178, 1977.
After a brief background history, the problem of rural-urban migration in Iran is examined. Some of the developments relevant to this migration such as the effect of the land reform program, increase in oil revenues, and land speculation are discussed.

858 Ahrens, Peter Georg. Die Entwicklung der Stadt Teheran: Eine Städtebauliche Untersuchung Ihrer Zukünftigen Gestaltung. Opladen: Leske, 1966.
Tehran's urban problems are discussed.

859 Ajami, Ismail. "Social Classes, Family Demographic Characteristics and Mobility in Three Iranian Villages." Sociologia Ruralis. 9(1):62-72, 1969.
Results of a sociological study of three Iranian villages demonstrating the effects of the social classes of the rural households on the family demographic characteristics.

860 Arasteh, Reza. Man and Society in Iran. Leiden: E.J. Brill, 1964.
In this sociological study of Iranian culture and civilization, the author attempts to analyze man and culture in Iran which might serve as a model for the study of other cultures. The book is divided into three major sections: "Man in Traditional Iranian Society"; "Man in Contemporary Iranian Society"; and "A Measure for the Future."

861 Askari, Hossein and Cummings, John Thomas. "The Middle East and the United States: A Problem of 'Brain Drain.'" International Journal of Middle East Studies. 8(1):65-90, 1977.

Examines the Middle Eastern migration to the United States and the problem of "brain drain." Several countries including Iran are used as examples.

862 Bagley, F. R. C. "Technocracy in Iran." Der Islam. 44:230-249, 1968.
Focuses on advances made in technocratic administration in Iran after the Second World War.

863 Banani, Amin. "The Role of the Mass Media." In: Yar-Shater, Ehsan (ed.), Iran Faces the Seventies. New York: Praeger, 1971. Pages 321-340.
Discusses the evolution of mass media in Iran and their role in the political process and social change. The problem of censorship is also examined.

864 Bémont, Frédy. Les Villes et l'Iran, des Cités d'Autrefois à l'Urbanisme Contemporain. Paris: L'auteur, 1969.
Urbanization in Iran and social and economic developments of major Iranian cities are examined.

865 Besharat, Ali Reza. "The Role of Local Government in Social Development: Iran." Ekistics. 28:435-439, 1969.
Social change related to Iranian local government systems is analyzed and problems involved in this area are discussed. The problem of resistance to change is also examined.

866 Bharier, Julian. "The Growth of Towns and Villages in Iran, 1900-66." Middle Eastern Studies. 8(1):51-62, 1972.
A demographic study of Iranian towns and villages. Internal migration and other issues are discussed.

867 Bill, James A. "Social and Economic Foundations of Power in Contemporary Iran." Middle East Journal. 17(4):400-418, 1963.
An analysis of Iran's social and economic structure. The appearance of middle and urban working classes in response to modernization and the role of various classes are examined. It is concluded, however, that power is still held by the traditional ruling elements.

868 "Current Mohammedan Newspapers and Magazines in Persia." Moslem World. 17:86-87, 1927.
Provides a list of newspapers and magazines published in Iran during the early career of Reza Shah. The list is subdivided by location.

869 Elwell-Sutton, L. P. "The Iranian Press 1941-1947." Iran. 6:65-104, 1968.
Studies the development of the Iranian press during this period.

870 _____. "The Press in Iran Today." Journal of the Royal Central Asian Society. 35:209-219, 1948.
Examines the Iranian Press from 1941 to 1948. After a brief history, a description of the papers published at that time, their circulation, and quality of news is given. The Iranian Press Law and government's suppression of the press are also discussed.

871 Farmanfarmaian, Khodadad. "Social Change and Economic Behaviour in Iran." Explorations in Entrepreneurial History. 9(2):178-183, 1956.
Examines the economic behavior of the ruling or "privileged" group in the Iranian society. Asserts that the primary motivation of this group is acquisition of money.

872 Fischer, Michael. "Persian Society: Transformation and Strain." In: Amirsadeghi, Hossein (ed.), Twentieth-Century Iran. New York: Holmes & Meier, 1977. Pages 171-195.
Reviews the structural changes of the Iranian society in the twentieth century. The issues discussed include tribal and urban communities, the bazaar, and religion in modern Iran.

873 Florea, Aurelia. "Indagine Sulla Povertà: Informazione Sociale e Partecipazione Popolare Nell'Iran." Revue Internationale de Sociologie. 10(2-3):156-184, 1974.
A study of the Iranian society and its problems. The emphasis is on the lack of popular participation in Iran. One of the main reasons offered for this problem is the absolutist and paternalistic system of government.

874 Gable, R.W. "Culture and Administration in Iran." Middle East Journal. 13(4):407-421, 1959.
The author discusses his experience as a public administrator working in Iran. The relationship between Iranian cultural life and the way administration is performed in Iran is analyzed.

875 Gudarzi-Nejad, Shahpur. "A New Phase in the Evolution of Urban Centers in Iran." Durham University Journal. 70 (1):53-58, 1977.
A statistical analysis of urban development in Iran in the 1960's. The problem of urban migration of farmers is examined and its causes are described.

876 Hemmasi, M. "Tehran in Transition: A Study in Comparative Factorial Ecology." Journal of the Regional Cultural Institute. 6(3-4):159-176, 1973.
Discusses the growth of Tehran since the eighteenth century and examines its present socioeconomic status.

877 Jacobs, Norman. "Economic Rationality and Social Development: An Iranian Case Study." Studies in Comparative

International Development. 2(9):137-141, 1966.
A sociological discussion of the relations between economic rationality and social development. The author attempts to demonstrate the process in which the demands of economic rationality collide with and are defeated by the demands of local vested interests.

878 Jamei, Abbas. "Some General Observations on the 1966 Census." Tahqiqat-e Eqtesadi. 5(13-14):17-33, 1968.
Reviews the 1966 Iranian census and offers suggestions for future demographic studies.

879 Kazemi, Farhad. Poverty and Revolution in Iran: The Migrant Poor, Urban Marginality and Politics. New York: New York University Press, 1980.
Studies the migration of the poor rural inhabitants of Iran to the urban centers and its relation with the 1978/79 Iranian revolution.

880 Mozafari, Mehdi. "Transformations Sociales et Problèmes Politiques en Iran." Politique Etrangère. 43(5):557-578, 1978.
Discusses social change and political problems in Iran. Iranian reforms, the Shah's power, and the role of religious leaders in Iranian society are examined.

881 Nakhshab, Mohamed. Civil Service Reform and Social Environment in Developing Nations with Special Reference to Iran. Ph.D. dissertation, New York University, 1966.
Discusses the application of the Western public administration theory and practice to the administrative conditions of the developing countries. Parts IV and V examine the civil service in Iran and its administrative problems.

882 Naraghi, Ehsan. "Les Classes Moyennes en Iran." Cahiers Internationaux de Sociologie. 22:156-173, 1957.
After pinpointing the difficulties of a workable definition for the Iranian "middle class," the author studies the situation of the professional classes.

883 _____. "Elite Ancienne et Elite Nouvelle dans l'Iran Actuel avec une Note sur le Système d'Education." Revue des Etudes Islamiques. 69-80, 1957.
The situation of the traditional as well as the new elite emerging due to modernization is discussed. The Iranian educational system is surveyed.

884 Rassekh, Shahpour. "Coûts Urbains et Conséquences Sociales du Développement Economique en Iran." Revue d'Economie Politique. 83(1):16-25, 1973.
Although rapid industrialization and urbanization have taken place in Iran, many shortcomings exist in this country's pattern of urbanization.

Social Conditions

885 _____. "Planning for Social Change." In: Yar-Shater, Ehsan (ed.), Iran Faces the Seventies. New York: Praeger, 1971. Pages 143-165.

Examines the effect of Iran's four development plans on Iranian society ranging from demographic changes to economic growth.

886 Razi, G. H. "The Press and Political Institutions of Iran: A Content Analysis of Ettela'at and Keyhan." Middle East Journal. 22(4):463-474, 1968.

Contents of two major Iranian newspapers during three government administrations are analyzed in order to investigate the role of the press in Iranian politics.

887 Rotblat, Howard J. "Social Organization and Development in an Iranian Provincial Bazaar." Economic Development and Cultural Change. 23(2):292-305, 1975.

Studies the Iranian bazaars and their impact on economic and social development of the country. Business practices in Iran and the role of provincial bazaars are analyzed.

888 Rudolph-Touba, Jacqueline. "Impact of Societal Institutional Changes on the Iranian Family." International Journal of Sociology of the Family. 3(1):61-69, 1973.

A sociological study of changes in the Iranian family.

889 Savory, Roger M. "Social Development in Iran During the Pahlavi Era." In: Lenczowski, George (ed.), Iran Under the Pahlavis. Stanford, California: Hoover Institution Press, 1978. Pages 85-127.

An overview of social changes in different sectors of the society during the Pahlavi regime. Following a brief comment on the social conditions of the pre-Pahlavi era, this essay discusses the changes brought about in the legal system, education, health, status of peasants, and women's emancipation during both Reza Shah's reign and that of his successor, Mohammad Reza Pahlavi.

890 Wilson, Arnold T. "National and Racial Characteristics of the Persian Nation." Asiatic Review. 25(82):298-311, 1929.

A personal view of the Iranians' characteristics and values.

ETHNIC AND RELIGIOUS MINORITIES

891 Aliev, S. M. "The Problems of Nationalities in Contemporary Persia." Central Asian Review. 14(1):62-70, 1966.
Abridged translation of an article in Russian by the same author. Discusses the development of Iranian Nationalism and sociopolitical issues related to different nationalities in Iran.

892 Barth, Frederik. Nomads of South Persia: The Basseri Tribe of the Khamseh Confederacy. New York: Humanities Press, 1965.
A description of a nomadic tribe in Southern Iran based on fieldwork conducted in 1957 and 1958. The political structure of the tribe is described and a general discussion of factors aiding its maintenance as a unit offered.

893 Black-Michaud, Jacob. "An Ethnographic and Ecological Survey of Luristan, Western Persia: Modernization in a Nomadic Pastoral Society." Middle Eastern Studies. 10(2): 210-228, 1974.
Includes a study of history and the effects of forced sedentarization. The agrarian problems and the effects of the land reform laws of 1962 on these problems are examined.

894 Catudal, H. M. "The War in Kurdistan: End of a Nationalist Struggle?" International Relations. 5:1024-1044, 1976.
Traces the roots of the Kurdish conflict. The consequences of the 1975 agreement between Iran and Iraq on the Kurdish struggle are examined. This agreement, which normalized the relations between Iran and Iraq and ended the border disputes, was responsible for the Iranian government's decision to withdraw its support from the Kurdish separatist movement inside Iraqi territory.

895 Destrée, Annette. "Le Développement des Etats du Moyen-Orient et la Crise du Nomadisme." Revue de l'Institut de Sociologie. 2:263-282, 1969.
Nomadism and tribalism in the Middle East and problems associated with them are discussed. A description of the characteristics of the forced sedentralization of Iranian nomads in 1925-1940 is given.

896 Digard, Jean-Pierre. "Histoire et Anthropologie des Sociétés Nomades: Le Cas d'une Tribu d'Iran." Annales. Economies, Sociétés, Civilisations. 28(6):1423-1435, 1973.
An anthropological study of the Bakhtiari tribe of Iran. Analyzes the social and economic changes and evolution of this particular tribe and other nomadic tribes in general.

897 Eagleton, William. The Kurdish Republic of 1946. London: Oxford University Press, 1963.
History of the short-lived Kurdish Republic of Mahabad or the Komala Kurdish Republic formed in 1946 with the Soviet Union's support.

898 Elphinstone, W. G. "Kurds and Kurdish Question." Journal of the Royal Central Asian Society. 35:38-51, 1948.
Examines the origins and history of the Kurds in the Middle East including Iran. Discusses Reza Shah's policy regarding the Kurds in Iran and briefly touches upon the situation after World War II.

899 Garthwaite, Gene R. "The Bakhtiyari Ilkhani: An Illusion of Unity." International Journal of Middle East Studies. 8(2):145-160, 1977.
Discusses the disappearance of the Ilkhani institution, the major chief of the nomadic Bakhtiari tribe, because of government interference.

900 Harris, George S. "Ethnic Conflict and the Kurds." Annals of the American Academy of Political and Social Science. 433:112-124, 1977.
The condition of the Kurds in Iran, Iraq, and Turkey is examined. Analyzes the reasons behind their failure to achieve independence.

901 Helfgott, L. "Tribalism as a Socioeconomic Formation in Iranian History." Iranian Studies. 10(1-2):36-61, 1977.
"Aims at developing a theory that can situate pastoral nomadism within the overall movement of Iranian history."

902 Kopellowitz, Jehudah. "The Jews of Persia." Menorah Journal. 18(1):42-51, 1930.
Summarizes the status of Iranian Jews in 1930 describing their demographic distribution, social, and economic status.

903 Loeb, Laurence D. "Dhimmi Status and Jewish Roles in Iranian Society." Ethnic Groups. 1(2):89-105, 1976.
The economic and social survival of Iranian Jews through the ages and up to the 1970's is surveyed. Iranian Jews are considered to have dhimmi or the protected minority status under the Islamic law.

904 _____. Outcaste: Jewish Life in Southern Iran. New York: Gordon and Breach, 1977.

An anthropological study of the Jewish community of Shiraz, a city in Southern Iran. Based on field research in Iran from August 1967 through December 1968, this work is a contribution to the ethnography of Iranian Jews. The condition of the Jewish community of Shiraz is traced through the ages including the Pahlavi era. Contains a useful appendix on Iranian Jewish history.

905 Murray, Andrew. "The Kurdish Struggle." Patterns of Prejudice. 9(4):31-36, 1975.
   The Kurdish nationalist movement in Iran, Iraq, Syria, and Turkey is studied.

906 Richards, J.R. "Baha'ism in Persia Today." Moslem World. 21(4):344-351, 1931.
   Examines the status of the Baha'i religion in Iran in the 1930's.

907 Roosevelt, Archie. "The Kurdish Republic of Mahabad." Middle East Journal. 1(3):247-269, 1947.
   See entry 101.

908 Rosman, Abraham and Rubel, Paula G. "Nomad-Sedentary Interethnic Relations in Iran and Afghanistan." International Journal of Middle East Studies. 7(4):545-570, 1976.
   Report of a study conducted in the central Mazarjat of Afghanistan and in the central Zagros Mountains of Iran. Nomad-Sedentary relations are studied in terms of exchange.

909 Salzman, P.C. "Adaptation and Political Organization in Iranian Baluchistan." Ethnology. 10(4):433-444, 1971.
   Explores the factors related to political structure and organization in Iranian Baluchistan.

910 _____. "Continuity and Changes in Baluchi Tribal Leadership." International Journal of Middle East Studies. 4(4):428-439, 1973.
   Discusses the effect of modernization on the leadership of Iranian Baluchistan. The political systems of several Baluchi tribes are compared.

911 _____. "National Integration of the Tribes in Modern Iran." Middle East Journal. 25(3):325-336, 1971.
   Argues that it is often profitable to assist nomadic tribes to adapt in their traditional forms rather than breaking with them. Concludes that this approach has been taken in Iran.

912 Tosco, Franco. "Problemi del Nomadismo oggi in Iran." Quaderni di Sociologia. 25(1):56-82, 1976.
   Studies the problems of nomadism in present-day Iran. Recommendations and solutions to some of the problems are offered.

Social Conditions

913 Ullens de Schooten, Marie T. <u>Lords of the Mountains: Southern Persia and the Kashkai Tribes.</u> London: Chatto and Windus, 1956.
 A useful guide to the nomadic Qashqai tribes of Iran. One of the several appendices lists the tribes and families of Qashqais in Iran.

914 Wilson, Arnold T. "The Bakhtiaris." <u>Journal of the Royal Central Asian Society.</u> 13:205-225, 1926.
 Describes the nomadic tribes of the Bakhtiari, their origin, organization, and customs. Their role in recent Iranian history is briefly outlined.

WOMEN AND THEIR STATUS

915 Amirian, A. M. Condition Politique, Sociale et Juridique de la Femme en Iran. Paris: Libraire de Recueil Sirey, 1938.
Examines the status of women in Iran at the time of Reza Shah.

916 Arasteh, Reza. "The Struggle for Equality in Iran." Middle East Journal. 18(2):189-205, 1964.
Discusses the status of Iranian women in contemporary Iran and their role in the reconstruction of the country.

917 Bagley, F.R.C. "The Iranian Protection Law of 1967: A Milestone in the Advance of Women's Rights." In: Bosworth, E.C. (ed.), Iran and Islam. Edinburgh: Edinburgh University Press, 1971. Pages 47-64.
The Family Protection Law of 1967 which provided Iranian women with more equality, restricted polygamy, and made certain improvements in divorce laws is discussed.

918 Boyce, Annie Stocking. "Moslem Women in the Capital of Persia." Moslem World. 20(3):265-269, 1930.
See entry 47.

919 Chatterjee, Staindra Mohan. "Persian Womanhood." Modern Review. (Calcutta) 49(2):199-202, 1931.
Outlines the status of women in Iran throughout history and the efforts of Reza Shah to improve their social and political status.

920 Fischer, Michael. "On Changing the Concept and Position of Persian Women." In: Beck, Lois and Keddie, Nikki R. (eds.), Women in Muslim World. Cambridge: Harvard University Press, 1978. Pages 189-215.
Inquires into changes in the position of the Iranian women and relates them to the changes in the old social patterns. The role of the government as a "major force" of change is also considered.

921 Mirvahabi, Farin. "The Status of Women in Iran." Journal of Family Law. 14(3):383-404, 1975/76.
A historical background on the status of Iranian women

is presented. Modern Iranian Family Protection Law, social and political rights of women, and their employment are subjects discussed in this article.

922 Pakizegi, Behnaz. "Legal and Social Positions of Iranian Women." In: Beck, Lois and Keddie, Nikki R. (eds.), Women in Muslim World. Cambridge: Harvard University Press, 1978, Pages 216-226.
Examines the legislative changes made in regard to the status of women in Iran and their relation to social change. The author contends that the laws equalizing the status of women and men often contradict each other. The existing gap between the legal system and social customs is also mentioned.

923 Rahmani, Mahin. "Evolution of Iranian Women's Role in Society." Revue Internationale de Sociologie/International Review of Sociology. 8:93-100, 1972.
After presenting a historical background of the legal and social position of Iranian women, a discussion of developments in educational, technical, economic, and legal status of women in the early 1970's is given.

924 Sedghi, Hamideh and Ashraf, Amad. "The Role of Women in Iranian Development: Dynamics of Women's Condition in Iran." In: Jacqz, Jane W. (ed.), Iran: Past, Present and Future. New York: Aspen Institute for Humanistic Studies, 1976. Pages 201-210.
Maintains that modernization has changed the position of Iranian women in society. The role of women in the economy and their participation in the political process are discussed.

925 _____. "Women in Iran." In: Iglitzin, Lynne B. and Ross, Ruth (eds.), Women in the World: A Comparative Study. Santa Barbara, California: Clio Press, 1976. Pages 219-228.
A brief discussion of the position of women in Iranian history and changes that occurred in their status during the Pahlavi regime.

926 Touba, Jacqueline R. "The Relationship Between Urbanization and the Changing Status of Women in Iran, 1956-1966." Iranian Studies. 5(1):25-36, 1972.
A study of the relationship between education and the employment of women in urban areas. Fields of employment of women in urban and rural areas are compared.

927 Woodsmall, Ruth Frances. Moslem Women Enter a New World. London: George Allen and Unwin, 1936.
Studies the feminist movement in Iran under Reza Shah and examines its relation with other such movements in the Middle East.

928 Yarshater, Latifeh. "Iran." In: Patai, Raphael (ed.), Women in the Modern World. New York: Free Press, 1967. Pages 61-81.

A discussion of the status of women in Iranian history with an emphasis on the Pahlavi period beginning with the abolishment of the veil in 1935 by Reza Shah.

MODERNIZATION AND ITS OBSTACLES

929 Alimard, Amin and Elahi, Cyrus. "Modernization and Changing Leadership in Iran." In: Jacqz, Jane W. (ed.), Iran: Past, Present and Future. New York: Aspen Institute for Humanistic Studies, 1976. Pages 217-225.
Discusses the political leadership and sociopolitical change in Iran due to modernization. The role of the monarchy and the Shah's central role in the political process are also examined.

930 Banani, Amin. Impact of the West on Iran, 1921-1941: A Study in Modernization of Social Institutions. Ph.D. dissertation, Stanford University, 1959.
Concentrates on the impact of European influence on Iran during this period.

931 _____. The Modernization of Iran, 1921-1941. Stanford, California: Stanford University Press, 1961.
Although restricted to the Reza Shah period, this study is valuable for understanding the process of modernization in Iran. See also entry 44.

932 Bayne, E.A. Four Ways of Politics: State and Nation in Italy, Somalia, Israel, Iran: The Dynamics of Political Participation as Exhibited in Four Countries Caught Up in the Process of Modernization. New York: American Universities Field Staff, 1965.
An attempt to examine the modernization process in four countries. The last chapter is devoted to Iran and is entitled: "Monarchy and Nation: Iran's Dialectic."

933 Bémont, Frédy. L'Iran Devant le Progres. Paris: Presses Universitaires de France, 1964.
Iran's problems in dealing with modernization are discussed. Problems in various areas such as agriculture, transportation, industrialization as well as education and culture are examined.

934 Bill, James A. "Class Analysis and the Dialectics of Modernization in the Middle East." International Journal of Middle East Studies. 3(1):417-434, 1972.

Examines the interaction of class relationships and movements with the modernization process in the Middle Eastern countries including Iran.

935 _____. The Politics of Iran: Groups, Classes and Modernization. Columbus, Ohio: Merrill, 1972.
Analyzes Iran's quest for modernization and its relationship with various social classes and groups. The emerging middle class is discussed and its relationship with other groups is outlined.

936 Bonine, Michael E. and Keddie, Nikki R. (eds.). Modern Iran: The Dialectics of Continuity and Change. Albany, New York: State University of New York, 1981.
A collection of essays focusing on the effect of modernization on the Iranian culture and society. The persistence of the Iranian culture is demonstrated throughout these essays.

937 Doerr, Arthur H. "National Schizophrenia: The Case Study of Iran." Social Studies. 63(2):79-82, 1972.
Maintains that an analysis of Iranian national life shows the conflict Iranians have between the traditionalism and modernization.

938 Gastil, Raymond D. "Middle Class Impediments to Iranian Modernization." Public Opinion Quarterly. 22:325-329, 1958.
Discusses the behavior of middle-class Iranians and views their skepticism and individualistic attitudes as obstacles to modernization.

939 Lambton, A. K. S. "The Impact of the West on Persia." International Affairs. 33(1):12-26, 1957.
Traces the history of Iran's contact with the West. The rise of nationalism and constitutionalism are examined and their impact on Iran discussed.

940 Miklos, Jack C. The Iranian Revolution and Modernization: Way Stations to Anarchy. Washington, D. C.: National Defense University Press, 1983.
Studies the effect of modernization on Iranian society and its contribution to the revolution of 1978/79.

941 Pahlavi, Mohammad Reza. The White Revolution of Iran. Tehran: Imperial Pahlavi Library, 1967.
Useful for studying the theory and objectives of the Shah's modernization efforts.

942 Paydarfar, Ali A. "Modernization Process and Demographic Changes." Sociological Review. 15(2):141-153, 1967.
Examines the changes in population as a result of modernization in Iran and concludes that "the diffusion

Social Conditions

of various aspects of modernization has been between cities rather than throughout whole provinces."

943 _____. "The Modernization Process and Household Size: A Provincial Comparison for Iran." Journal of Marriage and the Family. 37(2):446-452, 1975.
A sociological study of family size as inversely related to modernization.

944 Pfaff, Richard H. "Disengagement from Traditionalism in Turkey and Iran." Western Political Quarterly. 16(1): 79-98, 1963.
Discusses the Westernization and reform in Turkey and Iran and examines problems associated with this process. Analyzes the effect of Mossadeq's fall and the Shah's land reform on Westernization of Iran. Also reprinted in: Rivlin, Benjamin and Szyliowicz, Joseph S. (eds.), The Contemporary Middle East: Tradition and Innovation. New York: Random House, 1965. Pages 417-428.

945 Ramazani, Rouhollah K. "Cultural Change and Intellectual Response in Algeria, Tunisia and Iran." Comparative Studies in Society and History. 6(2):219-229, 1964.
The intellectual's response to emerging Westernization in Iran, Tunisia, and Algeria is examined. Nationalistic ideologies in these countries are also discussed.

946 Rivlin, Benjamin and Szyliowicz, Joseph S. (eds.), The Contemporary Middle East: Tradition and Innovation. New York: Random House, 1965.
A collection of essays focusing on the transition of the Middle Eastern countries from traditionalism to modernity. Two chapters are specifically related to Iran. In Chapter Four of Part IV, Leonard Binder discusses nationalism in Iran. (See entry 219). And in Chapter One of Part VI, Richard Pfaff examines the modernization process in Iran (See entry 944).

947 Sadrai-Najafi, A. A Study of the Nature and the Roles of the Forces Influencing the Process of Change in Iran. Ph.D. dissertation, Ohio State University, 1975.
Results of a study conducted in Iran to determine the role of sociocultural, financial, political, and educational forces in operationalizing a set of proposed reforms.

948 Sarraf, Tahmoores. The Effectiveness of Patrimonial Rule as a Means to Modernization: A Study of Contemporary Iran. Ph.D. dissertation, University of Washington, 1972.
Iranian socioeconomic and political structure are examined and the relationship between an authoritarian political regime and the policies by which this regime carries out the task of modernization is analyzed. The ineffectiveness of such a condition is discussed.

949 Shafii, Forough. Educational Development and Other Correlates of Modernization in Iran: A Descriptive Profile. Ph.D. dissertation, Catholic University of America, 1971.

An attempt to show the relationship between education and some economic-demographic variables such as urbanization, industrialization, etc. The study is based on the 1956 and 1966 national censuses of Iran.

950 Taheri, Amir. "Internal Political Dynamics." In: Amirie, Abbas and Twitchell, Hamilton A. (eds.), Iran in the 1980's. Tehran: Institute for International Political and Economic Studies, 1978. Pages 41-85.

Criticizes Westernization and advocates finding Iranian solutions to problems facing Iran.

ISLAM AND POLITICS

951 Akhavi, Shahrough. Religion and Politics in Contemporary Iran: Clergy-State Relations in the Pahlavi Period. Albany: State University of New York Press, 1980.
The relationship between religion and politics during the Pahlavi dynasty is discussed. This study, which was originally based on a research carried out for the "Islam and Social Change" seminar at the University of Chicago, attempts to study the clergy's (ulama) "competition and cooperation with the state in the overall processes that affect the shaping of decisions and policies regarding education, ideology, ethics, and matters of social justice as a whole." Chapter Six analyzes interclergy relations and also reviews the main themes in Ayatollah Khomeini's book Islamic Republic.

952 Algar, Hamid. "The Oppositional Role of the Ulama in Twentieth-Century Iran." In: Keddie, Nikke R. (ed.), Scholars, Saints, and Sufis: Muslim Religious Institutions in the Middle East Since 1500. Berkeley, California: University of California Press, 1972. Pages 231-255.
In this essay the author attempts to trace the causes of the persistent opposition of the ulama to monarchical absolutism. The main focus is on the expression of this opposition in the 1960's in Iran. Includes a discussion of Ayatollah Khomeini's opposition to the Shah's regime.

953 Ayoob, Mohammed. "Two Faces of Political Islam: Iran and Pakistan Compared." Asian Survey. 19(6):536-546, 1979.
Explores the relationship between Islamic religion and politics in Iran and the neighboring Pakistan. The author asserts that it was the revolutionary side of politicized Islam which led to the fall of the Iranian monarchy.

954 Bagley, F.R.C. "Religion and the State in Modern Iran." In: V^e [i.e. Cinquième] Congrès International d'Arabisants et d'Islamisants. Bruxelles, 31 Août-6 Septembre 1970. Actes. Bruxelles: Publications du Centre pour l'Etude des Problèmes du Monde Musulman Contemporain, 1971. Pages 75-88.
The relation between religion and State in Iran is discussed. The emphasis is on the twentieth century. The

conference was organized by the Union Européene des Arabisants et Islamisants and this document contains materials in French, English, German, Italian, and Spanish.

955 Batra, Ravi. Muslim Civilization and the Crisis in Iran. Dallas: Venus Books, 1980.
Attempts to explain the revival of Islam as well as the overthrow of the Pahlavi dynasty and its replacement by an Islamic Republic. The analysis is based on a philosophy of history developed by Indian scholar, P.R. Sarkar.

956 Binder, Leonard. "The Proofs of Islam: Religion and Politics in Iran." In: Makdisi, George (ed.), Arabic and Islamic Studies in Honor of Hamilton A.R. Gibb. Cambridge, Massachusetts: Harvard University Press, 1965. Pages 118-140.
A study of the political role of the ulama in Iran. Originally a paper presented at the University of Chicago. One of the issues discussed is that ulama of Iran are more centrally organized in terms of formal institutional status roles than are Sunni ulama.

957 Eliash, Joseph. "Misconceptions Regarding the Juridical Status of the Iranian 'Ulama.'" International Journal of Middle East Studies. 10(1):9-25, 1979.
Studies the notions of contemporary Western and Shiite scholars on the juridical status of the Iranian ulama.

958 Faghfoory, Mohammad Hassan. The Role of Ulama in Twentieth Century Iran with Particular Reference to Ayatullah Haj Sayyid Abul-Qasim Kashani. Ph.D. dissertation, University of Wisconsin, 1978.
This study focuses on the role played by Kashani, the organizer of the Fadayan-i Islam, in Mossadeq's regime.

959 Ferdows, Adele Kazemi. Religion in Iranian Nationalism: The Study of the Fadayan-i Islam. Ph.D. dissertation, Indiana University, 1967.
A study of the Fadayan-i Islam, a political/religious group, and its role in the nationalist movement of 1951-1953. This dissertation also examines the role of religion in Iranian politics in general.

960 Fischer, Michael. Iran: From Religious Dispute to Revolution. Cambridge: Harvard University Press, 1980.
Examines the role of religion in social and cultural transformation of Iran. Religious education and its effects on individuals are emphasized. The Iranian revolution of 1978/79 and its religious elements are also discussed.

961 Frye, Richard N. "Islam in Iran." Muslim World. 46(1):5-12, 1956.
A study of different branches of Shiism in Iran. The future of Islam in Iran is discussed.

Social Conditions

962 Garoussian, Vida. The "Ulema" and Secularization in Contemporary Iran. Ph.D. dissertation, Northern Illinois University, 1974.
The relationship of religion and modernization in Iran is examined. The role of the Shiite clergy in Iranian politics is studied and examples offered.

963 Jacobs, Norman. "La Religion et le Développement Economique: Le Cas de l'Iran." Archives de Sociologie des Religions. 15:43-48, 1963.
In this sociological study of religion, the author examines the interrelationship between religion and politics in Iran as well as between the religious leaders and social change. The effect of religious values on economic development is also examined. Iran is taken as a case study in this investigation.

964 Keddie, Nikki R. Iran: Religion, Politics, and Society: Collected Essays. London: F. Cass; Totowa, New Jersey: Biblio Distribution Center, 1980.

965 _____. "The Origins of the Religious-Radical Alliance in Iran." Past and Present. 34:70-80, 1966.
Attempts to trace the historical roots of the alliance between religious and radical elements in Iran in opposition to the central government.

966 _____ (ed.). Religion and Politics in Iran: Shi'ism from Quietism to Revolution. New Haven: Yale University Press, 1983.
A collection of papers dealing with the development of religious ideologies and movements in Iran and their interaction with Iranian society and politics. The role of religion in the Iranian revolution of 1978/79 is studied.

967 _____. "The Roots of the Ulama's Power in Modern Iran." Studia Islamica. 29:31-53, 1969.
A historical survey of the causes behind the clergy's influence in Iran. The increase in the power of the ulama is mainly attributed to the weakness of the Qajar governments in the nineteenth century and later to the doctrine of the illegitimacy of the state which exists in the Shiite sect of Islam.

968 Lambton, A.K.S. Islamic Society in Persia: An Inaugural Lecture Delivered on 9 March 1954. London: School of Oriental and African Studies, University of London, 1954.
Attempts to survey the structure of Iranian society throughout her past history. Useful in understanding the Islamic elements in a non-Arab country such as Iran.

969 _____. "A Reconsideration of the Position of Marja al-Taqlid and the Religious Institution." Studia Islamica. 20:115-135, 1964.

The conflicts arising from the Iranian government's attempts to control the religious institutions are discussed.

970 Ramazani, Rouhollah K. "'Church' and State in Modernizing Society: The Case of Iran." American Behavioral Scientist. 7:26-28, 1964.
The role of the clergy in Iranian politics is discussed. The conflict between the traditional Islamic hierarchy and successive Iranian governments is examined.

971 Salzman, P. C. "Islam and Authority in Tribal Iran: A Comparative Comment." Muslim World. 65(3):186-195, 1975.
The interaction of secular and religious authority in Southern and Northern Baluchistan in Iran since the 1930's is examined.

972 Spooner, Brian. "Religion and Society Today: An Anthropological Perspective." In: Yar-Shater, Ehsan (ed.), Iran Faces the Seventies. New York: Praeger, 1971. Pages 166-188.
Demonstrates the relationship between religious tradition and cultural change in urban, rural, and tribal communities in Iran.

973 Thaiss, Gustav. "The Bazaar as a Case Study of Religion and Social Change." In: Yar-Shater, Ehsan (ed.), Iran Faces the Seventies. New York: Praeger, 1971. Pages 189-216.
Discusses the interaction between religion and social change and the role played by the Iranian bazaar. The focus is on the 1960's.

974 _____. "The Modernization of Islamic Society in Persia." Nonaligned Third World Annual. 232-244, 1970.
The bazaaris' adaptation to modernization is studied as a case study.

HUMAN RESOURCES AND EDUCATION

975 Aghazadeh, Ahmad. Higher Education and Investment in Human Capital: The Case of Iran. Ph.D. dissertation, Florida State University, 1977.
An attempt to investigate the impact of Iran's emphasis on diversified investment in the development of human resources through education. The study focuses on the period 1965-1975.

976 Aminzadeh, F. "Human Resources Development: Problems and Prospects." In: Jacqz, Jane W. (ed.), Iran: Past, Present and Future. New York: Aspen Institute for Humanistic Studies, 1976. Pages 179-194.
An overview of Iran's human resources development, 1956-1972, describing the population, literacy, productivity, educational system, and employment. This overview is followed by a discussion of the fifth Development Plan and its provisions for the human resources sector and the problems affecting the growth and utilization of human resources.

977 Arasteh, Reza. Education and Social Awakening in Iran, 1850-1968. Leiden: E.J. Brill, 1969.
Various forms of education in Iranian society are studied and their impact on social change examined.

978 Askari, Hossein; Cummings, John T.; and Izbudak, Mehmet. "Iran's Migration of Skilled Labor to the United States." Iranian Studies. 10:3-35, 1977.
Attempts to discover the reasons behind the migration and suggests possible solutions to the problem. One of the recommendations includes the government's effort to produce highly skilled labor in order to counteract this problem.

979 Baldwin, George B. "The Foreign-Educated Iranian: A Profile." Middle East Journal. 17(3):264-278, 1963.
Result of a study to answer questions regarding various aspects of the foreign-educated Iranian. Their characteristics, geographical origins, occupational distributions, duration of stay, and the role of Iranian government in overseeing them are discussed.

980 Bartsch, William H. "The Industrial Labor Force in Iran: Problems of Recruitment, Training and Productivity." Middle East Journal. 25(1):15-30, 1971.
Based on the author's interviews as well as information from the U. N. advisors, labor experts, manpower planners, and economists, this article attempts to evaluate the factory sector of the Iranian industry. Reasons for the rapid industrial growth of Iran are briefly examined.

981 _____. Problems of Employment Creation in Iran. Geneva: International Labour Office, 1970.
Analyzes the employment condition and problems associated with it and offers possible solutions. Employment planning in various Iranian economic development plans is also examined.

982 Behkish, Mohammad M. Economics of Investing in Human Capital: The Case of Iran. Ph.D. dissertation, Indiana University, 1977.
Analyzes the rate of return on investment in education in Iran. This research study focuses on the year 1975.

983 Bill, James A. "The Politics of Student Alienation: The Case of Iran." Iranian Studies. 2(1):8-26, 1969.
A survey of a group of Iranian students' opinions shows that they consider injustice and the Iranian educational system to be problematic requiring solutions.

984 Birjandi, Amir. The Education Corps Project in Iran: A Work Plan for Rural Development. Tehran: Ministry of Education, 1965.
This is an official source on the activities of the Literacy Corps in Iran. The creation of the corps was a part of the Shah's reform program using educated youth in national service to raise the literacy rate.

985 Blandy, Richard and Nashat, Mahyar. "The Education Corps in Iran: A Survey of Its Social and Economic Aspects." International Labour Review. 93(5):521-529, 1966.
The activities of the Literacy Corps are evaluated in terms of their social and economic effectiveness in the life of the Iranian villagers.

986 Brammer, L. M. "Problems of Iranian University Students." Middle East Journal. 18(4):443-450, 1964.
Results of a study conducted to study the Iranian students' attitudes and values on various subjects. The study reveals the conflict in their traditional values and their Western beliefs.

987 Cass, James. "Iran's Race to Catch the Twentieth Century." Change. 9:16-18, 1977.
Iran's effort to modernize has led to the establishment

of several higher education institutions in order to train Iranians. Among these are the Iran Center for Management Studies, established with the assistance of the Harvard Business School.

988 Eilers, Wilhelm. "Educational and Cultural Development in Iran During the Pahlavi Era." In: Lenczowski, George (ed.), Iran Under the Pahlavis. Stanford, California: Hoover Institution Press, 1978. Pages 303-331.

After a brief examination of the educational system at the end of the Qajar dynasty, this essay gives an overview of the changes in the educational and cultural aspects of the Iranian society during the two Pahlavi kings. The discussion includes higher education, elementary and secondary schools, struggle against illiteracy, and educational administration.

989 Elkan, Walter. "Employment, Education, Training, and Skilled Labor in Iran." Middle East Journal. 31(2):175-187, 1977.

Examines Iran's labor market and its relation to economic development. Discusses the shortage of skilled labor in Iran and the government's efforts to seek help from abroad.

990 Hanna, Barbara. Der Kampf gegen das Analphabetentum im Iran. Opladen: C.W. Leske (Deutsches Orient-Institut), 1966.

The activities of the Literacy Corps are discussed.

991 Kuklan, Hooshang. "Civil Service Reform in Iran: Myth and Reality." Revue Internationale des Sciences Administratives. 43(4):345-351, 1977.

Studies the consequences of the implementation of position classification (based on American merit system) for organizing Iranian public personnel system.

992 Parhizgar, Kamal Dean. An Investigation of Organizational Structure and Administrative Positions of Academic Affairs of Selected Universities in Iran. Ph.D. dissertation, Northwestern University, 1972.

One of the findings of this investigation is that the Iranian government has full authority and power over the academic operation of the universities studied in this research.

993 Sadeghy, Ghafur. An Historical Analysis of the Development of the Administrative Structure of Higher Education in Iran from 1900 to 1971. Ph.D. dissertation, University of Oklahoma, 1972.

Traces the past and present structure of the Iranian higher education administration. European and American influences are examined. The emphasis of the study is on the universities.

994 Sadiq, Issa. Modern Persia and Her Educational System. New York: Columbia University, 1931.
Useful for the study of educational system of the Reza Shah period.

995 Street, Brian. "The Mullah, the Shahname and the Madrasseh." Asian Affairs. 62(3):290-306, 1975.
Based on a lecture given to the Society for Asian Affairs in London in March 1975, this article presents a historical survey of educational systems in Iran. It discusses the role of madrasseh, or the theological colleges, and compares them with more modern schools. The role of the Literacy Corps developed by the Shah to bring education to the rural areas and the consequences of this plan are also discussed.

996 Tibi, Bassam. "Die Iranischen Studenten im Ausland als ein Gesellschaftliches Veränderungspotential und ihre Stellung im Politischen System." Orient. (Opladen) 20(3):100-108, 1979.
The role of the Iranian students studying abroad in the political system of Iran and their potential for introducing change are discussed. Their contribution to the overthrow of the Shah is also examined.

997 Vafa, Javad. Liberal Nationalism and Educational Policies in Iran. Ph.D. dissertation, Indiana University, 1957.
This study attempts to evaluate some of the significant characteristics of the Iranian culture in relation to liberal nationalism. It also proposes a variety of educational policies for the advancement of liberal nationalism.

998 Yousefi, Mahmood and Ertek, Tumay. "The Problem of Manpower Shortage in Iran." Economic Analysis and Workers' Management. 11(1/2):108-114, 1977.
An examination of the manpower shortage in Iran especially at the skilled and semiskilled levels. The authors offer suggestions and possible solutions.

999 Zareian, Soleiman. An Investigation and Development of a Technical Curriculum for Technician Preparation in Agricultural Mechanization for Iran. Ph.D. dissertation, Michigan State University, 1969.
Results of a survey in order to formulate a curriculum for a two-year post-high school agricultural technician training program.

1000 Zonis, Marvin. "Educational Ambivalence in Iran." Iranian Studies. 1(4):132-148, 1968.
Examines the attitudes of the Iranian political leaders toward the educational system. These attitudes are considered to be vague and ambivalent.

1001 _____. "Higher Education and Social Change: Problems and Prospects." In: Yar-Shater, Ehsan (ed.), Iran Faces the Seventies. New York: Praeger, 1971. Pages 217-259.

Examines the problems of higher education in Iran within the social and political contexts. The educational systems as centers for political activities are also discussed. Includes several statistical tables.

LEGAL SYSTEM AND THE ADMINISTRATION OF JUSTICE

1002 Aghababian, R. L'analyse de la Législation Persane. Tehran, 1927.

1003 _____. Législation Iranienne Actuelle Intéressant les Etrangers et les Iraniens à l'Etranger. Tehran; Paris: Juris-Classeurs, 1939.
An outdated but valuable source as a compendium of Iranian legislation for the period covered. Its primary concern is with the laws affecting the status of foreigners. The administrative and judicial structure of Iran are also dealt with.

1004 Baldwin, Gordon B. "Legal System of Iran." International Lawyer. 7(2):493-504, 1973.

1005 Butler, William J. and Levasseur, Georges. Human Rights and the Legal System in Iran: Two Reports. Geneva, Switzerland: International Commission of Jurists, 1976.
These two reports are the result of investigations by the authors who visited Iran in 1975 on behalf of the International Commission of Jurists. In addition to the two reports, the book contains several appendices including the law which led to the establishment of SAVAK--the Security Organization Act of 1957.

1006 Habib, Mohammad. "The Administration of Justice in Modern Persia." Islamic Culture. 7:234-284, 1933.
A discussion of the structure of the Ministry of Justice during the Reza Shah's regime is followed by a brief background history on the constitutional provisions of the administration of justice in Iran.

1007 Lockhart, Laurence. "The Constitutional Laws of Persia: An Outline of Their Origin and Development." Middle East Journal. 13(4):372-388, 1959.
Reviews the Iranian constitutional history, the Majlis, and the changes in constitutional laws up to 1959.

1008 Matin-Daftari, Ahmad. La Suppression des Capitulations en

Perse: L'ancien Régime et le Statut Actuel des Etrangers dans l'Empire du "Lion et Soleil." Paris: Les Presses Universitaires de France, 1930.
    Contains materials on modern Iranian legislation and the problem of capitulations which was abolished by Reza Shah.

1009 Moazzami, Abdollah. Essai sur la Condition des Etrangers en Iran. Paris: Recueil Sirey, 1937.
    One of the few sources for the study of modern Iranian legislation especially the laws affecting the condition of foreigners.

1010 Naqavi, Sayyid Ali Reza. Family Laws of Iran. Islamabad, Pakistan: Islamic Research Institute, 1971.
    The family laws passed since 1928 are discussed. The Appendix presents the texts of the laws.

1011 "Recent Constitutional Changes in Iran." Journal of the Royal Central Asian Society. 36:265-266, 1949.
    A brief discussion of some changes in the Iranian constitution voted by a constituent assembly which was formed at the Shah's request. One of the changes, an amendment to Article 48, grants more power to the Shah in the dissolution of the Majlis (The Iranian Parliament).

1012 Tohidipur, M. "Das Werden und der Inhalt der Iranischen Verfassung." Verfassung und Recht im Übersee. 7(2): 189-206, 1974.
    Studies the development of the Iranian constitution since the constitutional movement of 1906.

REPRESSION, THE SECRET POLICE (SAVAK), AND OTHER VIOLATIONS OF HUMAN RIGHTS

1013 Abbas, Hossein. "White Terror." World Trade Union Movement. 2:14-16, 1978.
An account of the Iranian workers' political repression under the Shah's regime.

1014 Baraheni, Reza. "Censorship and the Plight of Iranian Writers." Intercontinental Press. 16:492, 495, 1978.
Discusses censorship and repression in Iran and the official sources responsible for them including the Iranian secret police (SAVAK).

1015 _____. The Crowned Cannibals: Writings on Repression in Iran. New York: Vintage Books, 1977.
Written by an Iranian poet, writer, and former professor at Tehran University, this book is an attack against the Shah, his regime, and repression created by him throughout Iran. The author recalls his experience as a political prisoner in Iran and his involvement with the secret police. It also contains brief accounts of other political prisoners of Iran.

1016 _____. Persia sin Máscara. Barcelona: Editorial Argos Vergara, 1978.
Spanish translation of the author's The Crowned Cannibals: Writings on Repression in Iran by H. González Trejo. See previous entry.

1017 _____. "The Shah's Executioner." Index on Censorship. 5(1):13-20, 1976.
An Iranian writer and poet, Reza Baraheni, recalls his experience as a political prisoner in Iran in 1973. The reason for his arrest, he asserts, was the publication of his book, Masculine History, and an article he wrote, "The Culture of the Oppressor and the Culture of the Oppressed" in which he had demanded cultural autonomy for Iran's ethnic minorities.

1018 Boini, Allan A. "SAVAK Guidelines." Index on Censorship. 9:50-52, 1978.

Social Conditions   165

         Discusses the suppression of the freedom of expression
         in Iran and outlines the strict guidelines enforced by the
         Iranian secret police.

1019 Butler, William J. "Civil and Political Rights in Iran."
     World Issues. 1(1):20-22, 1976.
         The violation of the civil and political rights of Iranian
         citizens is reported. Lack of freedom of the press and
         speech are discussed and the role of SAVAK examined.

1020 Committee Against Repression in Iran. Iran: The Shah's
     Empire of Repression. London: The Committee, 1976.

1021 Confederation of Iranian Students. Documents on the Pahlavi
     Reign of Terror in Iran: (Eyewitness Reports and News-
     paper Articles). Frankfurt am Main, Germany: Docu-
     mentation Centre of Confederation of Iranian Students Na-
     tional Union, 1971.
         A collection of materials, mostly articles from foreign
         periodicals, regarding the political oppression of the Iran-
         ian government and its violations of human rights. The
         materials are in various Western languages and arranged
         chronologically covering the period between 1954 to 1971.

1022 Cottam, Richard. "The Case of Iran." In: Gastil, Raymond
     D. (ed.), Freedom in the World: Political Rights and
     Civil Liberties, 1978. New York: Freedom House, 1978.
     Pages 88-108.
         Issues of freedom and human rights including the strat-
         egies for control used by the Shah's regime and the role
         of SAVAK (the Iranian secret police) are discussed. The
         emphasis is on the period from 1953 to the mid-1970's.

1023 Dehghani, A. Camarade, N'oublie pas le Vol, l'Oiseau est
     Mortel: Souvenirs d'une Révolutionnaire Evadée de la
     Prison du Chah d'Iran. Commission Conjointe des Peup-
     les Iraniens et Palestiniens, [between 1976 and 1979].

1024 _____. Torture and Resistance in Iran: Memoirs of
     the Woman Guerrilla Ashraf Dehghani. New Delhi(?):
     Iran Committee, New Delhi; available at Printox, 1978.
         Memoirs of a member of the Organisation of Iranian
         People's Fedai Guerrillas. She recalls the story of her
         involvement with the Iranian secret police (SAVAK) after
         her arrest in 1971 until her escape in 1973.

1025 Faroughy, Ahmad. "Repression in Iran." Index on Censor-
     ship. 3(4):9-18, 1974.
         Traces the history of repression in Iran since ancient
         times. However, the major emphasis is on the repres-
         sion during the Pahlavi period.

1026 Grossi, Gianaldo. "L'Iran Imperiale Senza Maschera." Ponte. 27(1/2):33-37, 1971.
Repression in Iran, political prisoners, and the activities of SAVAK, the Iranian secret police, are topics discussed in this article.

1027 Hanrahan, John D. "Foreign Agents in Our Midst." Progressive. 41:31-35, 1977.
Asserts that foreign espionage agencies including SAVAK, the Iranian secret police, harass their citizens residing in the U.S. without American government's interfering.

1028 Hottinger, Arnold. "The Shah and Iran's Constitution." Swiss Review of World Affairs. 28:14-15, 1978.
Describes the undermining of the Iranian constitution by the Pahlavi dynasty. Examines the oppositions' call for a return to constitutionalism.

1029 Irnberger, Harold. SAVAK: Oder, Der Folterfreund des Westens: Aus den Akten des Iranischen Geheimdienstes. Reinbek bei Hamburg: Rowohlt, 1977.
Detail of the activities of the Iranian secret police, SAVAK (Sazeman Etelaat va Amniat Keshvar), under the Shah. Contains reproductions of several original documents of SAVAK's activities abroad.

1030 "Justice, SAVAK Style." Impact International. 8:6, 1978.
Excerpts from Brian Wrobel's Human Rights in Iran: Testimony on Behalf of Amnesty International. See entry 1038.

1031 Lafue-Veron, Madeleine. Voyage au Pays de la Peur, Iran 1978. Genève: Comité Suisse de Défense des Prisonniers Politiques Iraniens, 1978.
This brief publication throws more light on the repression and lack of freedom of expression in Iran under the Shah's regime.

1032 Political Prisoners in the Oil States: Oman, Bahrein, Saudi Arabia, Iran. London: Gulf Committee, 1974.
This booklet provides some information on torture and imprisonment of political prisoners in four oil-producing countries. The last chapter is devoted to Iran. It gives a brief account of political oppression in Iran and discusses the role of SAVAK (the Iranian secret police). Translated from Arabic by the Gulf Committee.

1033 Ramon, Nithal. "Gholam Hoseyn Sa'edi." Index on Censorship. 7(1):40-42, 1978.
Profile of an Iranian intellectual, writer, and psychiatrist whose works have been censored by the Iranian secret police (SAVAK) for his statements about Iran's

worsening sociopolitical conditions. He has been imprisoned, threatened, and harassed many times.

1034 Salzberg, John P. "The Human Rights Program in Congress: Some Policy Implications from the 1977 Hearings." International Studies Notes. 4:1-4, Winter 1977.
Examines political repression in several countries including Iran which have been reported in congressional hearings. These hearings have resulted in the United States pressure on these countries regarding human rights.

1035 United States. Congress. House. Committee on International Relations. Subcommittee on International Organizations. Human Rights in Iran. Washington, D.C.: U.S. Government Printing Office, 1976.
This hearing was held before the Subcommittee on August 3 and September 8, 1976, ninety-fourth Congress, second session. Testimonies of the following individuals were heard in this session: William J. Butler, chairman of the International Commission of Jurists; Alfred L. Atherton, Jr., assistant secretary for Near Eastern and South Asian Affairs, Department of State; and Reza Baraheni, a former political prisoner in Iran. Political repression, torture and other violations of human rights in Iran as well as the role played by the Iranian secret police, SAVAK, were discussed. This document contains several appendices including a "Report by Amnesty International on Political Prisoners in Iran, August 12, 1976" and a "Report by Iranian Students Association in the United States, on the Violation of Human Rights in Iran, September 1976."

1036 _____. Human Rights in Iran. Washington, D.C.: U.S. Government Printing Office, 1977.
This hearing was held before the Subcommittee on October 26, 1977, ninety-fifth Congress, first session. The impact of amendments to the Code of Military Justice which were passed by the Iranian Senate in August 1977 on the Iranian legal structure and on the status of human rights situation in Iran in general were explored. The following testimonies were heard in this session: Testimony of William Butler, Chairman of the Executive Committee of the International Commission of Jurists; testimony of Richard Cottam, professor of Political Science, University of Pittsburgh; testimony of Thomas M. Ricks, professor of History, Georgetown University; and testimony of Charles Naas, Director of Iranian Affairs, Bureau of Near Eastern and South Asian Affairs, Department of State.

1037 Vieille, Paul and Banisadr, Abol Hassan. Pétrole et Violence: Terreur Blanche et Résistance en Iran. Paris: Editions Anthropos, 1974.

Contains a discussion of repression in Iran under the Shah's regime and opposition to this repression by various groups including the Shiite clergy.

1038 Wrobel, Brian. <u>Human Rights in Iran: Testimony on Behalf of Amnesty International.</u> London: Amnesty International, 1978.

Testimony before the Subcommittee on International Organizations of the Committee on International Relations, House of Representatives, United States Congress on February 28, 1978. The administration of justice in Iran, the nature and function of the Iranian secret police (SAVAK), procedure used by the Military Tribunal, violations of human rights, and breach of various international laws and standards are discussed.

V

THE FALL OF THE PAHLAVI DYNASTY

31
DISCONTENT, OPPOSITION, AND REVOLUTION

1039 Abdulla, Ahmed. <u>Iran's Revolution: Causes & Consequences.</u>
Karachi: Tanzeem Publishers, 1979.
Following a historical background on Iran, this brief publication attempts to trace the causes of the 1978/79 Iranian revolution. The author, a Pakistani with a background in journalism and public relations, considers the exploitation by foreigners and "attempt to de-Islamise Iran" as the two major causes of the Iranian revolution.

1040 Abidi, A. H. H. "The Iranian Revolution: Its Origins and Dimensions." <u>International Studies.</u> 18(2):129-161, 1979.
Background study of the Iranian revolution of 1978/79 which ended the Pahlavi dynasty.

1041 Abrahamian, Ervand. "The Guerilla Movement in Iran, 1963-1977." <u>Middle East Research & Information Project.</u> 86: 3-21, 1980.
Studies various guerilla activities in operation in Iran between 1963-1977 including the Fedaiyan-i Khalq and the Mojahedin-i Khalq. The author asserts that these guerilla activities were an extension of the 1963 riots which were severely suppressed by the Shah and went underground.

1042 _____. "Iran in Revolution: The Opposition Forces."
<u>Middle East Research & Information Project.</u> 75/76:3-8, 1979.

1043 _____. "Iran: The Political Challenge." <u>Middle East Research & Information Project.</u> 69:3-8, 1978.
Written while Iran was experiencing unrest in 1978, this article attempts to examine the roots of the opposition against the Shah and describes the various forces of opposition which he is facing. Anticipates that if the industrial working class joins the middle class in the opposition, a revolution is very likely to follow.

1044 _____. "Iran: The Political Crisis Intensifies." <u>Middle East Research & Information Project.</u> 71:3-6, 1978.
Describes the support of the urban wage earners and

their joining to the opposition against the Shah's regime and his government's response with repression and martial law.

1045 _____. "Political Forces in the Iranian Revolution." Radical America. 13(3):44-55, 1979.
Traces the causes of the 1978/79 revolution. Severe repression after the fall of Mossadeq in 1953 and the beginnings of unrest in 1977 are among the factors contributing to the revolution.

1046 _____. "Structural Causes of the Iranian Revolution." Middle East Research & Information Project. 87:21-26, 1980.

1047 An Alliance of Reaction and Terror ... : The Revealing Story of Anti-Iranian Activities Abroad. Tehran: Focus Publications, 1977.
This brief publication is a highly critical account of the anti-Shah activities of the Iranian students abroad. The book is published anonymously and the name of the author who was an ex-activist is not revealed. The author dismisses all such activities as "stage-managed by a single set-up-international communism." Contains brief biographies of some Iranian student activists abroad.

1048 Benab, Younes P. "Tabriz in Perspective: A Historical Analysis of the Current Struggles of Iranian Peoples." RIPEH/The Review of Iranian Political Economy and History. 2(2):1-42, 1978.
"Traces the historical developments of the democratic struggles of Tabriz primarily during the 1905-1945 period." Written on the occasion of the uprising of the people of Tabriz, a city in Northwest Iran, against the Shah in 1978.

1049 Bewaffneter Kampf in Iran. Iran-Komitee, 1975.
A brief discussion of the armed opposition against the Shah's regime.

1050 Bill, James A. "Iran and the Crisis of '78." Foreign Affairs. 57(2):323-342, 1978/79.
Analyzes the political crisis of 1978 which eventually led to the Shah's overthrow. Identifies the opposition forces and suggests that the Shah must take measures to liberalize if he is to survive. Asserts that the United States government has shown ignorance in analyzing the Iranian politics and society.

1051 Binder, Leonard. Revolution in Iran: Three Essays. New York: American Academic Association for Peace in the Middle East, 1980.
These previously published essays attempt to provide information on the background as well as the causes and consequences of the 1978/79 Iranian revolution.

1052 Chubin, Shahram. "The United States and Iran's Revolution: Local Soil, Foreign Plants." Foreign Policy. 34:20-33, 1979.
Analyzes some of the causes of the Iranian revolution of 1978/79 including the Shah's military buildup.

1053 Cockburn, Patrick. "Who Will Support the Shah?" New Statesman. 96:322, 1978.
Discusses the spreading opposition to the Shah's regime. Questions the degree of loyalty of the army to support the Shah.

1054 Cottam, Richard. "Goodbye to America's Shah." Foreign Policy. 34:3-14, 1979.
Examines the success of the Iranian revolution of 1978/79 and the fall of the Shah's regime. Argues that the Shah's lack of popularity and his downfall were directly linked to his continued association with the United States interests.

1055 Danesch, Mostafa. "Die Innenpolitische Entwicklung im Iran. 25 Jahre nach dem Sturz Mossadeghs." Blätter für Deutsche und Internationale Politik. 23(9):1112-1123, 1978.
Reviews the political evolution of Iran after the fall of Mossadeq in 1953. The Shah's dependence on the United States and forces of opposition to his regime are examined.

1056 Faroughy, Ahmad and Reverier, Jean-Loup. L'Iran Contre le Châh. Paris: J.C. Simoën, 1979.

1057 Fischer, Michael. "Protest and Revolution in Iran." Harvard International Review. 1(2):1-6, 1979.

1058 Forbis, William H. Fall of the Peacock Throne: The Story of Iran. New York: Harper & Row, 1980.
The bulk of this book is devoted to the Iranian history and the characteristics of the Iranian people. However, the purpose is to more fully understand the Iranian revolution of 1978/79 and the last chapter specifically deals with that subject.

1059 Golestan, Ali. "Cracks Begin to Appear in the Shah's Regime." Intercontinental Press. 16:304, 1978.
Questions the Shah's ability to cope with the oppositions and demonstrations against him in Qom and Tabriz.

1060 Goodell, Grace E. "How the Shah De-stabilized Himself." Policy Review. 16:55-72, 1981.
Attempts to understand reasons behind the overthrow of the Shah. Asserts that the extreme secularism advocated by the Pahlavi dynasty in addition to the Shah's haste in changing the Iranian society are among major factors contributing to his fall.

1061 Goodman, Raymond W. "Iran." In: A Compendium of European Theater Groups. Maxwell Air Force Base, Alabama: United States Air University, 1976. Pages 67-78.
A brief discussion of terrorist activities against the Iranian government and the Shah's regime. According to this research study conducted by career military officers studying at the U.S. Air University, Iranian terrorist groups constantly change their names and form various factions which make identification of specific groups extremely difficult.

1062 Green, Jerrold D. Revolution in Iran: The Politics of Countermobilization. New York: Praeger, 1982.
Attempts to study the Iranian revolution of 1978/79 which led to the dissolution of the Pahlavi dynasty. Social conditions which led to the revolution as well as the nature of participation in that event are examined.

1063 Halliday, Fred. Iran: Dictatorship and Development. Harmondsworth: Penguin, 1978.
"This book is intended to give a general introduction to contemporary Iran, and in particular to political and economic developments since the early 1960's." Chapter 4, "The Armed Forces and SAVAK," and Chapter 8, "The Opposition," attempt to examine the future of the Shah's regime in light of the 1978 crisis.

1064 _____. "Iran: Trade Unions and the Working Class Opposition." Middle East Research & Information Project. 71:7-13, 1978.
Surveys the history of working-class organizations in Iran and examines the Pahlavi regime's policy of suppressing such organizations.

1065 Hanks, Robert J. "Conflict in Iran." Conflict. 1(3):145-159, 1979.
Examines the negative consequences of the Iranian revolution of 1978/79 for the United States and Western Europe.

1066 Harney, Desmond. "Some Explanations for the Iranian Revolution." Asian Affairs. 67(2):134-143, 1980.
Factors contributing to the Iranian revolution of 1978/79 are analyzed and discussed. The clergy's opposition to secularization; the Iranian people's resentment of extreme corruption; and their dissatisfaction with soaring inflation, as well as the United States' lack of a clear policy toward the Shah are considered among the significant factors leading to the crisis.

1067 Heikal, Mohamed. Iran: The Untold Story: An Insider's Account of America's Iranian Adventure and Its Consequences for the Future. New York: Pantheon Books, 1981.

The views of a renowned Egyptian journalist on the Iranian revolution of 1978/79 and the role played by the United States.

1068 Hetherington, Norriss S. "Industrialization and Revolution in Iran: Forced Progress on Unmet Expectation." Middle East Journal. 36(3):362-373, 1982.
Argues against the view that the Shah's too rapid modernization programs were responsible for the Iranian revolution of 1978/79.

1069 Hirschfeld, Yair P. "Decline and Fall of the Pahlavis." Jerusalem Quarterly. 12:20-33, 1979.
Following a brief historical background on the establishment of the Pahlavi dynasty, some of the causes contributing to its fall including the socioeconomic problems and conflict with the religious leaders are discussed.

1070 Hoveyda, Fereydoun. The Fall of the Shah. New York: Wyndham Books, 1980.
Memoirs of the Shah's former foreign minister and the brother of former prime minister and minister of the court, Amir Abbas Hoveyda who was executed by the revolutionary government in 1979. He recalls the events which led to the Shah's downfall. This book is translated by Roger Liddell.

1071 Jabbari, Ahmad and Olson, Robert. Iran: Essays on a Revolution in the Making. Lexington, Kentucky: Mazdea Publishers, 1981.
Based on the symposium, "Iran: A Revolution in the Making," held at Centre College of Kentucky on June 15-17, 1979, this publication is a collection of papers dealing with various aspects of the Iranian revolution of 1978/79. Topics discussed include background to the revolution, ideologies behind it, and the economic factors contributing to it.

1072 Jazani, Bizhan. Armed Struggle in Iran: The Road to Mobilization of the Masses. London: Iran Committee, 1976(?).
The author was one of the theorists of a guerilla group known as the Fedaiyan-i Khalq, who was killed in the Shah's prison in 1975. This publication is translated by the Iran Committee and was first published in 1973.

1073 _____. Capitalism and Revolution in Iran: Selected Writings of Bizhan Jazani. London: Zed Press, 1980.
A collection of essays by a theorist of the Fedaiyan-i Khalq, a guerilla group who opposed the Shah's regime. Jazani was killed in prison in 1975. This publication is translated by the Iran Committee.

1074 Joseph, Ralph. "Iran: Mounting Campaign Against Guerillas." Middle East. 23:18-20, 1976.
    The Guerilla activities against the Iranian government and their origins are briefly discussed. The author asserts that there appears to be some assistance from abroad involved in these activities.

1075 Kazemi, Farhad. "Economic Indicators and Political Violence in Iran, 1946-1968." Iranian Studies. 8(1-2):70-86, 1975.
    Evaluates the effect of various economic factors on the political violence in Iran.

1076 Keddie, Nikki R. "Iran: Is 'Modernization' the Message?" Middle East Review. 11(3):55-56, 1978.
    Argues that the 1978/79 opposition movement in Iran was not necessarily a reaction to a hasty modernization. Analyzes the effects of modernization on Iran and some of the causes of the opposition against the Shah's government.

1077 _____. "The Midas Touch: Black Gold, Economics and Politics in Iran Today." Iranian Studies. 10(4):243-266, 1977.
    Examines the relationship between the increase in oil income in Iran and the growth of social tension and opposition to the Shah's regime.

1078 _____. Roots of Revolution: An Interpretive History of Modern Iran. New Haven: Yale University Press, 1981.
    Surveys the social, economic, and political conditions in modern Iranian history during the Qajar (1796-1925) and the Pahlavi (1925-1979) dynasties in order to analyze major causes of the 1978/79 Iranian revolution which brought an end to the Pahlavi era and the Iranian monarchy. Chapter Eight is a useful review of the modern Iranian political thought by Yann Richard.

1079 Kermalec, Jean. "L'Iran à la Croisée des Chemins." Orient. (Paris) 4th trim. : 69-75, 1960.
    Analyzes the causes underlying the widespread discontent which forced the Shah to annul the 1960 national elections.

1080 Koury, Enver M. and MacDonald, Charles G. (eds.), Revolution in Iran: A Reappraisal. Hyattsville, Maryland: Institute of Middle Eastern & North African Affairs, 1982.
    A collection of essays attempting to study the nature and implications of the 1978/79 Iranian revolution. The last chapter deals with the reaction of the Middle Eastern countries to the revolution.

1081 Ledeen, Michael A. and Lewis, William H. "Carter and the Fall of the Shah: The Inside Story." Washington

Quarterly. 3(2):3-40, 1980.
Critical of the Carter Administration's policy toward Iran during the Iranian crisis of 1978/79. The human rights policy is particularly emphasized.

1082 Moran, Theodore H. "Iranian Defense Expenditures and the Social Crisis." International Security. 3(3):178-192, 1978/79.
Argues that the Shah's defense expenditure and the Carter administration's lack of attention to this subject are among the causes of the Iranian crisis of 1978/79 and that country's government inability to deal with the political dissatisfaction.

1083 _____. "Still Well-Oiled?" Foreign Policy. 34:23-28, 1979.
This article concentrates on the effect of the 1978/79 Iranian revolution on the international oil market.

1084 Moss, Robert. "The Campaign to Destabilise Iran." Conflict Studies. 101:1-17, 1978.
Written at the time when the Iranian revolution of 1978/79 was in progress, this article attempts to study the relationship between that crisis and the Soviet interests in the region. The author maintains that a pro-Soviet regime may be established in Iran and examines the consequences of such a government for Western European countries.

1085 Najafi, Parvin. "Growing Dissatisfaction Among Iranian Masses." Intercontinental Press. 16:538-539, 1978.
A brief discussion of political and religious opposition to the Shah's government in 1978 which eventually led to a full-blown revolution against the monarchy.

1086 Nirumand, Bahman. Iran: The New Imperialism in Action. New York: Monthly Review Press, 1969.
Translated by Leonard Mins, this is the English version of the author's Persien, Modell eines Entwicklungslandes: Oder, Die Diktatur der Freien Welt. See next entry.

1087 _____. Persien, Modell eines Entwicklungslandes: Oder, Die Diktatur der Freien Welt. Reinbek b. Hamburg: Rowohlt, 1967.
A critical account of the Western World's attempts to Westernize Iran. The Shah's foreign policy and his alliance with the West are attacked. Chapter 4 is entitled: "Shah M.R. Pahlavi: Emperor by the Grace of America."

1088 Nobari, Ali-Reza (ed.). Iran Erupts. Stanford, California: Iran-America Documentation Group, 1978.
A collection of articles and interviews previously

published in the press related to the revolutionary upheaval in Iran in 1978 and while it was in progress. Many of the articles are from the French newspaper, Le Monde.

1089 Pahlavi, Mohammad Reza. Réponse à l'Histoire. Paris: A. Michel, 1979.
This is the Shah's last autobiographical account written in exile before his death. In Chapter 13, he gives his views on the events which took place in Iran after his departure due to the opposition to his regime. This book has been translated into English under the titles: Answer to History and The Shah's Story. See entries 190 and 196. See also entry 191.

1090 Petrossian, Vahe. "Crippling Oil Strikes Pose New Crisis for Shah." Middle East Economic Digest. 22:17, November 1978.
The political demands of the Iranian oil workers and their strike are examined and the effect of the strike on the Iranian economy and several other countries is briefly described.

1091 _____. "New Cabinet's Concessions May Draw Opposition into Dialogue." Middle East Economic Digest. 22:3-4, September 1978.
Installation of a new prime minister, Jaafar Sharif-Emani, by the Shah is seen as a possible initiation of dialogue between the Shah and the opposition in the 1978 crisis.

1092 Pouyan, A. P. and Mani, M. Iran: Three Essays on Imperialism, the Revolutionary Left and the Guerilla Movement. Florence: Edition Mazdak, 1971?
The three essays contained in this book are: "Necessity of Armed Struggle"; "American Imperialism in Iran"; and "The Left and Revolutionary Struggle--an Historical Appraisal." In these essays, the authors outline the activities and the ideologies of the leftist revolutionary movement in Iran, born out of the Tudeh party and after the 1963 opposition.

1093 Ricks, Tom. "Iranian People Challenge Pahlavi Arms and American Support." Middle East Research & Information Project. 8:18-19, 1978.
Asserts that despite the Shah's suppression of the demonstrations and riots against his regime, his fall is certain.

1094 "Riots Will Revive Interest in Long-Term Security Questions." Middle East Economic Digest. 22:16, February 1978.
Riots, demonstrations, and increase in opposition against the Shah's regime in 1978 and the concern of his government are discussed.

1095 Saikal, Amin. The Rise and Fall of the Shah. Princeton, New Jersey: Princeton University Press, 1980.
   A scholarly book which attempts "to provide an in-depth, macro-level analysis of the Shah's rule...." The author contends that "the Shah's goals and policies were full of inherent contradictions and weaknesses" which led to the 1978/79 revolution, ended the Pahlavi dynasty, and founded the Islamic Republic.

1096 Salvini, Gianpaolo. "Motivi e Aspetti della Crisi in Iran." Aggiornamenti Sociali. 29(12):741-754, 1978.
   Analyzes the underlying causes of the crisis in Iran in 1978 which led to the overthrow of the Pahlavi dynasty.

1097 "SAVAK Chief's Dismissal Hints at Compromise." Middle East Economic Digest. 22:17, June 1978.
   Discusses the removal and replacement of Nematollah Nassiri, head of the Iranian secret police--SAVAK. This action is interpreted as a signal for possible compromise between the Shah and his opponents.

1098 Schoenbaum, David. "Passing the Buck(s)." Foreign Policy. 34:14-20, 1979.
   A critical examination of the position of the United States government during the Iranian revolution of 1978/79.

1099 Semkus, Charles Ismail. The Fall of Iran, 1978-1979. New York: Copen Press, 1979.

1100 Stemple, John D. Inside the Iranian Revolution. Bloomington: Indiana University Press, 1981.

1101 Sullivan, William H. "Dateline Iran: The Road Not Taken." Foreign Policy. 40:175-186, 1980.
   The author, who was the United States ambassador in Iran during the Iranian revolution of 1978/79, criticizes the U.S. foreign policy toward Iran at that time. The effect of the Carter administration's policy regarding human rights during the Iranian crisis is also discussed.

1102 Zabih, Sepehr. Iran's Revolutionary Upheaval: An Interpretive Essay. San Francisco: Alchemy Books, 1979.
   Examines the sociopolitical conditions in Iran before the revolution of 1978/79. Inquires into some of the factors leading to this major event in Iranian history, such as the alienation and lack of political participation of Iranians under the Shah's rule, economic factors, and policies of the regime during its last two years in power.

1103 Zu den Ökonomischen Hintergründen des Aufstandes und der Krise des Schahregimes im Iran. Herausgeber, Confederation of Iranian Students (N. U.). Frankfurt: CISNU, 1978.

Discusses the economic background of the Iranian revolution of 1978/79 which led to the eventual overthrow of the Pahlavi dynasty.

VI
GENERAL SOURCES OF INFORMATION

GENERAL AND BIBLIOGRAPHICAL SOURCES

1104   Abolhamd, Abdolhamid and Pakdaman, Nasser. Bibliographie Française de Civilisation Iranienne. Téhéran: Presses Universitaires de Téhéran, 1972-1974.
This three-volume general bibliography covers French materials related to Iran since the sixteenth century. Volume 2 includes a section on the Pahlavi dynasty. This bibliography is not annotated.

1105   American University (Washington, D. C.). Foreign Area Studies. Iran, a Country Study. Washington, D. C.: U. S. Government Printing Office, 1978.
Edited by Richard F. Nyrop, this volume supersedes the Area Handbook for Iran published in 1971. It covers all aspects of Iran including history, culture, economy, politics, and government and is a useful guide in studying the Pahlavi period of government.

1106   Amirie, Abbas and Twitchell, Hamilton A. (eds.). Iran in the 1980's. Tehran: Institute for International Political and Economic Studies, 1978.
A collection of essays based on papers presented at a symposium held in Washington, D. C. in October 1977, sponsored by the Institute for International Political and Economic Studies (Tehran, Iran) and Stanford Research Institute (Menlo Park, California). The Iranian participants who included scholars as well as government officials discussed various subjects related to Iran's development goals and policies. The American participants covered the same topics for the United States. The future of Iran-U. S. relations was also discussed.

1107   Amirsadeghi, Hossein (ed.). Twentieth-Century Iran. New York: Homes & Meier, 1977.
This book consists of eight chapters by various contributors. The essays deal with political, economic, strategic, and social factors of modern Iran. The first chapter is devoted to "The Last Years of the Qajar Dynasty" and the remaining chapters discuss various issues related to the Pahlavi dynasty.

1108 Andrews, Robert Hardy. "Iran: The Persian Empire That Refused to Die." Mankind. 5(3):22-27, 60-63, 1975.
A survey of the Iranian military and political history from the sixth century B.C. to 1974. The influence of the West in the sixteenth century as well as the Shah's political power in the twentieth century are among subjects explored.

1109 Arfa, Hassan. Under Five Shahs: An Autobiography. London: J. Murray, 1964.
Biography and reminiscences of a former Iranian army officer and political figure. Part I deals with the last Qajar Shahs. Part II is devoted to Iran under Reza Shah. Part III discusses the Iran of the post-World War II period (1941-1946) and Part IV, the last section of the book, is devoted to Mohammad Reza Pahlavi's period up to 1963.

1110 Armajani, Yahya. Iran. Englewood Cliffs, New Jersey: Prentice-Hall, 1972.
A selective and interpretive history of Iran. Chapter One, "Contemporary Iran," and Chapters Eight and Nine, entitled respectively "The Resurgence of Iran" and "Struggle for Power," deal with the events which occurred during the Pahlavi dynasty.

1111 Atiyeh, George N. The Contemporary Middle East, 1948-1973: A Selective and Annotated Bibliography. Boston: G.K. Hall, 1975.
This bibliography lists selective publications (books as well as journal articles) dealing with all countries of the Middle East and North Africa. A section is devoted to Iran (pages 525-554) which contains entries on political conditions. The majority of the citations are in English. This is basically a social science bibliography but a small section on literature and the arts is included. A well-executed work with excellent index.

1112 Avery, Peter. "Iran: A Culture Challenged." Contemporary Review. 233(1354):243-249, (1355):298-303, 1978.
A survey of the Iranian history and culture from ancient times until 1978.

1113 _____. Modern Iran. New York: Praeger, 1965.
Intended primarily for the general reader, this book is a contemporary history of Iran with an emphasis on the Pahlavi dynasty.

1114 Bartsch, William H. and Bharier, Julian. The Economy of Iran, 1940-1970: A Bibliography. Durham: University of Durham, 1971.
This bibliography contains monographs and periodical articles dealing with various aspects of the Iranian

economy. It is organized by broad subjects. Some of these subjects include "National Income and Its Components," economic development, labor, "Fiscal and Monetary Policy and Conditions," and manpower planning. The majority of the entries are in English and none are annotated. An author index accompanies the bibliography. Many of the entries are mimeographed reports not easily available.

1115 Bau, Milli. Iran, wie er Wirklich Ist. Munich: Bechtle Verlag, 1971.
A general book on Iran discussing a variety of subjects ranging from history, economy, industry, education to water, land and traditional crafts. Contains useful information on the Pahlavi era.

1116 Bausani, Alessandro. I Persiani. Firenze: Sansoni, 1962.
A general history of Iran containing some useful information on politics and government of the Pahlavi period.

1117 _____. The Persians: From the Earliest Days to the Twentieth Century. New York: St. Martin's Press, 1971.
Translation of the Italian original, I Persiani, by J. B. Donne. See previous entry.

1118 Behn, Wolfgang. The Iranian Opposition in Exile: An Annotated Bibliography of Publications from 1341/1962 to 1357/1979 with Selective Locations. Wiesbaden: Harrassowitz in Komm, 1979.
A bibliography of underground materials published outside Iran in opposition to the Pahlavi regime. "Materials in this bibliography cover publications from all countries except the Soviet Union from 1341/1962 to 1357/1979."

1119 _____. Power and Reaction in Iran: A Supplement to the Bibliographies: The Iranian Opposition in Exile and Islamic Revolution or Revolutionary Islam in Iran, with Brief Annotations. Berlin: Adiyok, 1981.

1120 _____. Twenty Years of Iranian Power Struggle: A Bibliography of 951 Political Periodicals from 1341/1962 to 1360/1981 with Selective Locations. Berlin: Adiyok, 1982.

1121 Bryson, Thomas A. United States/Middle East Diplomatic Relations, 1784-1978: An Annotated Bibliography. Metuchen, New Jersey: Scarecrow Press, 1979.
This selective bibliography is a useful source for studying Iran-U.S. diplomatic relations. It is arranged chronologically by era and, to some extent, by subject within eras. The last chapter is devoted to doctoral

dissertations. Only English language materials are listed.

1122 Conférence Olivaint de Belgique. Essor de l'Iran. Bruxelles: Conférence Olivaint de Belgique, 1969.
This two-volume work contains the papers and reports of the conference held July 24 to August 22, 1968. Rich in information on almost all aspects of Iran.

1123 Ehlers, Eckart. Iran: Ein Bibliographischer Forschungsbericht: Mit Kommentaren und Annotationen [A Bibliographic Research Survey: With Comments and Annotations]. München; New York: K. G. Saur; Detroit, Mich.: Distributed by Gale Research Co., 1980.
Although this bibliography addresses itself to the professional geographer, it contains a section on contemporary Iranian history (pages 191-209) with entries related to the politics and government during the Pahlavi dynasty. While some of the other sections contain annotations in German and English, this particular section is not annotated.

1124 Elwell-Sutton, L. P. (ed.). Bibliographical Guide to Iran: The Middle East Library Committee Guide. Sussex: Harvester Press; Totowa, New Jersey: Barnes & Noble Books, 1983.
This is a bibliographical guide to publications dealing with pre-Islamic and Islamic Iran. Its structure is based on a thematic classification and very brief annotations which accompany some of the entries serve to indicate the usefulness and scope of each item and do not provide information about the contents of the entries. Entries lack full bibliographic data. A section on government and politics is included (pages 384-394) which contains some entries related to the Pahlavi period. Other sections cover subjects ranging from languages and the arts to geography and literature.

1125 ———. A Guide to Iranian Area Study. Ann Arbor, Michigan: Published for the American Council of Learned Societies by J. W. Edwards, 1952.
Although it needs updating, this guide is a valuable source of information on Iran. Includes a chronology of events up to 1951 and an extensive bibliography.

1126 Evans, Hubert. "Recent Soviet Writings on Iran." Central Asian Review. 15(3):238-251, 1967.
Reviews and analyzes twenty articles on Iran written in Russian by Soviet writers.

1127 Farman, Hafez F. Iran: A Selected and Annotated Bibliography. New York: Greenwood Press, 1968.
Originally prepared for the General Reference and

Bibliography Division, the Library of Congress, and printed in 1951, this bibliography is now outdated. It lists general materials on Iran available at the Library of Congress. A small section entitled "Politics and Government" (pages 30-36) contains some entries relating to the Pahlavi period of government. Entries are accompanied by brief annotations.

1128 Farmayan, H. "Observations on Sources of the Study of Nineteenth and Twentieth-Century Iranian History." International Journal of Middle East Studies. 5(1):32-49, 1974.
Contains comments on major sources for the study of twentieth-century Iran including the Pahlavi period.

1129 Furon, Raymond. La Perse. Paris: Payot, 1938.
The author, a former professor at the University of Tehran, gives a broad historical and geographical survey of Iran including the Reza Shah period.

1130 Gehrke, Ulrich. Iran: Natur, Bevölkerung, Geschichte, Kultur, Staat, Wirtschaft. Tübingen; Basel: Erdmann, 1975.
A general work on Iran covering a wide variety of subjects from history and culture to economy, population and state. Includes numerous illustrations and plates.

1131 Girard, Robert. "L'Iran et Son Avenir." Revue de Défense Nationale. 28(5):788-800, 1972.
A general survey of Iranian contemporary history. Modernization of Iran as well as social, economic and political changes during the twentieth century are outlined. The author concludes that Iran has great potential in becoming a leader in the Third World.

1132 Groseclose, Elgin Earl. Introduction to Iran. New York: Oxford University Press, 1947.
An introductory source on Iran dealing with the Iranian history including the Reza Shah's period of power.

1133 Handley-Taylor, Geoffrey. Bibliography of Iran. Chicago: St. James Press, 1969.
This general bibliography on Iran is not a useful source for surveying Iranian politics and government during the Pahlavi period. The number of entries devoted to this area is insignificant. Arranged alphabetically by author under several broad subject headings, this bibliography contains approximately 400 entries dealing with ancient as well as modern Iranian history, culture, etc. Only books are included in this source and there are no annotations. No index provides access to the entries.

1134 Holler, Frederick L. Information Sources of Political Science. Santa Barbara, California: ABC-Clio, 1984. The first edition of this publication appeared in 1971 and the fourth edition is to be published in 1984. It is a valuable source of information for identifying reference tools in political science including sources related to Iran and Iranian politics.

1135 Iran Almanac and Book of Facts. Tehran: Echo of Iran, 1961.
Although a useful source, especially regarding statistics on various areas of the Iranian government and society in general, the data is not always accurate or reliable and must be used with caution. Almost all aspects of Iran are covered.

1136 Irani, Ghobad and Ashraf, Fereshteh. Iranian Foreign Relations, 1941-1974: A Selective Bibliography. Tehran: Institute for International Political and Economic Studies, 1976.

1137 Jacqz, Jane W. (ed.). Iran: Past, Present and Future: Aspen Institute/Persepolis Symposium. New York: Aspen Institute for Humanistic Studies, 1976.
A collection of addresses given in a symposium held in Persepolis near Shiraz, Iran in September 1975. The symposium was sponsored by a grant from the Pahlavi Foundation. A variety of subjects including the economy, foreign policy, culture, and human resources are covered. The addresses are followed by discussions and comments.

1138 Kazemi, Asghar. Iran-Bibliographie: Deutschsprachige Abhandlungen, Beiträge, Aufsätze, Bücher, Dissertationen. Tehran: Universitäts Deuckerie [sic], 1970.
A general bibliography listing German materials published on Iran. Chapter XII, entitled "Politik," is a brief section dealing with internal and external Iranian politics. Other chapters cover topics such as literature, religion, geography, etc. Contains numerous typographical errors. No annotations are included.

1139 Keddie, Nikki R. "An Assessment of American, British, and French Works Since 1940 on Modern Iranian History." Iranian Studies. 6(2-3):152-172, 1973.
Several works are reviewed and the difficulties of documentation that stand in the way of more adequate studies of Iranian history are pointed out.

1140 Lambton, A.K.S. "Persia Today." World Today. 17:76-87, 1961.
Surveys various subjects including the rivalries of the superpowers in Iran, the Iranian economic situation, and changes in the social structure of the country.

General Sources of Information

1141 Larteguy, Jean. Visa Pour L'Iran. Paris: Gallimard, 1962.
A French journalist's informal report on Iran.

1142 Lenczowski, George (ed.). Iran Under the Pahlavis. Stanford, California: Hoover Institution Press, 1978.
Edited by an authority on Iran, this book contains twelve chapters written by an international team of scholars. The essays, all dealing with the Pahlavi dynasty, cover a variety of subjects from "Social Development in Iran During the Pahlavi Era" (Chapter 3) to "Iran's Foreign Policy in the Pahlavi Era" (Chapter 10). The purpose of the book, as stated in its Preface, is "an attempt to portray and evaluate the changes that have occurred in Iran since the coming to power of the Pahlavi dynasty."

1143 Lyautey, Pierre. Iran Secret. Paris: R. Julliard, 1963.
Written by a journalist, this book gives a historical background on Iran as well as her place in the Middle East. The evolution of modern Iran including the Pahlavi period is covered.

1144 Mahdi, Ali-Akbar. "Women of Iran: A Bibliography of Sources in the English Language." Resources for Feminist Research. (Canada) 9(4):19-24, 1980/81.
The status of women in modern Iran is surveyed in this short bibliography involving largely works written in the 1970's.

1145 Marlowe, John. Iran: A Short Political Guide. New York: Praeger, 1963.
Deals with the twentieth-century Iran and includes useful information on the history and politics of the Pahlavi era.

1146 Mirheydar, Dorreh. Geographic Factors in the Political Viability in Iran. Ph.D. dissertation, Indiana University, 1962.
This study attempts to demonstrate that Iran has been a victim of her geographic location, a fact which manifests itself in the political history of this country during the nineteenth and the first half of the twentieth century. Economic and cultural factors are also examined.

1147 Nahavandi, H. L'Iran, 1940-1980: Crise, Révolution et Tragédie. Paris: IREP, 1980.

1148 Nawabi, Y.M. A Bibliography of Iran: A Catalogue of Books and Articles on Iranian Subjects Mainly in European Languages. Tehran: Iranian Cultural Foundation, 1969-
This general bibliography plans to cover various aspects of Iranian history and culture in several volumes. However, so far two volumes have been released.

1149 Regional Cooperation for Development. Secretariat. Bibliography of Publications on Public Administration and Management. Tehran, 1967.

1150 Saba, Mohsen. Bibliographie Française de l'Iran: Bibliographie Méthodique et Raisonnée des Ouvrages Français Parus depuis 1560 jusqu'à Nos Jours. Téhéran: Imprimerie de l'Université de Téhéran, 1966.
A general bibliography of French materials published on Iran. A small section entitled "Sciences Politiques et Sociales" includes some entries related to the Pahlavi period. Books as well as articles are included and arranged under broad subject headings.

1151 _____. English Bibliography of Iran. Tehran: Bank Melli Iran Press, 1965.
The number of entries related to politics and government in Iran under the Pahlavis is not significant in this general bibliography. Subjects cover a wide variety of areas including literature, fine arts, philology, etc. and are arranged according to the Dewey decimal classification system. Some of the entries are briefly annotated.

1152 Sahebjam, Freidoune. L'Iran des Pahlavis. Paris: Editions Berger-Levrault, 1966.
A detailed discussion of Iran under the Pahlavis follows a short general history of Iran. The focus is on the achievements of the Pahlavi dynasty. The Preface is written by the Shah, Mohammad Reza Pahlavi.

1153 _____. L'Iran vers l'An 2000: Document. Paris: J. C. Lattes, 1977.

1154 Savory, Roger M. "Persia Since the Constitution." University of Toronto Quarterly. 29(2):243-261, 1960.
A brief description of political, economical and social events in Iran from the constitutional revolution until 1960.

1155 United States Department of State. Library Division. Point Four: Near East and Africa: A Selected Bibliography of Studies on Economically Underdeveloped Countries. New York: Greenwood Press, 1969.
This outdated bibliography is a reprint of the 1951 edition. It was "aimed primarily at assistance in the planning and development of the President's Point Four Program." The entries deal with basic economic studies and are not annotated. Only three pages (89-91) are devoted to Iran.

1156 Upton, Joseph M. The History of Modern Iran: An Interpretation. Cambridge, Massachusetts: Distributed for the Center for Middle Eastern Studies of Harvard

University by Harvard University Press, 1960.
Major development in Iran up to 1941 is discussed. Focusing on the twentieth century, Iranian history and society as well as political and economic elements underlying events are described.

1157 Wilbur, Donald Newton. Contemporary Iran. New York: Praeger, 1963.
A historical survey of contemporary Iran. Most of the book is a description of the Mossadeq's era. The struggle for power in Iran between the U.S. and the U.S.S.R. is also discussed.

1158 _____. Iran: Past and Present. Princeton: Princeton University Press, 1976.
First published in 1948, this monograph attempts to briefly survey the history and culture of Iran. Modern Iran is emphasized and the Pahlavi era is also covered.

1159 Wilson, Arnold T. A Bibliography of Persia. Oxford: Clarendon Press, 1930.
This general bibliography covers sources in European languages dealing with Iranian history, archeology, geography, etc. All entries are arranged in alphabetical order and in dictionary form. Some entries deal with Reza Shah's period but their number is not significant. There is no index to this bibliography and since there is no subject arrangement, access to specific information is very difficult. No annotations accompany the entries. Needs updating.

1160 Yar-Shater, Ehsan (ed.). Iran Faces the Seventies. New York: Praeger, 1971.
Proceedings of a conference held at Columbia University in November 1968. The papers deal with a variety of subjects such as economic conditions, land reform, and foreign affairs as well as the arts and literature.

NAME INDEX

Abbas, Hossein 1013
Abbeg, L. 117
Abdulla, Ahmed 1039
Abidi, A. H. H. 375, 591, 1040
Abolfathi, Farid 363
Abolhamd, Abdolhamid 1104
Abrahamian, Ervand 210-213, 248, 856, 1041-1046
Achoube-Amini, Rahmatollah 376
Adamiyat, Fereydoun 401
Adibi, Hossein 857
Adli, Abolfazl 756
Afkhami, Gholamreza 249
Afshar, Kamran 656
Agabekov, G. 1, 450
Agah, Manouchehr 757
Aghababian, R. 1002-1003
Aghababoff, R. See Aghababian, R.
Aghazadeh, Ahmad 975
Ahmadi, Ashraf 166
Ahrari, Mohammed E. 700
Ahrens, Peter Georg 858
Ajami, Ismail 801, 859
Ajdari, Ahmad 802
Akhavan, Soheil 616
Akhavi, Shahrough 951
Akhtar, Shameem 377
Akrami, Reza 592
Alaolmolki, Nozar 402
Alavi, Bozorg 214-216, 593
Alexander, Yonah 510
Algar, Hamid 952
Ali, Mehrunnisa 511, 575
Aliev, S. M. 891
Alimard, Amin 929
American Society of International Law 130
American University (Washington, D. C.). Foreign Area Studies 1105

Amini, Ali 758
Aminzadeh, F. 976
Amiralai, Chamseddine 701-702
Amirian, A. M. 915
Amirie, Abbas 311, 337, 378, 403-404, 522, 545, 563, 677, 694, 757, 760, 800, 851, 950, 1106
Amirsadeghi, Hossein 17, 40, 179, 325, 344, 724, 783, 878, 1107
Amouzegar, Jahangir. See Amuzegar, Jahangir
Amouzegar, Parviz 42
Amuzegar, Jahangir 512-513, 617-619, 679, 703, 759-760
Andrews, Robert Hardy 1108
Andrews, William R. 70
Anglo-Iranian Oil Company, Ltd. 118, 704-706
Anjuman-i Naft-i Iran 707
Ansari, Hormoz 489
Arasteh, Reza 860, 916, 977
Arcilesi, Salvatore Alfred 514
Arfa, Hassan 803, 1109
Arfa, Prince 43
Armajani, Yahya 1110
Artzt, P. 761
Ashraf. See Pahlavi, Ashraf
Ashraf, Ahmad 250, 924
Ashraf, Fereshteh 1136
Ashrafi, Jamshid 657
Ashrafi, Mehdi 217
Asia Development Corporation 762
Askari, Hossein 680, 763, 861, 978
Asopa, Sheel K. 594
Asrari, Reza 708
Atiyeh, George N. 1111
Atyeo, Henry C. 119

192

Name Index

Avery, Peter 251, 1112-1113
Ayoob, Mohammed 576, 953
Azadeh, Behrouze 252
Azami-Zangueneh, Abd al-Hamid 709

Badii, Rabi 681
Bagley, F.R.C. 804, 862, 917, 954
Baharna, H. al- 405
Bahrampour, Firouz 338
Bala, Mirza 451
Baldwin, George B. 620, 979
Baldwin, Gordon B. 1004
Banani, Amin 44, 863, 930-931
Banisadr, A.H. 218, 253, 682, 1037
Bank Markazi Iran 658
Baraheni, Reza 1014-1017
Barth, Frederik 892
Bartsch, William H. 980-981, 1114
Batra, Ravi 955
Bau, Milli 1115
Bausani, Alessandro 1116-1117
Bayne, E.A. 120, 167, 309, 339, 932
Beaumont, Peter 683
Beck, Lois 920, 922
Beck, Peter J. 710
Bedore, James M. 698-699
Behkish, Mohammad M. 982
Behn, Wolfgang 1118-1120
Beladíez, E. 490
Beloff, Max 452
Bémont, Frédy 864, 933
Benab, Younes P. 453, 1048
Benedick, Richard Elliot 659
Bennett, Margaret N. 632
Berner, Wolfgang 454-455
Berry, John A. 456
Besharat, Ali Reza 865
Bharier, Julian 600, 621, 866, 1114
Bhattacharya, Anindya K. 711
Bildner, Robert 673
Bilen, I. 226
Bill, James A. 168, 254-256, 305, 867, 934-935, 983, 1050

Binder, Leonard 219, 257-258, 956, 1051
Birjandi, Amir 984
Black-Michaud, Jacob 893
Blanch, Lesley 169
Blandy, Richard 985
Blücher, Wipert von 3
Boini, Allan A. 1018
Boisen, Ingolf 491
Bonine, Michael E. 936
Bonn, A.G. 45
Bonnell, Helen Marie 622
Borzoui, Farzin 457
Bosworth, E.C. 917
Bourke-Burrowes, D. 46
Boyce, Annie Stocking 47, 918
Brammer, L.M. 986
Braun, Ursula 406
Brewer, William D. 407
Brooks, Michael 712
Brun, Thierry A. 805-806
Bruton, Henry J. 623
Bryan, William 713
Bryson, Thomas A. 515, 1121
Bullard, Reader 4, 71, 121
Burrell, R.M. 340-341
Burt, Richard 310
Butler, William J. 1005, 1019

Cadman, Basil Cadman 750
Campbell, John C. 714
Canat, Frédéric 342
Carey, Andrew G. 684, 716, 807
Carey, J.P.C. 684, 715-716, 807
Carrère d'Encausse 122, 259
Cass, James 987
Catudal, H.M. 894
Chahidzadeh, Hossein 492
Chandler, Geoffrey 717
Chatterjee, Staindra Mohan 919
Cheng, B. 123
Chidfar, Z.M. 660
Childs, James Rives. See Filmer, Henry
Choudhary, L.K. 379
Chowdhury, A.H.M. Nuruddin 595
Chubin, Shahram 311-312, 343-345, 577, 1052
Churchill, Winston L.S. 72

Clapp, Gordon R.   624
Clark, Peter M.   346
Clawson, Patrick   661
Cockburn, Patrick   1053
Collin, Richard O.   309
Committee Against Repression in Iran   1020
Conat, Melvin A.   525
Confederation of Iranian Students   1021
Confederazione Generale dell'Industria Italiana   764
Conference Olivaint de Belgique   1122
Connell, John   765
Conolly, Violet   48, 458
Cooper, A. R. C.   718
Cottam, Richard   73, 220-221, 516, 1022, 1054
Cottrell, Alvin J.   313-314, 347, 408-409
Courtois, V.   222
Craig, Daniel   808
Croizat, Victor J.   315, 410
Cumming-Bruce, N.   662-663
Cummings, John T.   763, 861, 978

Daftary, Farhad   626, 664
Danesch, Mostafa   1055
Darvich-Kodjouri, Djamshid   348
Davenport, Robert Wesley   459
Davidian, Zaven   260
Decker, Donald James   517
Dehghani, A.   1023-1024
Delavallé, J. P.   809
Denman, D. R.   810-811
D'Ermé, Giovanni   223
Destrée, Annette   261, 895
Dhanani, Gulshan   380
Diba, Farah. See Pahlavi, Farah
Digard, Jean-Pierre   896
Djalili, Mohammad Reza   349, 381, 411-412
Djazaeri, Chams-ed-Dine   766
Djourabtchi, Hassan   767
Doenecke, Justus D.   74-75
Doerr, Arthur H.   937
Doeval, Hans   768
Doroudian, R.   812
Dougherty, James E.   314

Duclos, L. J.   719
Dumont, René   805
Dupree, L.   316, 382

Eagleton, William   76, 897
Ebrahimzadeh, Cyrus   685
Edmonds, C. J.   383
Edmonds, I. G.   170
Efimenco, N. M.   125
Ehlers, Eckart   1123
Eilers, Wilhelm   988
Eisenhower, Dwight D.   126, 518
Elahi, Cyrus   249, 350-352, 929
Eliash, Joseph   957
Elkan, Walter   989
Elm, Mostafa M.   627
Elphinstone, W. G.   898
Elwell-Sutton, L. P.   6-7, 77, 224-225, 720, 869-870, 1124-1125
Engler, Robert   127, 721
Entessar, Nader   578
Ertek, Tumay   998
Esfandiari, Soraya   171-173
Eskandari, Iradj   226
Esmaili, Malek   413
Essad, Bey   8-9
Evans, Hubert   1126

Faghfoory, Mohammad Hassan   958
Fallaci, Oriana   174-175
Fallah, R.   686, 722
Farahmand, Sohrab   628
Farboud, Homayoun   78
Fardanesh, Mohammad Ali   262
Fardi, Mohsen A.   769
Farman, Hafez F.   1127
Farmanfarma, Ali-Naghi   665
Farmanfarmaian, Hafez   10
Farmanfarmaian, Khodadad   723, 871
Farmayan, H. F.   263, 1128
Faroughy, Abbas   414
Faroughy, Ahmad   1025, 1056
Fartash, Manoutchehr   596, 629
Fateh, Moustafa Khan   770
Fatemi, Faramarz   460
Fatemi, Nasrollah S.   128
Fawzi, Abd al-Sattar   415

Name Index

Fekrat, Ali 619, 630
Ferdows, Adele Kazemi 959
Ferrier, Ronald 724
Fesharaki, Fereidun 666, 725
Filippani-Ronconi, Pio 264
Filmer, Henry 11
Firoozi, Fereydoon 519-520, 667-668
Fischer, Louis 461
Fischer, Michael 872, 920, 920, 960, 1057
Fishburne, Charles Carroll 521
Fisher, C. B. 813
Fisher, Charles A. 397
Fisher, Commodore S. 176
Fleming, D. F. 79
Fleury, Antoine 494, 597
Florea, Aurelia 873
Foot, Rosemary 579
Forbes, Rosita 49
Forbis, William H. 1058
Ford, Alan W. 129
Foroughi, Mahmoud 522
Fort, Raymond 523
Foster, Austin T. 130
Fredborg, Arvid 131
Freivalds, John 814
Frescobadi, D. 265
Friedman, Bruno 177
Frye, Richard N. 567, 961
Fucito, Guido 771
Furlong, R. 317
Furon, Raymond 772, 1129
Fürstenau, G. 50

Gable, R. W. 266, 874
Gallagher, Nancy E. 158
Ganji, Manouchehr 631
Gardner, Lloyd C. 524
Garoussian, Vida 962
Garthwaite, Gene R. 899
Gastil, Raymond D. 938, 1022
Gehrke, Ulrich 1130
George, Patrick Cyril 598
German, Clifford 205
Geyer, Dietrich 462
Ghadimipour, Fatemeh 384
Ghavami, Taghi 385
Ghazanfarpour, A. 253
Ghazanfarpour, S. 218, 253
Ghoreichi, Ahmad 463
Ghoreyshi, Ahmad 351-352

Ghosh, Sunil Kanti 132
Gil Benumeya, R. 178, 353, 416
Giniewski, Paul 267
Girard, Robert 1131
Gittinger, James Price 815
Gold, Fern R. 525
Golestan, Ali 1059
Goodarzi, Manucher 268
Goodell, Grace E. 1060
Goodman, Raymond W. 1061
Gordon, Edward 417
Graefe, Axel von 51
Graham, Robert 269
Gray, F. A. G. 773
Great Britain. Central Office of Information 80
Great Britain. Foreign Office 133
Greaves, Rose 179
Green, Jerrold D. 1062
Green, Thomas F. 319
Gregory, Lois 180
Greussing, Kurt 816
Grey, W. G. 12
Grifith, William E. 354
Groseclose, Elgin Earl 1132
Grossi, Gianaldo 726, 1026
Grué, B. 320
Grunwald, K. 687
Gudarzi-Nejad, Shahpur 875
Gun, Nerin E. 270
Gupta, Raj Narain 727, 774
Guyer, R. E. 134

Haas, William S. 13
Habib, Mohammad 1006
Hadary, Gideon 817
Hadley, Guy 599
Hale, W. M. 600
Halliday, Fred 418, 775, 1063-1064
Hammeed, Kamal A. 632
Hamzavi, A. H. 81-83
Handley-Taylor, Geoffrey 1133
Hanks, Robert J. 1065
Hanna, Barbara 990
Hanrahan, John D. 1027
Harbutt, Fraser J. 84, 526
Harding, Clifford H. 14
Harney, Desmond 1066
Harris, F. S. 527
Harris, George S. 900

Hashemi, Fazlollah 271
Hashmi, Zia 601-602
Hayden, Lyle J. 818
Heikal, Mohamed 1067
Hekmat, Hormoz 528
Helfgott, L. 227, 901
Hemmasi, M. 876
Hendershot, Clarence 529
Hensel, Howard M. 464
Heravi, Mehdi 530
Hess, Gary R. 85
Hesse, Fritz 52, 495, 728
Hetherington, Norriss S. 1068
Hetrick, Kenneth Lee 603
Hidayati, Muhammad Ali 135
Hindus, Maurice 86
Hirschfeld, Yair P. 87, 496, 1069
Hobbs, John A. 819
Hoeppner, R. R. 497, 729
Holden, David 419
Holler, Frederick L. 1134
Hollist, W. Ladd 321
Hooglund, Eric J. 820-822
Hopper, Bruce 53
Hoskins, Halford L. 531-532
Hottinger, Arnold 1028
Housego, David 272
Hoveyda, Amir Abbas 273
Hoveyda, Fereydoun 136, 1070
Hoyt, Edwin Palmer 181
Hueber, Reinhard 498
Hugessen, Hughe Montgomery Knatchbull 15
Huici Poyales, F. 137
Hull, Cordell 533
Hurewitz, J. C. 322, 355

Iglitzin, Lynne B. 925
Imhoff, Christop von 420-421, 465
Imperial Government of Iran.
   Plan Organization 633
Inlow, Edgar Burke 274
International Chamber of Commerce. Iranian Committee 776
International Court of Justice 138
International Labour Office 730

Iran. Embassy. United States 139
Iran Financial and Commercial Service 275
Iran. Ministry of Foreign Affairs 88
Iran Press Services 183
Iran. Prime Minister 140
Iran. Vizarat-i Ittilaat va Jahangardi 182
Iran. Vizarat-i Umur-i Kharijah 386
Irani, Ghobad 89, 534-536, 1136
Irnberger, Harold 1029
Issawi, Charles 634, 778-779
Izbudak, Mehmet 978
Izzi, Khalid Yahya al- 388

Jabbari, Ahmad 1071
Jacobs, Norman 877, 963
Jacqz, Jane W. 88, 366, 630-631, 666, 674, 722, 769, 785, 798-799, 801, 812, 924, 929, 976, 1137
Jain, H. M. 389
Jamei, Abbas 878
Jandaghi, Ali 276
Jazani, Bizhan 1072-1073
Jones, J. H. 732
Joseph, Ralph 1074
Just, A. W. 537

Kaiser, Karl 604-605
Kappeler, D. 499
Karanjia, Rustom Khurshedji 185
Kassin, A. M. 16
Katouzian, Homa 780
Katouzian, Homayoun 228
Katouzian, M. A. 823-824
Kaviani, Bijan 277
Kazemi, Asghar 1138
Kazemi, Farhad 879, 1075
Kazemi, Parviz 781
Kazemian, Gholam H. 538
Kazemzadeh, F. 323
Kazemzadeh, Hossein 90, 606
Keddie, Nikki R. 278, 825, 920, 922, 936, 952, 964-967, 1076-1078, 1139
Kelly, J. B. 422

Name Index

Kemp, Norman 141
Kennedy, Edward M. 423
Kermalec, Jean 1079
Kermani, Taghi 539
Kerwin, Harry Wayne 540
Khabiri, Cyrus 356
Khadjenouri, M. 357
Khalatbary, Abbas 607
Khaleeli, Abbas 358
Khamsi, Farhad 826
Khosrovi, K. 827-828
Kia, Abbas Chamseddine 688
Kiani, Manutschehr 669
Kingsley, R. 279
Kirk, George E. 142
Klare, Michael T. 324
Knapp, Wilfrid 17
Kochwasser, Friedrich 500
Kohn, Hans 18
Kolko, Gabriel 541-542
Kolko, Joyce 542
Kopellowitz, Jehudah 902
Korby, Wilfried 689
Koszinowski, T. 390
Koury, Enver M. 1080
Kovac, John Eugene 91
Kristjanson, Baldur H. 829
Kuklan, Hooshang 280, 991
Kuniholm, Bruce Robellet 92
Kurth, Hanns 186
Kuschiar, Amir Hossein 733
Kutuzov, V. 466

Labrousse, H. 424
Lacoste, Raymond 467
Lafue-Veron, Madeleine 1031
Laing, Margaret 187
Lambton, A.K.S. 93-95, 830-833, 939, 968-969, 1140
Laqueur, Walter 468
Larteguy, Jean 1141
Lateef, Abdul 425
Laurent, François 469
Lauterpacht, E. 391
Lavrent'yev, A.K. 143
Ledeen, Michael 543, 1081
Lee, Lester A. 54
Lenczowski, George 7, 229, 255, 264, 281, 313, 354, 470, 544-546, 634, 637, 752, 811, 988, 1142
Lentz, W. 144-146
Levasseur, Georges 1005

Levy, Walter J. 147
Lewis, William 543, 1081
Lindt, A.R. 426
Lockhart, Laurence 148, 1007
Lockwood, Rupert 149
Loeb, Laurence D. 903-904
Long, D.E. 427
Looney, Robert E. 635-636, 670, 782
Lotz, J.D. 651
Lyautey, Pierre 1143

Macciocchi, Maria Antonietta 150
McCrea, William S. 151
MacDonald, Charles G. 1080
McLachlan, Keith 783
MacLeod, A. 428
Maczynski, Michal 501
Magnus, Ralph 152, 547, 734
Mahdavy, Hossein 834
Mahdi, Ali-Akbar 1144
Mahrad, Ahmad 19-21, 96, 502-504
Majidi, Abdol-Majid 735
Majin, Shohreh 680
Makdisi, George 956
Malek, Hossein 835
Malek-Mahdavi, Ahmed 282
Malekpur, Abdollah 784
Mani, M. 1092
Mark, Edward M. 97
Marlowe, John 429, 1145
Martin, Laurence 325
Martín de la Escalera, C. 430
Martini, Aldo 690
Marwah, Onkar 431
Massudi-Toiserkan, Schapur 736
Matin-Daftari, Ahmad 1008
Matthews, Michael 608
Mattison, Georgia 188
Mehner, Harald 637
Mehnert, K. 471-472
Mehran, Hassan Ali 785
Meister, Irene W. 473
Melamid, Alexander 392, 737
Melikov, O.S. 5
Melzig, Herbert 22
Menon, Rajan 474
Mesbah Zadeh, Mostafa 609
Meyer-Ranke, Peter 475
Migliorini, Elio 56

Miklos, Jack C. 940
Milani, Abbas 631
Miller, William G. 230, 836
Millspaugh, Arthur C. 23, 549-550, 671
Minai, Ahmad 638
Mirheydar, Dorreh 1146
Mirvahabi, Farin 921
Missen, David 205
Moarefi, Ali 639
Moazzami, Abdollah 1009
Mochaver, Fazlollah 672
Moghadam, Gholam Reza 786
Moghaddam, Reza 837
Moghari, Mohammad 738
Moghtader, Hushang 432, 640, 787
Mohammadally, Safia S. 393
Mohammadi-Nejad, Hassan 283
Mohammad Reza Pahlavi, Shah of Iran. See Pahlavi, Mohammad Reza
Mojdehi, Hassan 551
Mojtahedi, Ahmad 691
Molavi, M. A. 641
Monterisi, Mario 24
Moran, Theodore H. 739, 1082-1083
Moss, Robert 1084
Mossadegh, Mohammed. See Mossadeq, Mohammad
Mossadeq, Mohammad 153
Motter, Thomas Hubbard Vail 98
Moulvi, A. M. 25
Mowlana, Hamid 346
Mozafari, M. 231, 360, 880
Mughisuddin, M. 431
Müller, Kurt 476
Müller, Wilhelm 642
Müllers, Horst 643
Murray, Andrew 905

Naamani, Israel T. 154
Nabavi, J. 232, 581
Nahavandi, H. 233, 284, 1147
Najafi, Parvin 1085
Najmabadi, F. 692
Nakhai, M. 285, 740
Nakhshab, Mohamed 881
Nanes, Allan 510
Naqavi, Sayyid Ali Reza 1010
Naraghi, Ehsan 882-883

Nashat, Mahyar 985
Nava, Santi 505
Navai, M. 477
Nawabi, Y. M. 1148
Nazari, Hassan 741
Neuman, Stephanie 326
Nikgohar, Abdolhossein 838
Nikitine, Basile 234
Nikitine, R. 788
Nirumand, Bahman 1086-1087
Nobari, Ali-Reza 1088
Nollau, Günther 478
Noorani, A. G. 479
Noori, Hossein Shiekh-Hosseini 155
Nowshirvani, Vahid F. 673
Nyrop, Richard F. 1105

Olson, Robert 1071
O'Neill, Bard E. 552
Oppenheim, V. H. 742
Overseas Consultants, Inc., New York 644
Owen, R. P. 433

Pahlavi, Ashraf 286
Pahlavi, Farah 189
Pahlavi, Mohammad Reza 26-29, 190-199, 287, 361-362, 743, 941, 1089
Pakdaman, Nasser 1104
Pakizegi, Behnaz 922
Panahi, Bahram 744
Paolini, M. 434
Parhizgar, Kamal Dean 992
Park, Tong-Whan 363
Partin, Michael Wayne 553
Parvin, Manoucher 327, 480
Patai, Raphael 928
Paydarfar, Ali A. 942-943
Pedrazzani, Jean-Michel 200
Peretz, Don 394
Perroux, François 745
Pesaran, M. H. 674, 790
Petrossian, Vahe 1090-1091
Pfaff, Richard H. 944
Pfau, Richard 554-556
Pfeffer, Karl Heinz 610
Pirayech, Purandocht 481
Pirnia, Hossein 693, 791
Plan Organization. Statistical Centre of Iran 792
Polacco, Angelo 58

Name Index

Pour Homayoun, Ali Asghar 675
Pouyan, A. P. 1092
Price, Philips 156
Pryor, Leslie M. 328
Puri, Rakshat 583

Quester, G. H. 329
Quintana Pali, Santiago 839

Rad-Serecht, Farhad 793
Rahmani, Mahin 923
Rajput, A. B. 794
Ramazani, Rouhollah K. 99, 201, 364-368, 435-436, 557, 584, 611, 945, 970, 1033
Rashidi, Ramezan Ali 482
Rassekh, Shahpour 884-885
Razi, G. H. 235, 886
Razwy, A. A. 157
Regard, J. 747
Regional Cooperation for Development. Secretariat 1149
Reinhard, George M. 437
Remba, Oded 612
Remick, William C. 330
Reppa, Robert B. 585-586
Reverier, Jean-Loup 1056
Rey, Lucien 236
Rezun, Miron 32
Richard, Yann 1078
Richards, J. R. 906
Richter, Gunter 763
Ricks, Thomas M. 237
Ricks, Tom 1093
Ringer, B. B. 238
Ritter, Wolfgang 239
Rivlin, Benjamin 219, 944, 946
Rondot, Philippe 438
Rondot, Pierre 439
Roosevelt, Archie 101, 907
Roosevelt, Kermit 158, 558
Rosenberg, J. Philip 102
Rosenberg, Robert L. 748
Rosman, Abraham 908
Ross, Ruth 925
Rossi, Ettore 61
Rossi, Pierre 395
Rossow, Robert 103
Rotblat, Howard J. 887

Rouhani, Fuad 749
Rouzbeh, Khosrov 240
Rowland, John 750
Royal Institute of International Affairs 104
Rubel, Paula G. 908
Rubin, Barry 559
Rubio García, L. 288
Rudolph-Touba, Jacqueline 888
Rumney, Mason P. 331

Saba, Mohsen 1150-1151
Sabeti, Houshang 694
Sablier, E. 159
Sadeeg, Javad 241
Sadeghy, Ghafur 993
Sadiq, Issa 994
Sadjady, Mohamed 289
Sadr, Anoushirvan 271
Sadrai-Najafi, A. 947
Sadri, Amir 645
Sadr-Nabawi, Rampur 105
Safari, H. 242
Sahebjam, Freidoune 202, 1152-1153
Saikal, Amin 1095
Saklatvala, Phiroz D. 35
Sale, Richard 560
Saleh, Ali Pasha 561
Salvadori, Massimo 795
Salvini, Gianpaolo 1096
Salzberg, John P. 1034
Salzman, P. C. 840, 909-911, 971
Samadi, Hadi 695
Sandjabi, Karim 841
Sanghvi, Ramesh 203-205
Sarraf, Tahmoores 948
Savory, Roger M. 290, 889, 1154
Sayre, Joel 106
Sazman-i Barnamah 646-649
Scarcia, B. M. 291
Scarcia, Gianroberto 107, 292, 396, 483, 842
Scarcia Amoretti, B. 293
Scharlau, K. 650, 751
Schirazi, Ali 843
Schoenbaum, David 1098
Schulz, Ann T. 332, 440, 696
Schulze-Holthus, Bernhard 108-109
Sedehi, Abolghassem 294-295

Sedghi, Hamideh 924-925
Semkus, Charles Ismail 1099
Setoudeh, Hassan 62
Sevian, Vahe J. 397
Shafaq, Rezazadeh 651
Shafii, Forough 949
Shah, S. A. 333
Shahid, Hushang 676
Shamim, Ali Asghar 206
Shaoul, Eshagh Emran 369
Shapiro, Walter 334
Sheean, Vicent 36
Sheehan, Michael Kahl 562
Sherwen, Douglas S. 110
Shoko, Okazaki 845
Shoraka, Jalil 677
Shwadran, Benjamin 160
Sills, D. L. 238
Simmonds, S. 796
Simonet, Pierre A. 846
Sinclair, Angus 161
Singh, K. R. 370, 441
Siyassi, Ali-Akbar 63
Skrine, Clarmont P. 111
Smith, Douglas L. 37
Sober, Sidney 563
Soheily, Hossein 697
Sohrab, Siawusch 506
Soraya. See Esfandiari, Soraya
Speiser, E. A. 564
Spooner, Brian 972
Spuler, Bertold 296
Sreedhar 335
Stauffer, Thomas R. 797
Steinbach, U. 297, 371, 422
Stemple, John D. 1100
Steppat, Fritz 112
Sternberg-Sarel, Benno 847
Stevens, Willy 587
Stobaugh, Robert B. 752
Stocking, George W. 162
Street, Brian 995
Studiengesellschaft für Wirtschaftliche Entwicklung 507
Stürzenacher, Walter 64
Sullivan, William H. 565, 1101
Sykes, Edward 652
Szyliowicz, Joseph S. 219, 944

Tabari, Keyvan 566

Tabriztchi, S. 295
Tachau, Frank 307
Taheri, Amir 950
Tahir-Kheli, Shirin 398
Tardow 848
Tavallali, Djamchid 298
Tekiner, Suleiman 484
Thaiss, Gustav 973-974
Thoman, Roy E. 443-444
Thomas, Lewis V. 567
Thompson, W. J. 65, 113
Thorpe, J. A. 114, 568
Tibi, Bassam 996
Tofigh, Firouz 798
Tohidipur, M. 1012
Tomasek, R. D. 399
Tosco, Franco 912
Touba, Jacqueline R. 926
Touchais, Bernard 208-209
Towliat, Mohsen 445
Tripet, François 207, 849
Tully, Andrew 163
Tuma, Elias H. 850
Turner, Louis 698-699
Twitchell, Hamilton A. 311, 337, 522, 545, 563, 677, 694, 757, 760, 800, 851, 851, 950, 1106

Ule, Wolfgang 243
Ullens de Schooten, Marie T. 913
United Nations. General Assembly 115
United States. Congress. House 569, 1035-1036
United States. Congress. Senate 336, 570
United States. Department of State 571-572, 1155
United States. Petroleum Administration for War 753
Upton, Joseph M. 1156

Vafa, Javad 997
Vahidi, Iraj 851
Vakil, Firouz 799-800
Van Wagenen, Richard W. 116
Vasiu, Alex 508
Vassenhove, L. van 66, 372
Veccia Vaglieri, Laura 754
Vieille, Paul 218, 253, 299,

Name Index

682, 852-853, 1037
Villiers, Annick de 208-209
Villiers, Gérard de 208-209
Viotti, Paul R. 552

Waltman, Jerry 573
Ward, Gordon H. 854
Ward, Michael 363
Warne, William E. 574
Wasserberg, Arlyn B. 485
Watt, D. C. 613
Weaver, Paul E. 486-487
Weinbaum, M. G. 244, 300, 588, 855
Westwood, A. F. 301-302
Wilber, Donald Newton 38, 303, 614, 1157-1158
Williamson, John W. 755
Wilson, Arnold T. 39, 67-68, 890, 914, 1159
Wilson, Dunning S. 158
Woodsmall, Ruth Frances 927
Wriggins, Howard 589
Wright, Denis 447

Wright, George Ernest 653
Wrobel, Brian 1038
Wymar, Benno 615

Yaganegi, Esfandiar B. 678
Yapp, Malcolm E. 40
Yar-Shater, Ehsan 263, 355, 618, 778, 863, 885, 972-973, 1001, 1160
Yarshater, Latifeh 928
Young, Richard 590
Young, T. C. 69, 116, 164, 304, 488
Yousefi, Mahmood 998
Yusuf, Kaniz Fatima 400

Zabih, Sepehr 165, 245-247, 345, 373-374, 448, 1102
Zadé, Sultan 509
Zampa, Leone 449
Zarbafian, Shamseddin 654
Zareian, Soleiman 999
Zelli, M. Manoutchehr 655
Zonis, Marvin 305-308, 1000-1001

Ref Z 3366 .G58 1985   SEP 1 7 1985
Gitisetan, Dariush.
Iran, politics and
 government under the